THE ADVOCATE ADVISER

THE
ADVOCATE
ADVISER

by Pat Califia

*America's most popular gay columnist
tackles the questions that the others ignore*

Boston ♦ Alyson Publications, Inc.

Copyright © 1991 by Pat Califia.
Cover design copyright © by Darrell Buell. All rights reserved.
Typeset and printed in the United States of America.

This is a paperback original from Alyson Publications, Inc.,
40 Plympton St., Boston, Mass. 02118.

Distributed in England by GMP Publishers,
P.O. Box 247, London N17 9QR England.

First edition, first printing: June 1991

5 4 3 2 1

ISBN 1-55583-169-9

Library of Congress Cataloging-in-Publication Data

Califia, Pat.
   The Advocate adviser : America's most popular gay columnist
tackles the questions that the others ignore / by Pat Califia. —
1st ed.
    p.   cm.
  ISBN 1-55583-169-9 : $8.95
   1. Gays—United States—Social life and customs. 2.Gays—United
States—Sexual behavior. 3. American newspapers—Sections, columns,
etc.—Advice. I. Title.
HQ76.3.U5C35 1991
306.76′6′0973—dc20
                91-2928
                CIP

*This book is dedicated
to the memory of Robert I. McQueen
(March 5, 1942–October 8, 1989)*

*Or perhaps it would be more appropriate to refer to him as
RIM Queen, his favorite sobriquet. Robert's willingness to
publish controversial material in* The Advocate *made it much
easier for me to become a writer. His scathing wit, dark
passions, and creative spirit remain an inspiration.*

Acknowledgments

The following people gave me invaluable assistance in the preparation of this book: S. Bryn Austin, Beth Brown, Jan Brown, and Michael Shively.

Contents

A brief history of the Advocate Adviser

I was sitting at my desk in *The Advocate*'s office, trying to come up with a way to start a book review without saying, "This book is about..." Naturally, I was wearing nothing but black. Since my first contact with the magazine had been writing an article about lesbian S/M ("A Secret Side of Lesbian Sexuality," in 1979), when I actually came to work there, I felt I had to hold up the side for the pervs, even if that meant people frequently asked me, "Are those the same clothes you wore on Monday?" I was sulking because the ventilator shaft was blowing cold air on me, and I secretly suspected I had ruined my tough image forever by complaining bitterly about its effect on my delicate sinuses at the last staff meeting. Also, I had dyed my punk pigtail the night before, and helpful folks kept telling me my neck was blue.

In stalked Robert McQueen, our tall and suave editor, rubbing his hands together in a merry fashion. I had not been there for long, but I knew that Robert got that twinkle in his eye only when he was about to make somebody suffer. We had certain things in common, Robert and I did.

"Did you come to borrow office supplies?" I said. "Because I am going to put a note up on the bulletin board about that. I want people to stop rummaging in my desk every time they run out of pens, Liquid Paper, envelopes, or staples. It's a lot of trouble for me to keep my desk well organized, and it isn't fair of them to keep fucking it up."

Robert cocked an eyebrow. "Well, dear," he said archly, "can we help it if the entire supply cabinet seems to have moved into your drawers? That's not really why I came to see you, but since you reminded me, I'm out of memo pads."

I grudgingly handed them over. The masthead and the signature line on my paycheck both tended to confirm that he was, after all, the boss.

He graciously accepted them and then announced, "You're going to write an advice column for our pink pages!" (In those days, *The Advocate*'s classified ads were printed on pink paper, to make them easier for subscribers to find when they pulled them out and threw the rest of the magazine away. It also made them easier for people's mothers to find when they were tidying up their single sons' apartments.)

"Robert, I'm too busy."

All I got was a blank look. Robert, myself, and so many other people on the staff had been raised in the Church of Jesus Christ of Latter-Day Saints that "the Mormon Mafia" was an office joke. Gay Mormons are not that different from straight Mormons. They just plug "the movement" into the slot formerly occupied by "the church." Mormons think nothing of learning a new language in six weeks so they can go on a two-year mission to preach the gospel in a foreign country, coming home to get married and procreate, working a full-time job, going to church twice on Sunday, having family home evening once a week, going to either priesthood meetings (for men) or Relief Society meetings (for women), working on the church farm, amassing a six-months' supply of food, water, and other necessities for use in case of an emergency, and donating ten percent of their income to the Lord. My mother was always telling me, "Working too hard is not nearly as sad as having no work at all." None of the Mormon Mafia (except me) put in any less than a ten-hour day. They all felt guilty about taking vacations. "Too busy" was a non sequitur.

"I'm not qualified."

He laughed, politely, behind his hand. "Well, you keep running around here telling everybody except the janitor how to do fisting, and you're always consoling the receptionist about her latest operation" (our receptionist was a transsexual), "and you told the boy in the mail room he probably had crabs and gave him a list of eighteen different medications. The lesbian couple in payroll now have an open relationship, thanks to your sage counsel, and have been late to work every day this week. And you have the typesetter putting tit-clamps on her boyfriend. I think the lady doth protest too much."

Hmm. Well, I had done the volunteer training for San Francisco Sex Information and worked on their staff, had a bachelor's degree in psychology, and I'd written a sex manual for lesbians (*Sapphistry*, Naiad Press). I spent most of my spare time either reading about or talking about sex. I didn't discriminate. Pleasure — mine, other people's, our ancestors', that of future generations, leaders of the New Right, and space aliens — fascinated me. Maybe I was qualified. How did you get certified to be an advice columnist, anyway? Who gave Ann Landers or Dear Abby a license?

"Well, I'll want to include some questions from lesbians." Surely, I thought, this would kill it. No self-respecting editor of a national gay news magazine would want Q&A about tits and clits appearing next to classified ads for "Hunky Horny Hung Homo Honky Seeks Same. Narcissists need not apply."

But Robert disappointed me. He refused to be a bigot. "Gee, that'll make it very interesting," he said. "This is not a request," he added. "This is an order."

That cinched it. "Well, maybe it will be fun," I grumbled.

"I'm sure it will be. You can always eroticize feeling persecuted. Oh, did you know your neck was blue?"

After I went to the ladies' room and scrubbed most of the color off of my neck and out of my hair, I went back to my desk and banged out a memo requesting questions for my new column. I got only one written response — an extremely complicated question about a very idiosyncratic aspect of one male's sexual functioning that is still in my files, unanswered. I spring it on any new doctor I'd like to use as a resource to see if they can give me a clue.

But people did start slinking into my office and inviting me to lunch. In one week, I learned that the secret lives of the people I worked with were at least as complicated as my own. Somebody we all thought had a bad case of tearoom knees turned out to be impotent. Somebody else had done a threesome with his lover and was worried about the "emotional consequences." He thought lesbians (because of our vast experience with group sex?) would have handled it better. Another person had a collection of ladies' underwear and wanted to know how the hell you got a bra on over your head. Yet another person had no interest in sex at all unless he was in love, and had just about given up meeting another man with the same fetish.

I carefully explained to everyone that I was going to use this material in my column, that I would disguise identities, but I should not be told anything confidential. Everyone said okay. Then the first column hit print, in the April 30, 1981 issue, and my sources dried up. In fact, for a little while, everyone stopped speaking to me. If I went to the coffee machine and we were out of Cremora and sugar, nobody would even tell me where we kept the surplus. So when I found it, I had to move it into the overhead bin of my cubicle, next to my extra office supplies.

Luckily, letters started to pour in. I had a lot of anxiety about writing the column. Would gay men confide in a lesbian? Was there really anything about sex, health, or relationships that gay people (who were surely more sophisticated than our heterosexual counterparts) didn't know already? This flow of mail seemed to confirm that there was a need for "The Advocate Adviser," or at least that people found it fun to write to her. (Although I sometimes wonder how many of my readers realize I'm a lesbian. Every week, I get letters addressed to "Dear Mr. Califia." My favorite, which I received after writing a column defending size queens, begins, "Dear Sir, I would love to sit on all of your throbbing eight inches.")

I have never, oddly enough, gotten an irate letter from someone questioning my right to pronounce on male sexuality. This may be because I often read my letters (minus the names) to gay male friends and listen to their reactions before I write my own response. It may also be because I am a very peculiar sort of lesbian, a leather dyke who got taken in by a group of dissipated and extremely kinky leathermen who thought it was amusing and important to show me as much of the Folsom Street (and alley) lifestyle as possible. My own gender identity is a little confusing, even to myself, since dressing for a hot date can mean anything from a strapless fifties prom dress with crinolines and seven-inch steel-heeled spikes to a rubber wetsuit with a gas mask to impersonating a well-endowed (if short) leatherman to my birthday suit, latex gloves, and a thin coating of water-based lubricant containing at least 5 percent nonoxynol-9.

The pansexual nature of "The Advocate Adviser" has been one of its most important features. Lesbians and gay men can work together (sometimes) on (very) pressing political issues, we can share the same dance bars (if we have to), but often there is a pervasive tone of hostility, suspicion, and contempt when we must deal with one another. I believe that the reasons for this alienation are not all that different from the reasons straight people hate "queers": ignorance, fear of difference, and an assumption that what you like and are used to (especially in bed) is morally superior to what other people prefer. One sex-crazed lezzie columnist is not going to change every fool's mind. But the more we know about each other's vulnerabilities, our need for love, and the frustrations we experience when we try to meet our most private needs, the easier it is for lesbians and gay men to see each other as people with common ground.

If I didn't know it before, writing "The Adviser" has taught me that in matters of sex, you can take nothing for granted and you can't judge anything, either. The process of coming out does not automatically inform gay people about how our bodies function, nor does it eradicate shame. It's been a century since the Victorian era ended, but I still get letters asking me about the harmful consequences of masturbation. I get letters asking me what the prostate gland is, what a venereal disease is. Gay sex education is not an oxymoron. When we talk loosely about "the gay community," we are referring to a group of people with a variety of erotic tastes, drives, and fantasies. I have come to believe that sexual morality is not a matter of what you do to get off — or what you'd like to do. No erotic act is inherently immoral if it is performed with consent and is mutually pleasurable, and precautions are taken to preserve the participants' physical and emotional well-being. Rudeness disturbs me much more than deviance. This may be why perfect strangers tell me secrets they've never told their lovers.

I'm always being asked if I get tired of writing "The Adviser." The answer is no. Every month I get a letter that deals with something I've never thought about before. (See "Most Outrageous Questions.") And no matter how many times I get a sad letter from someone who just can't seem to find true love (see "Most Common Questions"), each of these letters comes from an individual whose grief is not diminished by the fact that the Lonelyhearts Club is the biggest gay group in town. Furthermore, every time I answer a sticky question, I know it will upset someone. (See "Most Controversial Columns.") I like the angry mail I get as much as I like the fan mail. It proves that people are reading the column. How will I know I've made a mistake if someone doesn't point it out? (However, there is no list of "The Adviser's Biggest Bloopers." Let bygones be bygones, I always say.)

The only thing I sometimes wish for is a secretary, so that I could provide personal answers to everyone who writes in. Anybody who wants to defect from Ann, Abby, or Miss Manners's staff should let me know. There's no money in it, but you'll get to read about things that are a lot more interesting than inconsiderate in-laws who drop by at dinnertime without an invitation or where to seat your divorced parents at the wedding.

Most outrageous questions

• A man who managed a horse boarding stable that had several gay customers wrote in. He was sure his customers were having sex with the horses, and he wanted to know if this could expose his staff to AIDS when they groomed the animals, or if other men who had sex with the same horses could get AIDS. I told him no to the first question, recommended condoms and a burglar alarm, and scolded him a bit for having such an exotic fantasy about his gay customers. I then got three letters from men who wanted to know where the stable was located.

• An indignant reader sent me a clipping alleging that gay men were showing up in emergency rooms because they had stuffed gerbils up their tushes. He wanted to know if there was any truth to this heinous rumor. I was able to report that I had been unable to find a shred of hard evidence to document this folktale. Furthermore, I contended that the real news was that most people who wind up in the hospital having something odd removed from their heinies are straight men who are too ignorant or embarrassed to go buy a good dildo. Wives of America, arm yourselves!

• I printed a letter from a straight man with AIDS whose doctor did not tell him how to have safe sex with his wife. His hope was that perhaps the diagnosis was wrong. He did not see how he could have been at risk with AIDS because when he had sex with other men, he was always the "inserter." And Reagan officials blocked a mass mailing of AIDS information to American households for months! It's enough to make you want to become a tax resister.

• A naughty lesbian wrote to say that ever since she had encountered Andrea Dworkin's anti-porn spiel, she had been masturbating to the image of "splayed vaginal lips," and was there a safe way to permanently spread labia? After laughing so hard I peed, I advised against Krazy Glue.

• A man who was having an affair with his father, whom he had seen very little of as a child, wrote in to inquire about his legal status. I advised caution, if only because too many of his friends would be terminally jealous if they found out he had a real Daddy!

• A letter from a white man who bought tons of porn featuring black models, but did not have a clue how to pick up a handsome black man in his favorite bar, made me seethe. Not at the reader — it's not his fault we all grow up in a racist culture — but at the color line that continues to divide a bunch of outcasts from one another.

• A reader described in great detail his adventure with a truck driver who stuck a cigar up his ass, and coyly asked, "Is this any threat to my health?" While acknowledging that there was some risk, I was understandably reluctant to send this gentleman to Smokenders. I also wondered where this supposedly simple piece of blue-collar trade got such a wild idea. Are they selling *Drummer* at Phillips 66 truck stops now?

Most common questions

• How to find a lover. This is the runaway number one most frequently asked question. It's an index of how isolated we still are. Sometimes I think it won't be solved until every television and VCR in the country blows up, and people *have* to go out and talk to one another. I also sometimes wonder if people are really just looking for love, or if they want to be transformed into Someone Fascinating and Important by the Stud of their Dreams. Bottom line is, if you are willing to listen, you can always find someone to talk to, and if you are willing to give care and affection, you will never lack for a relationship.

• I am still getting tons of questions about basic safe sex. There seems to be tremendous resistance to condoms. Many of my readers prefer being celibate to using a rubber. It's obvious to me that *explicit* safe sex education about how to use (and enjoy) condoms is imperative, whether we have federal funds to do it or not. The condom manufacturers also need to redesign their product. There's no excuse for this "one size fits all" canard. Men who have encounters that present no risk of disease transmission get anxious enough to write and ask me if there was any way they could have caught something after (for example) a mutual J/O session in the shower. So it's obvious that we can't repeat the basics about safe sex often enough.

• Penis size is another popular topic. I get about the same number of letters from readers who feel their penises are too small and readers who feel it's too big. And lots of questions about whether or not penis enlargement devices work.

• I've always gotten a lot of questions about how to make anal sex feel good, and whether or not getting fucked is bad for your asshole. Since the AIDS epidemic, I am getting many more questions about whether or not anal toys are safe, how to decide which toys to buy, and how to use them. There's still a lot of misinformation — in our own community — about anal sex.

• Obscenity laws intimidate many gay people. I am frequently asked, Can I receive gay magazines (even nonpornographic publications) or X-rated videos at my home? And several women write in every year to ask where they can find lesbian porn. Recently, another question about porn is often asked — are porn models having safe sex? Many viewers find it difficult to enter the fantasy world of a videotape if they see high-risk behavior on the screen.

• Gender issues are another popular topic. I get lots of letters from transvestites looking for places to buy clothes and people to dress up with, transsexuals who want to know why their bodies feel wrong to them and what they can do about it, and lesbian readers asking me about the etiquette and practice of butch–femme role-playing.

• The problem of the older gay person who has lost their life partner, or is simply finding it more difficult to continue to have an active sex life as they age, or has worries about money, makes it clear to me that we urgently need more social services and outreach to gay seniors. There are even fewer resources for differently abled gay men and lesbians.

Most controversial columns

• I once made a reference to "the criminal origins of our wealthy classes," and later on, quoted a Bible scripture about how hard it is for rich people to get into heaven. This column garnered more nasty letters than any of the other ones below. Believe me, J. P. Morgan wasn't that sensitive, fellas.

• One column included a letter from a reader who was horrified by scat. I told him that if this bothered him so much that he had to write a letter deploring it, he was obviously fascinated as well as repulsed. Many readers who shared his negative feelings and resented the implication that they were closet shit-eaters wrote in to complain. I stand firm in my belief that moralizing about other people's vices is no more than a safe way to titillate yourself.

• A column in which I discussed whether or not fisting put people at special risk for AIDS and how to do it as safely as possible got many letters, pro and con.

• When I told a lonely prison inmate that he should not be surprised that people "outside" were reluctant to become close to him, I got letters from men who had met their ideal mate by corresponding with prisoners, people who were ready to offer their homes to discharged inmates (sight unseen), and angry letters from folks who had been ripped off by convict scams. Apparently there's a lot of fascination with the forced, all-male environment of prison — and not enough caution about getting close to the real thing.

• When it was first discovered that nonoxynol-9 killed the AIDS virus and it was suggested that it might be used during anal sex as a backup for condoms, my column relaying this information met with a rash of letters saying (properly) that not enough research had been done on the long-term effects of this chemical on the rectum. This research has still not been done, but nonoxynol-9 is being used more and more often in lubricants and condoms.

• A very early column on how to be a good cocksucker was controversial, at least around *The Advocate* office, apparently because nobody could figure out how I knew what to say. You boys are no Einsteins, are you? You couldn't recognize a Woman with a Past if she hit you on the nose with a rolled-up newspaper.

• A plaintive reader asked why tricks will ask for your name and phone number if they don't want to see you again. Rarely has a column gotten so much mail, both from slighted men with a similar problem and from well-meaning gents who asked for a phone number when they really meant to say, "This was fun to do — once."

THE ADVOCATE ADVISER

Meeting people
and finding partners

Q. I'm 30, single, and friends say quite attractive. The problem is, I keep going to bars and discos and don't seem to find the hunks I see out in public. When I do, I freeze up as I begin to make the approach, then just stand there frozen until the person walks away. I usually go home angry at myself, lonely, and depressed. I do not consider myself a shy person.

A. Those vivacious people at a bar or disco are dancing and drinking to distract themselves from the horrid fear that no one else is going to Make the First Move and save them from the onerous task of figuring out how to meet a handsome stranger without spilling something on him.

You probably aren't a shy person. Or, rather, you aren't any more shy than the rest of us. The typical hunk who sails by you is crushed by the fact that you didn't say something, *anything* ("He was staring at me all night long, I thought maybe he was really attracted, what did I do wrong?") and is going to go home alone, angry at himself, and depressed.

Some people give up cruising bars and discos altogether, and only cruise public places (like baths or tearooms) where a man's mere presence signals that he is horny, and you don't have to talk at all, just grope and hope your hand doesn't get slapped. But there are fewer places like this than there used to be, and you can't guarantee that the hunk (let alone the husband) of your dreams will be in the next clump of bushes, either.

Classified ads don't cause as much stage fright as walking onto the dance floor, but they don't give you a chance to check someone out in person, either. If you want anything more intimate than a pen pal, sooner or later you have to meet and (gulp) *talk* to your "GM BB sks FA, GP, CBT, long walks on the beach and quiet evenings at home in front of the fireplace."

The value of the witty opening line has been overestimated. Chances are, if you come up with a unique and clever approach, anyone who overhears it will steal it, and by the next weekend, it will be a cliche. Since you really have no reason to speak to a stranger in a public place unless you want to make his acquaintance, any question, remark, or comment will do. If he replies and gives you an opening for a response, he is interested. If he grunts, walks away, or says something cutting, he is probably not a real boy, anyway, just a magical talking dildo that got misplaced by a Fairy Godmother on too many designer drugs.

You can ask an attractive fella where the men's room or the cigarette machine is, who the deejay is, if there are any more like him at home, or where there is a better/different/smaller place. You can tell him you like the music, ask him if you can buy him a drink or dance with him or play pool or a video game, or ask for (or offer) a light.

Make it your goal to say something to three strangers the next time you go out. You don't have to persuade somebody to go home with you, just speak with a few men you don't know already. Then pat yourself on the back or give yourself a more material reward. Before long, you will find that bantering with other people at the bar comes more naturally, and eventually you will train yourself to pick people up.

Don't be deterred by those Ice Queens who can crush your ego, possibly even send you into long-term psychotherapy, with a one-liner, the way Hell's Angels crush beer cans with one hand. If ships continued to put out to sea after the Titanic, you can don your Mae West life-saving vest and venture forth again. Most people would rather snuggle up to a warm body than work on their Oscar Wilde imitation. Do them a favor — give them a chance to get to know you!

✍

Q. How can you tell if a straight woman is really straight? There's this really pretty girl in my English literature class (I'm getting my bachelor's degree by going to night school). She always smiles and says hello to me, and we've had some great conversations about the class. She's so sensitive to women's issues that I think even if she's not a lesbian maybe she could be. I think about her a lot, especially at work, and I'm afraid I'm going to slip and let some of my fantasies show.

A. Ouch. This is a tricky situation. Lesbian bars and lesbian organizations are important, not just because lesbians like to drink or do political work, but because we need a way to tell which women are safe to approach and which ones are not. Women have been trained to be so sexually passive that if there was no external method for sorting the heterosexuals out from the bisexuals and the lesbians and the curious, we would all sit on separate ends of the Love Seat of Life and sip our Pink Ladies and never lay a finger on a real, live pink (or brown or red or yellow) lady.

One time-honored method is to ask her if she has a boyfriend. (However, I know very few lesbians who at one time in their lives didn't have — or claim to have — a relationship with a man.) You can also mention an author (Virginia Woolf, perhaps, since this is a class in English literature) and say, "I remember reading somewhere that she had several affairs with women." George Sand is another good one for this. Or you can drag in the whole polymorphously perverse Bloomsbury Group. If she doesn't turn green or jump out of her skin, you can assume that lesbianism is at least safe as a topic of conversation.

But many women who are liberal or sophisticated enough to say the word "lesbian" without losing some teeth are not ready to take their clothes off to the accompaniment of Sappho's lyre. If she demurely refuses to admit to any "tendencies" herself, the only way to get the subject out in the open is to come out to her and tell her you have a crush on her. Ideally, these should be two separate conversations, but revelations of this nature tend to come out like a gusher, all or nothing.

Should you ask her to go out with you? That depends. Perhaps you are fantasizing about her because your job is boring and you don't know any single lesbians. Can she be trusted to keep a secret, even if she does not return your affections? How badly would it hurt you if the worst possible thing happened and she rejected you completely? Are you strong enough about your gay identity to feel good about yourself even if she tells you you're sick and awful?

Develop more of a social life with other out-of-the-closet lesbians. Even if you become lovers with your friend, the two of you will still need a gay social life. More experience will help you measure the seriousness of your crush and give you a source of support if it doesn't work out.

If you do decide to come out to this woman, wait until the class is over, so you won't risk flunking out because you have to avoid her. Try not to put any pressure on her; that's a certified turnoff. Ideally expressed, a proposition is a compliment — "You are beautiful and desirable, and I respond to that" — and creates no obligation in the recipient — "We can make love if you think you would enjoy that, but in no case will I cease to admire you and seek your company."

✍

Q. Recently some very horrible things have happened in my life. In December, I was diagnosed with generalized lymphadenopathy and subsequently tested positive for the HIV antibody. Also in December, my family discovered that I'm gay and as a consequence, they hardly speak to me. I've not told them about my exposure to the AIDS virus.

My psychiatrist thinks I'm very emotionally and psychologically strong, but I often blame my gayness for my situation. If I were straight, I wouldn't have these problems. I have lots of friends but no lover. In light of the situation with my parents, I feel very alone. I really need a special person in my life, but who would have me now? If the average person with my condition has had upwards of a thousand different partners I doubt I'd be interested in him. What time has he had to cultivate himself? Would he be interested in or capable of carrying on a monogamous relationship?

I'm 23, bright, and attractive, but I've been alone for over five years. My greatest fear is that I will grow old alone or die of AIDS. This fear becomes more vivid each time a new negative piece of information about AIDS surfaces. Sometimes I feel happy and content, but when I think of love and sex, I feel like such a loser. I've tried to continue with the other aspects of my life as if nothing were wrong, but stress has decreased my productivity. My problems seem insurmountable.

A. It doesn't sound like your psychiatrist understands the stress you are under right now. An assurance that you are "very emotionally and psychologically strong" is no help at all when your gut experience is that your world is falling apart. Call your local AIDS foundation and get a referral for some more effective counseling. It might be especially good for you to be in a group of other HIV-positive men. It's very difficult to be at risk for a debilitating, often fatal illness. This is *not* business as usual. No wonder you can't carry on like a happy little worker bee.

Once you get hooked into more support, contact your family and tell them your bad news. There's nothing wrong with a little judicious emotional blackmail to help our loved ones get over their bullshit. It could be your family regrets being nasty to you and is looking for a face-saving occasion to get back in touch. Many families pull together in a crisis like this, but of course I can't promise you that yours will be loving and kind. If they are still rejecting, write them off. You don't have time to waste on people who aren't going to be good to you.

I understand why you want the security of a long-term relationship. But if you haven't had a monogamous relationship before now, it will take major changes for you to be able to find and keep an exclusive lover. Is it romance and love you want, or is it a live-in attendant, in case you get sick? I don't think the latter is a good reason to become one-half of a couple. Do you have any energy left over from your own problems to be able to help him with his?

I'm not saying you shouldn't be looking for a lover. I'm just raising a few hard issues that you should think about because they will come up if you become involved with someone. This is probably the best time ever to be looking for a lover. Gay men are more willing to consider committed relationships now. While the stress of the health crisis can make us all do some crazy things, it can also make us drop some of the pettiness, vanity, and selfishness that interferes with intimacy, and force us to try harder to stay close to the people we love.

Don't blame your problems on your sexual orientation. Straight people also get AIDS, you know. If you were straight you could be enmeshed in a messy divorce case fighting for custody of your six kids. You could be unemployed and unable to take care of your wife and ailing mother-in-law. You could be disabled from an accident on the job.

The fact is, you do not have AIDS and you are not alone. You do have friends. Friends are sometimes more reliable and giving than a lover or parents or the welfare state. If you concentrate on giving love to your friends and allowing them to care for you and make you feel better, the man of your dreams might turn out to be one of them — or a friend of a friend.

Q. I've been going to Alcoholics Anonymous meetings for the last eight months. My group is small, only six including me. When I first started going to AA, I was quiet and didn't want to be noticed. Now I really want to get to know these guys, but maybe I waited too long. Sometimes during these meetings, they talk about what they did together during the week, and I feel left out.

A. This is an appropriate subject to bring up in the group. If you want to stay sober, you need to learn how to socialize without alcohol.

Everyone is shy. We all need company, and we're all afraid we'll be left out in the cold. Some people deal with this by being quiet, some by being gregarious, and some by snubbing anyone who asks for their attention.

Vulnerability is much more appealing than making accusations. So don't tell your group, "I need people who are clean and sober to spend time with me, and you guys are denying me an experience I need to make a full recovery!" This would just make everybody defensive. Instead, tell them how much the group has meant to you, that you've appreciated the space they gave you to be withdrawn, but that you feel safer now and would like to be more available within and outside the group. Then tell each person something that you have come to notice and appreciate about him.

If this doesn't break the ice, consider changing to another group where you can make a fresh start.

✍

Q. I'm a 19-year-old lesbian. Lately I've been going to the only bar here that seems to be mostly for women. There are also some mixed bars in town where a few women go dancing. But I don't like to dance. Can you tell me how to meet other women? I guess I assumed there would be more of a welcoming atmosphere. Any advice you can give me would be very appreciated. *The Advocate* is the only gay paper I can buy here.

A. You're probably going to get some weird attitude from the older lesbians at the bar until somebody has "brought you out" — i.e., the first time it becomes clear to them that you've had sex with another woman. Some old-fashioned lesbian communities have a rule (usually unspoken) that it is not proper to take responsibility for another woman's homosexuality by being the one to introduce her to lesbian sex.

Thank heaven, there are individual lesbians who don't feel this way. Somebody will take you under her wing either because she's adventurous and horny or because she sees you as a potential lover. Once the dangerous patina of the novice has worn off you, everybody will loosen up. You may be more likely to meet an available woman in the mixed bars. Besides, you need to learn how to be social in different environments.

In the meantime, try to learn how to dance. Or play pool. Or pinball. Or dice with the bartender. It's not important that you be particularly good at any of these activities, but these are the things you do in bars so you have a way to start conversations with other women. Just don't learn how to drink a lot. That's very bad for your social skills.

Many gay women use personal ads to find friends and lovers. Check the resource list in the back of this book for lesbian publications where you can advertise.

✍

Q. A couple of years ago, I placed some personal classified ads and got a lot of responses, all of which I answered. I met some nice people, and we had a good time. I even met one guy I see at least once a week. I'd like to place some more ads, correspond, or meet for whatever is satisfactory to both of us. Getting mail at a private box has become almost an obsession with me. My question is, what's legal? How far can you go in what you say? Are there cases of postal authority interference in explicit letters in answer to letters received or to other personal ads?

A. Go ahead and rent a post office box and have fun placing and answering ads. There's nothing illegal about writing explicit letters. Nude photos are also not illegal. Of course, you should be sure to use opaque envelopes and address your letters carefully, so your correspondence doesn't go astray.

There's one exception to this. The authorities have been known to use the mail to entrap people into breaking the laws about child pornography. It's a serious crime to circulate material involving minors. Be cautious of any correspondent who tries to send you this type of material or asks you for it.

There's a slight possibility that photographs of people having sex might be considered obscene. The laws that define obscenity are, unfortunately, vague. So exercise caution about sending anything more raunchy than a solo shot through the mail.

✍

Q. Could you please tell me what the abbreviations in ads mean?

A. Here's a list of the abbreviations I've seen in frequent use, but I can't guarantee that this is what any particular advertiser means. I'm always seeing new abbreviations I can't decipher, and being startled by the meanings attributed to old ones.

There are usually two types of abbreviations, the ones people use to describe themselves and the ones they use to describe what kind of sex they're looking for.

Descriptive Abbreviations

    BB = Bodybuilder
    Bi = Bisexual
    Bl/hz = Blond hair, hazel eyes
    Br/br = Brunette, brown eyes
    Dom = Dominant
    G/S = Gay, single
    GBM = Gay, black man
    GWM = Gay, Caucasian man
    GOM = Gay, Oriental man
    GJM = Gay, Jewish man
    M = Married
    NS, ND = No smoking, no drugs
    Sub = Submissive
    U/C = Uncut
    Vers = Versatile
    Y/O = Years old

Sexual Abbreviations

    B&D = Bondage and discipline
    BJ = Blowjob (oral sex)
    C/B = Cock and balls
    C&B/T = Cock-and-ball torture
    FA = French active (wants to give head)
    F/F = Fistfucking
    FP = French passive (wants to receive oral sex)
    GA = Greek active (wants to fuck, not get fucked)
    GH = Gloryholes
    GP = Greek passive (wants to be penetrated anally)
    JO = Jerking off (can mean either masturbation or hand jobs)
    S/M = Sadomasochism
    S/S = Safe sex
    T/T = Tit torture
    V/A = Verbal abuse
    W/S = Watersports (playing with piss)

✍

Q. Is it ipso facto evidence of poor self-esteem or of a desire for failure to be a black man exclusively attracted to white men? I already know it's unproductive, but does it also mean something's wrong with me?

I'm a good-looking, well-built professional, of middle-class values, tastes, and aspirations — including my taste in love/sex partners. The only lovers I've been able to attract so far have been dinge queens (or size queens) who were lacking in self-esteem or who have a fetish for "street blacks." Generally they're decent men, but I'm not needy enough to accept such relationships anymore. White peers rarely signal that they're emotionally available. When they do, they soon fade away, apparently unable to visualize me in their fantasies of a "power relationship."

Name an option and I've exercised it: bars, ads, Black and White Men Together, computer dating, gay organizations by the dozen, and various therapy groups. My white friends (who seem to adore me although they never date black men themselves) only try to matchmake me with other blacks. I've tried "reorienting" myself toward black men — with the same degree of success I got when I tried to reorient myself to prefer women.

Most of the black gay men I know recount the same frustrating history. Those few who have Anglo lovers invariably seem to have settled for men less attractive or less together than they are. A quick tally of the personals confirms that blacks are usually excluded (along with "fats, fems, and druggies") in even the most sensitively written ads.

Should I accept that as a black I just don't have the same relationship options as other gay men? Should I hold out for what I think I deserve? Or am I already getting it?

A. No, you're not getting what you deserve. You're feeling the effects of racism within the gay community (and the larger world). You also have some problems that are individual (and thus more easy to solve).

You want a financially secure relationship with an upwardly mobile, well-educated, middle-class man — someone who matches your own background, except for being Caucasian. But in my experience, that group of gay men is the least likely to be able to deal with the social consequences of crossing the color line. These negative consequences aren't imaginary, but they aren't insurmountable, and it's sad that prejudice can make anyone turn down a chance to be loved. If a white boy can take the heat for being gay, he should be able to take the heat for loving someone who is black.

Class and race are often conflated. Whites tend to assume that any black person they meet will be working-class or welfare-class. As you say in your letter, most white men who have eroticized black men have also, to some extent, eroticized a racially linked, lower-class background.

But some men have reasons other than erotic preference for seeking out a partner who is economically disadvantaged. Middle-class white men who are turned on to black men but want to keep their sexual preference a secret will prefer lower-class black men because they are less likely to demand an ongoing relationship. It's easier to hide your tricks than it is to hide your lovers.

I think the term "dinge queen" is offensive. But I leave you to judge if your use of it indicates any self-hatred or not. Regarding your friends, I will point out that if you are a member of a stigmatized and disenfranchised group, being able to look down on or even despise your lover if he is a member of the group that oppresses you provides some emotional compensation.

Be careful not to place yourself in the sexual conundrum of a man with a big dick who hates "size queens." Real love doesn't come along very often, but it has the power to transcend all limitations and achieve the unexpected and the unusual. There's probably an intelligent, good-looking, successful white man out there who is looking for you. But what will you do if he wants you to fulfill his *fantasy* of tricking with a tough, black street hustler? The fact that you're actually this very nice, middle-class person who is more likely to know his way around expensive department stores than the ghetto could be the very thing that makes him feel safe with you and want you.

If you're going to have an ongoing relationship with a white man, you're going to have to deal with his racism, his stereotypes, and all his fantasies about black men anyway. This can be a pain in the ass, but it can also be a lot of fun, if he's prepared to be your fantasy, too.

And what exactly would that be? You're very explicit about your disapproval of what other people want from a black-on-white sexual encounter or relationship, but there's nothing in your letter indicating what makes white men so fascinating for you. You had better be clearer about what you want if you're serious about getting it.

Q. Let me extol the joys of J/O. What can speak more directly to another man? It's the sexual ASCII code of all males "straight" or gay. Just note the ubiquitous come scene in all porno flicks. Then there's the look and feel of another man's penis. Nothing is more satisfying to me than orgasm whether it's my own or one I've helped induce in someone else. I give good hand. And I love a good cock. How can you make love to a cock or its owner when you're taking it up the ass?

J/O always seems to rate second best — a poor substitute for the more invasive methods: "All we did was jack off." In fact, I know a surprising number of men who are uncomfortable with masturbation alone and insist on "saving it" for "real sex."

Sheer exuberant joy of sex is as easy as dropping your drawers. Once, twice, three-plus times daily. I still marvel at this wonderful gift from nature. Most men report their most intense orgasms come from masturbation. Why not enjoy it? Also, I'm not worried about a congested or inflamed prostate, and my penis still thinks we're teenagers. J/O is both wholesome and healthy.

For me it's the very highest form of sex between men. What's more intimate than holding your buddy close while he's coming? You can feel him, taste him, shoot with him, milk him out, tend his balls, lick his ear, vibrate or massage his prostate, or whatever. And if it's just sexual camaraderie you seek, what's hotter than winding up as a group, cocks in all directions, and shooting load after hot load until each cock is squeezed dry? Whether it's videos, dirty talk, or just an impromptu jerk down, it's a great way for men to interact.

But men here are just too uptight. Several attempts to start J/O clubs locally have failed miserably. How can we make community J/O the great fun it should be?

A. Read on.

✍

Q. I'm all for home jack-off parties and wish there were some I could go to. But for some large-scale semipublic jacking off, available whenever anyone wants it, we need the power of capitalism. Please, some entrepreneur set up some erotic (safe sex) spaces and charge admission! Someone is going to make a lot of money as soon as the idea catches on. A starting point is masturbatory bathhouses or back rooms — with no total privacy and no total darkness. Anyone engaging in unsafe activities is thrown out and never allowed back. Anyone who observes unsafe activities and doesn't report it is thrown out for the evening.

Just think what it could do for the gay tourist industry. At the Circle J lodge, at night after dinner was cleaned up the fire would be made in the fireplace and all would strip down and start beating our meat. Or do it around the pool by moonlight. Or after we walk down to the beach to see the sunset. I'd sure like to go!

Why can't we have a gay video and jack-off festival?

I believe these activities, if done behind closed doors, are completely legal. But if someone wanted to be an activist, a masturbating civil disobedient, one could organize a modern version of the sixties smoke-in. Who would be willing to risk arrest in order to be part of masturbating leprechauns in a public park? Some police would ignore it unless forced to pay attention to it. Can you imagine the comment in the press? The publicity? What would the judge say?

Why can't we jack off (or jill off) in public toilets and rest stops? Who's going to be offended by that? Wouldn't it be *good* to offend them? There are a lot of guys that are real impatient for some promiscuous (safe) sex. Well, enough for tonight. Got to beat off.

A. The authorities have already closed down establishments where not a whole lot besides mutual J/O was going on. All it takes is some public pressure or a lying vice cop to make it look like the public welfare is being threatened. I think it's worth a struggle to try to open public J/O bathhouses, but it will take somebody with a lot of money and moral commitment to fight the legal battles.

As for jacking and jilling off in public toilets and rest stops ... I'm not sure it helps straight people to get over their sexual terror to be confronted by masturbating queers. Don't get me wrong, I've sometimes taken my pleasure with more luck than privacy. But I'd rather go to a J/O party where I know I'm not going to be interrupted or hassled by the uninitiated. Here's a quick list of suggestions for hosting a J/O party in your own home.

Cover furniture with sheets and put away breakables. Set out containers of lube (Crisco is good) and paper towels. If you don't have a VCR, rent one for the evening. Porn helps get things started. But screen it first, to make sure it has dick-hardening qualities. Taped music is also good. (You don't want to jump up every twenty minutes to change a record.) Make sure the room is warm.

Most hosts recommend a policy of no drugs or alcohol and no one under 18. Ask everybody to be there by a certain time, so you don't have to keep answering the door. In the beginning, you may want to let people get acquainted before they take their clothes off. But as people get more experienced, you may want to just give men who arrive a grocery bag for their clothes, and get everybody naked in a hurry. Lower the lights to signal that it's time to start getting sexy.

14

Keep your first party down to ten or so men. Invite a few more than that, because not everyone who RSVPs will show up. If you want to keep on doing parties, circulate a sheet of paper and get addresses or at least phone numbers so you can let the guys know when the next festivities will be held. You may want to ask somebody else who is there to host the next party.

You can set age limits or any other limit you want, but this doesn't encourage a friendly and open atmosphere. If you want more guys to come to your parties, make everybody welcome. You can also try advertising, although it's a good idea to rent a post office box instead of publishing your home address and telephone number. It's more discreet and safer to just ask your guests to bring their friends.

J/O parties work best if you have a core group of guys who enjoy manhandling each other's dicks and balls, talking nasty, tugging on each other's tits, etc., who will get carried away and hopefully inspire anyone who might be shy. Thinking filthy and acting healthy are social skills we have to teach one another!

✍

Q. I travel a lot and have trouble meeting people in strange cities. Is an escort service my answer? If so, could you give some tips on how to select, use, and find one? Just what's expected and do you confess to being a novice? Can you pre-select from a photograph?

A. Escort services stay in business by claiming that they sell nothing but nonsexual companionship. The fee you pay entitles you to nothing more than someone to talk to over dinner or at a show. This fee can be quite high. If the individual escort is willing to negotiate for more intimate activities, you will wind up paying an additional sum for the sex. Some escort services have photo books; most do not. They will ask you what your "type" is, and sometimes that's what they send you — sometimes it's not.

There's no way to tell in advance what kind of operation you're dealing with. If an escort service advertises in the gay press, and if they are polite on the phone, you can feel better about your chances of being satisfied than if you pick one out of the yellow pages. If you're not happy with your date, there isn't a whole lot you can do about it since they will probably take your credit card information over the phone before sending someone out to meet you.

Calling ads for models or masseurs is more direct. If you like someone when you speak to them on the phone, but you don't

15

like their looks when you show up for your appointment, all you have to do is leave. They won't be thrilled about it, but that's life.

The other traditional approach is to go to bars or neighborhoods that are frequented by hustlers and wait for somebody attractive to approach you and name a price. But it can be difficult to know where to go if you're from out of town. Bar and street hustlers are usually younger and have less security than guys with their own places, and are more likely to be on drugs or rip you off. Nevertheless, I have friends who have been dealing with hustlers for years without having any problems. It depends on how good you are at evaluating people, and whether you ask them to do things they will resent or let them think you can be victimized. Anybody who falls asleep with a hustler in his hotel room is an idiot.

You can tell the person you're hiring that you're a novice if it makes you more comfortable, but understand that they hear that kind of thing all the time and may not even believe you. What they care about is: (1) that you are clean and healthy, (2) that you will communicate your needs clearly, (3) that you are not a weirdo (which could mean anything from mutual oral sex to flogging, depending on the mores of the hustler), (4) will you pay up, and (5) will you come quickly so they can get back to whatever they were doing before you showed up. It's probably better to just ask, "What's the usual procedure?" and take care of business so you can have some fun.

✍

Q. There are a few bad telephone habits that are really depressing to me as a model advertiser. Would you please say a few words about telephone etiquette for clients?

1. There's a name on my ad for a reason. Please ask for that name when you call. I have mine coded, and it lets me know right away which ad you are calling about. I'm also a legitimate masseur and have an ad in the yellow pages. I give out less information to those callers than you might want. Advertisers who don't live alone will appreciate your discretion.

2. This business is based on trust. I confirm all my phone calls to help avoid teenage phone freaks and police entrapment. Please trust my discretion as much as I do yours. If you cannot, feel free to admit it. Don't give me a fake number.

3. Calling to get your rocks off over the phone or asking for a free meeting because I would enjoy it as much as you is the moral equivalent of shoplifting. There are fantasy phone lines. And of

course I enjoy my job. My customers could hardly enjoy themselves if I didn't.

4. Please have a fairly good idea of how much this is going to cost you. A session is going to run somewhere between $50 and $150. Offering me $20 insults my dignity and my product. Go get a street hustler. I've heard that's their going price.

5. Please don't hang up without saying good-bye. If someone walks into the room, it's much less suspicious to say you'll have to call me later. It also makes sense to say that if you mean to shop around. But if there's something about me that doesn't appeal to you and you're not interested in my services, please say so. It honestly hurts a lot less than getting no return call.

A. Many people feel angry about "having" to resort to the services of a professional and take this anger out on the person they call. A client with this attitude guarantees himself a halfhearted session, which will only make him feel worse, since he "wasted" his money.

Good manners are always appropriate. Someone who resents hiring a sex partner so much that he can't behave like a gentleman should spend his money on therapy or dancing lessons instead.

✍

Q. The first gay person I met was black, and ever since the sight of any black man makes my heart skip a beat. However, I live in Vancouver, Canada, where there are very few blacks. I have placed thirteen ads in local papers with no responses. I've thought of moving to some other part of the world where I'd have a better chance of success. Where do you think I should try? Since I'm HIV-positive, what countries would let me in?

A. New laws are always being passed regarding immigration and HIV antibody status. The Harvard School of Public Health says this rash of legislation is "unprecedented." About 45 percent of the countries that responded to their survey have discriminatory AIDS laws. America's policies are draconian. If you want to go someplace else, query that country's embassy about their policy.

You may have to stay where you are. You say there aren't many black men in Vancouver, but they do exist. It's very possible that personal contact will work a lot better than ads. When you're trying to cross a cultural or racial barrier, people want to check you out and make sure you're okay before they jump your bones.

You're within driving distance of Seattle, which has a large black community and many social opportunities for gay men. Spending an occasional weekend there would be a lot easier than changing your citizenship.

✍

Q. I'm a gay white male serving time in prison here in Illinois. I have no one to write to, and I've been using the personal columns in *The Advocate* to try and find someone caring enough to write back. I don't ask for money or anything. All I would like to have is a correspondence with someone. When I get out of here, I can travel anywhere in the U.S. of A.

I can't afford to place an ad. But I've answered a lot of them. I've had no response to any of my letters. Then I saw that warning about inmates taking advantage of gays. [Note: *The Advocate* runs a notice warning its readers to be cautious of financial scams run by inmates.]

Do you think that's why I get no responses to my letters? Like I said, I also am gay and I don't play games like that. I know there are people who do but they make it harder for people like me. What can I do?

A. It's a terrible thing to be lonely. It's possible that the warning, which recommends that readers throw away any mail they get from prisoners, made the people you wrote to reluctant to write back. But let's be real! You can't blame people for being cautious. It's reasonable to assume that if somebody is in prison, they did something wrong. If you want somebody to trust you, you'll have to prove yourself. Being defensive won't help. Check the resource list for organizations that help gay prisoners and papers that run free ads. There are a lot of gay men looking for companionship. I hope one of them will try being a prisoner's pen pal. Good luck to you!

✍

Q. Eight years ago I answered an ad in *The Advocate*. The man I wrote to was in prison at the time. I wrote to and visited him for four years, and when he was paroled I was there to meet him. We've been together ever since then, and I've never been sorry. I was never used in any sort of scam. I have a lover who is caring, and when he was out of work, worked harder getting a job than any other person I have ever known. He contributes every penny he makes to the household to make payments on my credit cards, keeps track of every penny we owe, knows exactly what we've paid in interest or doctor bills, and knows exactly what records to take to the tax people. I've never been so organized in my life, and I've never been happier. All because I answered an ad in *The Advocate* and started writing to a prisoner.

I'm aware that some prisoners are out to take advantage of people on the outside, and I guess I was lucky to find one that didn't take advantage of me. I also feel that it's unfair of you to judge all prisoners on the practices of a few.

A. Congratulations on your fine relationship. If you re-read my columns, I think you'll find that I don't say anywhere that *all* inmates are out to rip somebody off. You got to know your present partner by corresponding with him and visiting him for four years. He merited your trust enough to persuade you to wait for his parole. There's a big difference between that sort of courtship and the foolish chances some men take who are desperate for love. Too many gullible gay men fall prey to incarcerated con men who have come up with hard-luck stories calculated to extract cash from sympathetic correspondents. I've even had an elderly man beg me for the address of a prisoner who could (sight unseen) move into his home to keep him company when the inmate was released!

While many people in prison are eager to serve their time and "go straight," so to speak, let's not be naive enough to pretend that recidivism is not a big problem, or that some people are not too gullible to protect themselves. A prisoner who pretends to be surprised and hurt when non-inmates don't trust him has to be pulling my leg. Yeah, innocent people go to jail, but innocent or no, once you've done time, when you get out, you have to expect to prove yourself. I'm sure your lover didn't expect you to just pat him on the head and say, "There, there, nobody thinks bad of you." Without the hard work and scrupulous honesty he has shown, I doubt you would trust or love him. Nor should you.

Gay prisoners should get our help and support and an opportunity for a second chance, but it's no help to be presented with a big, fat temptation to fuck up again.

✍

Q. It's been a long time since I wanted to come out. Because my society doesn't accept gay life, I just kept everything to myself even though I've been wanting to be loved and love another man for many years.

The liberality of gay life in the U.S. made me dream of moving there, but when I started looking at gay ads all I could see is a white man looking for a white man too or a hunk looking for another hunk. This all the more discouraged me. Who would like an ordinary-looking Filipino who is not even average in his looks even if he is still a virgin at 40, even if he's looking 28 years old, even if he is the most honest, loyal, or true, monogamous man you could hope for?

A. Take a look at the resource list and check out some of the organizations that serve gay people of color. I get so many letters from men like you, who are older and looking for stable relationships, that I can't believe you couldn't meet the man of your dreams — regardless of the discrimination within the gay community — if you make yourself available. It isn't easy to meet new people. But if you make the effort to go out, join some groups, attend gay religious services, and smile, introduce yourself to people, make small talk, and be pleasant, you'll find that others respond. Very few gay people fit the stereotype that is making you feel inadequate.

You'll never be happy if you don't try to find what you know you really want. Isn't your happiness worth taking a few risks? Nobody can do this for you. But if you make a start, there will be people ready to welcome and help you.

✍

Q. I recently moved to another city and was relieved to discover it had a small but (apparently) congenial gay bar, where men and women mingled. The clientele included blacks as well as whites. I started dating a nice woman my own age who happens to be black. Suddenly, I find it much more difficult to get a table or get drinks. I thought I was making friends with local people, but now I feel like they're avoiding me. I'm afraid to discuss this with my new friend. What if I'm just imagining this? It just doesn't make sense to me.

A. I doubt this is all your imagination. Interracial relationships are still a big deal, even in the gay community. You're getting an education in how racism works. Unless you are the object of prejudice, you don't see it in operation — which gives most people in privileged groups the comfortable illusion that racism, sexism, homophobia, and other bigotry doesn't exist in their environment.

You'd better talk about this with your friend, soon, before she starts thinking she did something that put you uptight. She knows the community better than you do and can tell you if your dating is violating local mores. She can also introduce you to her friends. Hopefully you'll find people who will not be hostile to your new relationship.

If you've got the guts for it, pick the one person who was the friendliest to you, corner them, and demand to know what's going on. You might not like what you hear, but you'll find out where you stand.

And don't give in to the harassment. If the other gay people in town know you aren't going to repent or go sit in the back of the bus, there's a good chance the decent ones will get over their nonsense.

☞

Q. I don't make a big splash in the bars. I'm too shy to talk to strangers (getting drunk just makes me stutter), and I'm not gorgeous enough to motivate them to speak to me. I have a good job as a technical writer for a local banking firm, and I do some free-lance consulting on the side, but nobody seems to want to hear very much about my work. (A friend of mine once told me I was too much of a "computer nerd.") In a last-ditch effort to save my social life I volunteered for the fundraising committee of the gay hotline, but when they heard I had access to a computer, I was put in charge of the mailing list, which did not result in any hot dates.

Do you have any suggestions for me? I'm pleasant-appearing and a good listener. I like classical music and enjoy gourmet cooking on a modest scale at home. I have many straight friends, met primarily through work, who are very close and supportive, but I would really like to have a little more exciting contact with other gay men. If it's not too presumptuous of me, I'd even like to hope for romance and the chance to love someone special.

A. Since you're a "computer nerd" (what a classy phrase that is for a "friend" to use, about on a level with calling somebody "four-eyes"), I'm surprised that you haven't heard about BBSing. (A BBS is a computerized "bulletin board.") This is a great way to make contact with gay men who are a cut above the bar crowd. All you need is a modem (a device that lets computers talk to each other over the telephone lines) and a personal computer.

These systems range in complexity from boards that are only on-line a few hours every day and perhaps have only a few dozen users to 24-hour-a-day boards that have hundreds of subscribers and files of porn or other items of interest you can down-load, as well as lots of dishing, flirting, and cruising. The small boards are usually the personal hobby of a systems operator (sysop) and are free, but some of the larger boards charge a membership fee. In some areas, boards organize social events so members can meet in person as well as chatting on-line.

The only drawback is the long-distance phone bills, so try to find a system close to home. Being a sysop is not very difficult, especially for somebody with your level of computer skills; perhaps you'll eventually want to start your own board. See the resource list at the end of the book for more information.

✍

Q. I'm a handsome, muscular, all-American-looking, 28-year-old gay white male. I guess I could be called a "chubby chaser." I've always been attracted to ex-jocks who have put on a lot of weight. When I first came out and went to bars, if I pointed out a guy to my friends that I was interested in with larger than a 32-inch waist, they would tell me the guy was "fat and disgusting." I quickly became very uptight about pointing out when I was attracted to someone, because many were 300-plus pounds, and I could only imagine my friends' reactions.

I find it difficult to meet handsome fat guys in bars, but I have met some through personal ads. The problem is that I'm very hesitant to introduce these guys to my friends. I've "come out" about my interest in big guys to some friends, but they either don't believe it or assume I am talking about someone who is 18 pounds overweight. I don't think this prejudice against fat men is isolated to just my friends, either. I think it's very prevalent in the gay male community.

How do I have a fulfilling relationship with a fat man and at the same time feel comfortable including him in activities with my friends, just like they include their thin lovers in activities with me? By the way, most of the "friends" I refer to are intelligent, successful, and very educated people.

A. Once we've braved the scorn of the straight world to "come out," we're so terrified of not belonging in our own minority group that we become even more conformist than the most rigid, born-again homophobe. What are you supposed to do, I wonder?

Have sex with thin men who don't turn you on just because that would look right? If the emphasis is going to be on looking right, why be queer? I think you need a different set of friends, some who are more concerned about whether or not you're happy than whether or not you and your lover can wear the same-size shirts.

And I don't want to hear any blather from you borderline anorexics about how "unhealthy" it is to be fat. The contempt, hatred, ridicule, and discrimination that are heaped on fat people (and their friends and lovers) are so stressful that the net effect probably equals or exceeds any negative physical effects from fat alone.

Fat people who were accepted would be a lot happier and healthier than fat people who are stigmatized. Nobody knows why some people weigh more than others. Sometimes it's diet, sometimes it's metabolism, sometimes it's genetics. But for damn sure nobody ever lost weight because they hated themselves. And if you think all it takes is self-control to turn a fat person into a thin one, honey, I want to hear how many days *you* could go in a row feeling hungry every minute and defensive every time you had anything to eat besides a salad.

A wise old auntie with love handles out to Amarillo once told me, "Inside every thin person there is a fat person screaming to get out." Doesn't it rankle to see somebody who doesn't keep themselves on the short leash of public opinion, especially if that person looks like they have fun and great sex, too?

So — you handsome, muscular, all-American-looking 28-year-old gay white male! Yes, you! Get away from these brittle gym-queens and write or call the nearest club for big or heavy gay men and their admirers, listed in the resource guide. These clubs were formed to provide a place for fat men to meet the men who find them attractive and socialize away from the petty, bitchy attitude of fairies who are skinnier than their dicks.

And once you find yourself a boyfriend, or even just a hot fuck, reader of mine, you love and cherish that man and take him wherever you go. And if somebody can't be nice to him, cut that person out of your life. They may know your name, they may know your phone number, but I got their number, and they are *not* your friend.

✍

Q. I'm a man in my late 30s with very little sexual experience with men and no real feel for proper gay etiquette. A few weeks ago in a bookstore (nongay) I was cruised by a man I found extremely attractive, a first-time experience for me. I didn't know how to respond and eventually left the store, but he was very persistent, following me down the block and across the street to my bus stop. After about five minutes of him standing eight feet away, gazing intently at me and smiling, I gathered up my courage, walked over to him, and started a conversation.

We talked a long time (I let five buses go by that I could have taken home), and enough personal information was exchanged that both of us had to know the other is gay. I found him even more attractive intellectually than physically. However, I didn't really know what was "proper" or "expected" of me in this situation. I found an excuse to give him an outdated business card that has my name and unlisted phone number. As soon as he had my name and number, he told me his first name, said he was late for an appointment, and left. It's been three and a half weeks and I don't really expect to hear from him now, but I have some questions for future reference.

Does it sound as if I did or said anything out of line? Did I not do something? Should I have asked him for his number? What would be my reason? (We are in Utah, after all.) If I ever run into him downtown again, what would be proper? I'm planning on striking up a conversation and inviting him for coffee or a beer.

A. If you were in an adult bookstore (or even if you weren't, come to think of it, in Utah) the man who cruised you was probably looking for quick, anonymous sex — either in a movie cubicle or in your car, possibly at your house.

You didn't do anything out of line, you just misunderstood his intentions. If you were in a mood to have sex, you should have moved to a more secluded part of the bookstore and made your bod available, or if you were both outside, suggested a walk in the park, sitting in your car, or taking a taxi back to your apartment.

You told him that you were *not* looking for sex on the spot by giving him your name and phone number. Since he responded with no more than a first name, it would have been inappropriate for you to request his phone number. You had already given him sufficient opening to increase the intimacy of the interaction, and he rejected it, but in a way that was intended to communicate he liked you and was attracted to you.

If you run into him again, he may or may not again be in the mood for a bout of anonymous sex. If you want to trick with him, you have to move the interaction to a location where that can take place while protecting his (and your) anonymity. Don't forget to take a rubber or two with you!

If that is not your cup of Postum, by all means invite him out for something to drink. If he accepts and you take him to a bar, chances are he will talk to you for a while, then fade away again. But if you can persuade him to have a drink at your place, he might put something tastier than a cup of imitation coffee in your hand.

✍

Q. The problem that I need help in rectifying is one that we are all born with: virginity. Having concealed and suppressed my sexual longings for twenty-one years, I am unable to go through with sex whenever the opportunity arises.

At the risk of sounding vain, it's my nice looks that are inducing this difficulty. I'm not egotistical, but am embarrassed that I'm inexperienced. Being a six-foot-five masculine virgin is keeping me a virgin. The majority of my friends are not gay, and this leaves me with no one to turn to. Can you offer any words of wisdom?

A. Yes. Quit standing around thinking about how tall and handsome you are and start telling the hot-looking men around you how tall and handsome *they* are!

You say you are "unable to go through with sex whenever the opportunity arises." Does this mean that other men have approached you, and you've rejected them? Well, quit saying no! Or does this mean you're too shy to be able to approach others? If the bar scene is too overwhelming, call the local gay hotline and ask them what activities are available to help you meet other gay men.

A lot of us lose our virginity at age twenty-one or even later. Don't make such a big deal out of it. Doing it once isn't going to make you any good at it, anyway. That takes practice, practice, practice. And don't forget to use condoms on your first date, or I'll be even meaner to you than I'm being right now.

Don't be mad, honey — somebody has to push baby birds out of the nest or they'll never learn how to fly.

✍

Q. This is not a question as much as it is advice to others. For nearly a whole year, one of my coworkers (an attractive lady my own age) kept asking me to go out to lunch with her or stop after work for a cocktail and snack. Because I assumed she was heterosexual and was afraid of mixing my private life with my job, I always found one excuse or another to say no. Eventually she changed jobs, and I lost all contact with her.

Last week, I ran into her at the bar. She was dancing with another woman. She recognized me, and when the song was over, she came over and introduced her friend. After this woman excused herself to get us all drinks, my ex-coworker told me that she was very happy with her new lover, but she regretted the fact that I had never accepted her invitations when we were working for the same company and she was single.

I explained that I refused to go out with her because I thought she was straight. "What difference does that make?" she said. "I was being friendly. You can't have too many friends. And who knows what a friendship will develop into?"

I went home alone, as I often do, and the more I thought about it, the more I knew that she was right. I wonder how many other potentially rewarding relationships I've missed out on. We really *are* everywhere.

A. We do have some good reasons to be wary of people who aren't gay. Job discrimination is a reality. And one painful experience with unrequited love will teach most lesbians to avoid emotional entanglements with straight women. But this understandable attempt to protect ourselves can easily turn into a pattern of isolation and even paranoia. Thanks for writing. Better luck with the next "attractive lady your own age" who asks you out to lunch or cocktails.

✍

Q. I have a few comments about the personal ads in *The Advocate* and other publications. I've been in a gay relationship for over three years now. I personally don't think that's very long; however, in the gay world that seems to be quite a long-term relationship.

Some of the ads wanting relationships are unbelievable, such as ads about long evenings in front of the fireplace, cuddling in front of the TV after a long day at work, and now the big one seems to be "negative on the HIV antibody test"! We've had our nights in front of the fireplace and everywhere else in our apartment. But let's get a little realistic here. If this is all people are looking for it doesn't surprise me that gay relationships seem to be short-term.

There are those times when he can't stand your favorite meal, or when you're horny as hell and he's not (or vice versa). He has to work unexpectedly when you've cooked a good dinner for him, or you have to work over the weekend to repair the budget one of you

26

destroyed the month before buying something you really didn't need.

There are the times when he has to go out of town on a business trip for a week, and you think it sure would be nice to go to the baths and get fucked by someone different for a change (with a rubber, of course), but you don't because you don't want to hurt him.

And how about the times when you find out just how well the brakes in the car work because he's driving and sees someone walking down the street with a big basket and no shirt? Then you think he's having a heart attack, and you would swear that you were going to drown in the drool!

Then there's the plain, old-fashioned fight. I've been lucky. Neither one of us are yellers.

I really think I'm fortunate, because we met before the AIDS crisis was so widely reported, so I know that wasn't a factor in our deciding to become lovers. Since AIDS started getting the attention it deserves, I've noticed the ads for relationships have dramatically increased. I honestly believe that if two people are getting together out of fear of AIDS or out of convenience the relationship hasn't got a snowball's chance in hell. A lasting relationship takes a lot of work, patience, and acceptance on both sides. It takes an honest commitment, and people going into a relationship out of fear or convenience will be unable to make that kind of commitment.

There have been times when my lover has had the flu and I've waited on him hand and foot, not because I expect him to do the same for me when I'm sick (which by the way he has done), but because I've made a commitment to him that, God willing, will be for the rest of my life, and also because I love him and care about him more than anything else.

I wouldn't trade a moment of the time I've spent with my lover for anything else. Every moment is that special to me. I believe that's what makes a relationship work, not if you both are HIV-negative!

A. And thank *you* for a beautiful, accurate description of what it takes to keep the man of your dreams dreaming about you. The most frequent question I am asked is, "Why can't I find a lover?" You, sir, have answered it for me.

Relationships

Q. My lover and I have been living together for about two years and together nearly five. I really get into a great porn mag and a hot J/O session with myself now and again. My lover thinks this is awful, a sign that our sex life must not satisfy me. I've told him he's wrong and that our sex life is fantastic, but all I get is a sulk. I no longer do it when he's home or likely to arrive, 'cause I don't want to hurt him, but somehow I feel this is ridiculous. It's like listening for Mom's footsteps when I was 12 and the lights were out!

A. I sympathize. After two blissful decades of being a dyke (ahem), I'm still not sure which event requires more diplomacy — introducing a new lover to my family, or introducing a new lover to my vibrator. They never seem to think it's funny when I tell them they are better than a vibrator because I can take them anywhere without worrying about extension cords or batteries. It takes them about a year to believe that the Panabrator is going to stay plugged in by my pillow, and I am going to stay plugged into them. I just keep saying over and over again, "Masturbation is not better than sex with you, it's just different, but I still like it and want to be able to do it without feeling guilty. When did *you* stop masturbating?" (If they actually tell me they have, I start wondering what else they've been lying about.) I know I'm making some progress if: (a) I come home and find the vibrator lying in the middle of the bed, still warm, or (b) they let me watch while they get themselves off, or (c) we do it together and tell each other dirty stories or have a race.

Tell your lover he should start worrying if you *quit* masturbating, since that would indicate a lack of interest in sex in general. If you can't make yourself come, for damn sure nobody else is going to be able to get you off! Encourage him to join you or take his own time to enjoy his own body. Gently remind him that if he wants to keep your sex life hot, it would be wise not to remind you of your mother.

✍

Q. My lover is perfect in nearly every way — so perfect, in fact, that we've bought a house together, something I would *not* have done if our relationship was not completely stable. But lately he's taken to going back to church. He's going to mass at least once a week. This is especially irritating on weekends when I want to work on our house. It needs a lot of renovation. He's asked me to go with him a couple of times, but I've refused. Like him, I was raised Catholic, but it's clear to me the church has nothing but contempt for gay people, so it is no longer a part of my life. How can I get him out of the church and back to installing skylights?

A. Aren't you curious about why your lover has renewed interest in the faith of his childhood? Instead of fussing about the time he's wasting, ask him why he feels a need to attend church and what he gets out of it. Some gay people find, after waging bitter battles for independence and self-acceptance, that they still need some contact with certain aspects of their back-ground. Many Catholics who do not agree with the pope's sexual politics attend church with a good conscience. Your lover may simply be reaffirming who he is, refusing to be cut off from his family or his ethnic identity just because he's gay.

The need for spiritual solace and insight is understandable. Go to church with him at least once, simply to show you love and accept him. If you can't bring yourself to make it a regular event, at least accept his need to go. If there is a local congregation of MCC, perhaps you would feel more comfortable attending an ecumenical, gay-positive service.

✍

Q. The last time my lover had to work late at the office, I was doing some odds and ends of cleaning that usually get put off indefinitely. I came across one of those books full of blank pages, with a fabric cover. Only these pages were not blank. They were covered with my lover's handwriting. I had no idea that she kept a journal, and I was so surprised to recognize the handwriting that I somehow kept on reading it.

29

I've always assumed that the six years we've been together were happy ones. We've had periods of turmoil and conflict, but have always managed to compromise. I love her very much. But after reading her journal, I'm no longer sure that she loves me.

What can I do? I didn't go snooping deliberately. I was not spying on her. Since I found that damned diary and read it, she's noticed I'm withdrawn and irritable. She keeps asking me what the matter is. I feel as if I have a thousand questions I want to blurt out, but I'm afraid that if I do, she won't understand that it's not my fault that I obtained access to her hidden doubts and distress.

A. I'll forget everything I know about the power of the unconscious and let your statement that you "did not go snooping deliberately" pass unchallenged. However, the moment that you realized what you held in your hands *and kept reading anyway* was the moment you did, indeed, begin to spy on your lover. The only thing that's making you mind your tongue is the fear that she will understand only too well how you obtained the information that's making you uneasy.

That journal might be her safety valve — the place where she vents troubling thoughts that would be destructive to air with you. If that's the purpose it serves, you can hardly use it as an objective index for her feelings toward you. In any relationship, no matter how close it is, people have separate thoughts and different internal experiences of the events they share. Without that separation, one's sense of self vanishes. It would be cruel to expect your mate to experience partnership with you as bliss and sunshine every single minute of every single day.

The fact that you can't shrug this off indicates that *you* are having some doubts about the relationship. If you can clarify those and express them, that might make a useful starting point for a discussion. But once this gets started, it will probably be impossible for you to keep to yourself the fact that you read her diary and feel betrayed by what she said in it. It's barely possible that she hoped you would read it because it expresses opinions she can't voice directly. If so, maybe she can forgive you for violating her privacy. But I wouldn't count on it. So have the number of a couples counselor handy before you swallow hard and tell her to sit down so you can have a nice, long talk.

✍

Q. I moved in with my boyfriend after getting intense pressure from him and many promises that he would do everything to make me happy. I must admit, we get along better than I thought we would. Never having lived with a lover, I imagined I would feel crowded and claustrophobic. But I like having meals together, seeing more of him, etc. And of course it's nice to be able to cut back on expenses like the rent.

I knew I had some problems with allergies. In the past I've controlled this with over-the-counter antihistamines. But a few days after moving in I began to get severe attacks of shortness of breath. I believe it's due to living with a heavy smoker. He chain-smokes several packs of very rank cigarettes a day. I do not have problems breathing until he gets home from work in the evening.

I've told him about my fears, but he says I'm just being silly and nagging him. He's told me firmly there is no way he can ever quit smoking, he's just too addicted and needs it for his nerves. Do you think he loves his tobacco more than he loves me?

A. You need to see a doctor to get appropriate testing, diagnosis, and treatment for this problem. Your doctor might recommend allergy testing to make sure it's the cigarettes that are giving you problems — not pets, fungus, certain foods, etc. If it turns out that your lover's cigarettes are causing your asthma attacks, ask the doctor to explain this to him. If your lover hears a medical authority say that you are not making this up, he'll have a harder time denying there's a problem. And he may be more willing to quit smoking.

Asthma sometimes has a psychosomatic component. If you already have the condition, anxiety or stress can trigger it. Perhaps your body is expressing some problems with living with someone else. But it hardly matters, since you can't "will" an asthma attack away. If you're really this allergic to tobacco, either the cigarettes go, or you'll have to.

I feel sorry for your boyfriend because it really is tough to quit smoking. But several packs a day can't be good for his lungs (or his nerves, for that matter). Since he hasn't been able to quit for the sake of his own health, I hope he can abandon the evil weed for the sake of yours — not to mention preserving the domestic bliss of your new and happy home.

✍

Q. Most lesbians around here spend all their free time in the bar or have no social life at all. I never questioned it before. But recently I got involved with someone who I think has a drinking problem. I would like to spend some quiet evenings at home or go bowling, see a movie — anything but sitting at the same old table, guzzling beer, listening to the same songs on the jukebox over and over again, having the same conversations with the same old crowd. But my lover always claims it's "too much trouble" or she's "too tired." The last time we had a discussion about this, I told her it was a good thing the bar is within walking distance of her apartment, because she could never drive home. Well, it turns out she lost her license earlier this year for drunk driving!

The last time we were there, she wound up getting into a fight with some guy who wandered in and made a silly comment to her. We both got eighty-sixed from the bar. So maybe she'll listen to me now if I tell her I honestly wonder if she's an alcoholic. But how do you tell? She says it's just that the bar is the only place where she can be her true, gay self.

A. You need more information about Alcoholics Anonymous, Al-Anon, and Adult Children of Alcoholics. Check the resource guide for the addresses and telephone numbers of these organizations as well as other information about substance abuse.

Here's a list of questions someone can ask themselves to decide whether they are abusing alcohol (or any other drug).

1. Do you drink in the morning to get over the night before?
2. Do you have memory lapses or blackouts from drinking?
3. Do you find drinking affecting your work (for example, do you "call in sick" when you really have a hangover)?
4. Do you say "I'll have just one" and find that you can't?
5. Have you ever tried to stop drinking and found that difficult?
6. Do you drink to feel important, to relax, to solve problems?
7. Do you look for excuses to drink?
8. Have you ever stolen alcohol or stolen money to buy it?
9. Have you ever lost a job or a relationship because of drinking?
10. Do you find yourself drinking before a party or another event where you know there will be no alcohol?

If your lover won't listen to you, go to some twelve-step meetings by yourself and learn how you can stop helping her to be an alcoholic. She may never admit that she has a problem. But the fact that it bothers you means something is wrong. It may seem cruel to stop accompanying her when she goes out drinking, stop nursing her through hangovers, stop getting her out of trouble or making excuses for her. But that may get her to confront the problem. And it's the only way to keep it from becoming *your* problem.

$Q.$ I think my lover is turning into a workaholic. She always was very industrious and ambitious, never turned down overtime, etc. But since she got promoted to manager I hardly ever see her! When she does come home, she brings work with her. On weekends, she gets calls from the plant. I've tried to talk about this with her, but she says she has to work ten times as hard as a man to be half as successful. I'm getting worried about her. If I ask what she had for lunch she usually doesn't remember if she ate or not! We've postponed our vacation twice because "emergencies" came up that nobody else could handle. How can this much stress and overwork be good for somebody? Or for our relationship?

$A.$ Your lover is displaying a pattern not uncommon among professional women. There's a grain of truth in her statement about "having to work ten times as hard as a man to be half as successful" that makes it difficult to argue with her. I'm sure she's experienced enough discrimination and condescension to make her feel that she has to do this. Unfortunately, an employer will usually take as much from his or her employees as they can be cajoled or coerced into giving. A promotion is no compensation for an ulcer, a wrecked relationship, or being a worn-out husk by the time you retire.

Your partner has lost her perspective about what is a reasonable (or realistic) standard for job performance. She actually risks doing worse, not better, because people inevitably get tired when they overwork, then they make mistakes, which they then have to correct, which creates more exhaustion and more mistakes.

The problem is, how are you going to get her to listen? Do you have friends whose professional standing and judgment she respects? If so, have a talk with them, then invite them over for dinner, with the understanding that they will comment that your lover looks "under the weather." Give them space for a private talk about it.

It could also be that your lover is worried about maintaining a standard of living for you. Since you don't mention your own work, I don't know if she is supporting you or if the two of you split all expenses neatly in half. You might need to throw a minor tantrum, pull down some drapes, and tell her that material comfort doesn't mean as much to you as her health and happiness.

Overwork is a way to avoid other problems — a fear of getting old, sexual incompatibility or absence of interest in sex, anger at

33

parents for being inadequate providers, fear of being replaced by a competitor in the workplace, inability to delegate responsibility, repression of dislike for the job and of an urge to try something new and less secure, etc. Your lover sounds like somebody who doesn't express her feelings easily. It's a pain, but since she really does need to talk, for her own good, you must insist that she put all her papers back into her briefcase, turn off her beeper, and unburden her heart.

At a bare minimum, put your foot down about her bringing work home, postponing vacations, or getting calls at home. Even doctors don't do that any more — they have an answering service that can refer emergencies to another physician who is on call. If the place where she works operates twenty-four hours a day, seven days a week, she should delegate someone to handle things when she's not there. If she's that ambitious, I'm sure she wants to be promoted again, and the successful manager is always training her successor.

✍️

Q. I've been with my present mate for over five years. We were just able to move in together the last year. My lover has become increasingly despondent over the fact that I sleep in my bedroom, he in his. When we went shopping for an apartment, there was never any discussion over the fact that we'd get a two-bedroom unit. I think two adults need the space. We work together so the time apart, I believe, becomes even more important.

About a month ago, I agreed to try sleeping with him on a weekly basis — one night a week — to start. The first time out was largely sleepless for me because he snores amazingly loudly, and it took me about a day to recover. The subsequent two nights, I was really tired or had a headache, so I took sleeping pills. He began to hint about accelerating the process. Last night, one night before our agreed-upon night of tandem slumber bliss, he got very angry because I wouldn't sleep with him. I thought it was unfair of him to ask to move things up a night.

Am I being a monster? All our friends not only sleep together, but intertwined. I've told him that's a physical impossibility for me. I turn a lot and can't believe I wouldn't be cramped horribly. I do believe that eventually I can learn to sleep with another person from time to time.

I've known many couples that have separate sleeping arrangements. It works out just fine. I can't believe that our relationship can be wrapped up so tightly in the fact that we must be together while we're both unconscious.

34

Is it a personality disorder if someone *has* to have someone to sleep with, making that person — in my opinion — little more than a human substitute for the teddy bear they slept with as a child?

A. I don't understand how you and this other man could be lovers for five years without realizing that you had a conflict over this. Before you lived together, what happened when you finished fucking? Did he go home? Sleep on the couch? Or were you able to sleep with him as long as the two of you weren't roommates?

Most people assume that if a sexual partner cares deeply for them, that person will sleep with them. If you have sex with someone and don't sleep with him or her, the implication is that you have turned indifferent or hostile to the object of your lust. You can't possibly be ignorant of this. If you wanted your relationship to be the exception to this rule, you should have said something to your mate before you signed the lease.

Don't get me wrong — I have known a few loving couples who don't sleep together. This is especially true if one of them snores like a freight train or is a very light, restless sleeper. I personally would rather sleep alone most of the time. Everybody needs different amounts of privacy, time alone, and "air space" around their body. It's impossible to change something as personal and fundamental as this just to keep a lover. You can grit your teeth and try, but you will resent it bitterly, and resentment is the death of passion.

It would be great if your lover could see this and save the relationship by giving up his need to have your unconscious companionship. But he would surely resent doing without an experience he needs and feels entitled to receive. Martyr, martyr, who's the martyr?

This is the kind of thing that gets people pissed off enough to break up. Maybe some couples counseling is in order. It might help your lover to accept the compromise that you are offering — to try to learn to sleep comfortably with him some of the time. (Incidentally, was this offer sincere, or was it a ploy to prove that it really is impossible for you to sleep in his bed?) You need to find out if your lover really wants to turn you into a human teddy bear, with no choice about how you are used or handled. *That* accusation has implications that reach far beyond the Land of Nod.

✍

Q. About two months ago I finally found Mr. Right. Shortly after meeting and falling in love, we decided to get the HIV test at the public health department in our town together. We talked about a monogamous relationship, which is what we both want. We expected to both test negative, and then we'd never have to worry about AIDS.

We had sex together many times before the test. When the results came back, I was positive, and he was negative. The nurse explained that he would probably turn positive in a few months as it wouldn't show up in a month after exposure.

I feel awful that I could have infected him. The incredible thing is that he still loves me and says he still wants to move in with me and have our relationship. I want that more than anything, but I'm worried. Should we start taking precautions with each other? If he tests positive next month would it be necessary to use rubbers with each other? If he's still negative, I'm afraid I'll infect him. I'd make any sacrifice to keep him.

A. I'm not saying this to dump on you. But for the benefit of other readers who could avoid having this happen to them, let me remind everybody that true love does not protect you from STDs. Neither does being young and handsome and sleeping only with other young and handsome men. Even if you meet somebody you'd like to be monogamous with, unless you're both virgins who have never used IV drugs, you should have safe sex. Use rubbers.

Most health experts would recommend that the two of you start having safer sex. It's possible that your lover was not infected with the virus. You should have safe sex even if both of you test positive because some researchers believe that *repeated* exposure to HIV can cause full-blown AIDS to develop. Further, if your immune system is weakened, you don't want to be exposed to anything else the other person might have. Some microorganisms that can be present in a healthy person's body without ill effect will make an immune-deficient person get sick.

No one's done any research to find out how many couples who are both HIV-positive do, in fact, practice safer sex. That's too bad, because it would be helpful to know if abandoning safer sex has any significant impact on their health. I would guess that a lot of HIV-positive couples don't bother to use condoms. The potential, hypothetical dangers can seem very distant when compared to the consolation offered by uncomplicated, straightforward sex without latex barriers. And I can't honestly say I condemn anyone for making this decision. People in this situation should get the most up-to-date medical advice they can find, talk it over, and make their own choice.

Of course your partner still loves you! I'm glad his response to the test results was so reasonable. It would have been tragic if he'd abandoned an opportunity for a good relationship just because your test came back positive. Good luck to the both of you. I hope the home you're making together will be a happy, enduring one.

✍

Q. Recently I met a fellow who had placed an ad in the personal section of a local paper. He stated he was HIV-positive. I'm HIV-negative. After meeting we seemed to have much in common, and I hoped I might have met someone with whom to establish a relationship. From the start I made it clear the HIV results meant nothing to me. We could contend with that. Soon, however, my kind friend began to worry about infecting me, became distant, and finally decided that he would rather not pursue a relationship. Apart from the concern he has for my safety, everything was perfect. How can I help him overcome his fears? I respect his caution and concern, but my love for him is not diminished by the presence of that damned virus.

A. In an age where some PWAs die indigent and homeless because their lovers have abandoned them, a letter like yours is simply amazing.

It's very hard to talk about sex, especially in the context of a life-threatening illness. Perhaps you and your friend have not been completely honest with each other. Maybe he was hoping to find someone else who was HIV-positive, because he thought it would then be acceptable to dispense with "safer sex." Or perhaps he's not completely comfortable with whatever precautions the two of you have been taking. He may have been reluctant to burden you by asking you to go to even more trouble and limit the sex you were having even further. Or he may be using his HIV status as an excuse to end the relationship when there's another problem he doesn't want to discuss.

People who are frightened often withdraw. Make a concerted and firm effort to get him to talk to you. Isolating himself will not solve his problems. Even if he doesn't feel comfortable being sexual with anyone, he needs love and support in his life, and should not cut himself off from your friendship.

✍

Q. I'm involved with a very wealthy man, and initially I was really flattered by his attention and generosity. But at times I feel like he's trying to buy me. I feel like I can't measure up as I have not been nearly as successful in my own life. I also feel bad because I can't buy him the kind of expensive presents he gives me.

The gossip among our friends seems to be, what could he possibly see in me? We've been dating two years and have been talking about living together. I'm afraid that he'll eventually get tired of me and find someone prettier or younger, and by living with him, I'll become accustomed to a lifestyle I can't maintain on my own.

My lover was fairly experienced when we met, and he was the eighth man I ever slept with. Before him, the longest I was ever involved with another man was a brief four-month affair. We dated eight months before we slept together. At first the sex wasn't all that great. I was aroused by him and would have an erection, but I couldn't come. But I think that was just nerves because now this man has me coming like crazy.

He wants to pay for a nicer apartment for me and eventually buy me a condo as well as a fancier car, which he would register in my name. At first he wanted me to move in with him, but I made a fuss about it being *his* house, so now he wants to buy a new house that will be *ours* and in both of our names, though he'll buy it. He says this should prove how much he loves me because I'll have some protection should we eventually go our separate ways. For a while he wanted me to quit my job. But I won't, although it's not the greatest job.

Somehow I've avoided his giving me these major purchases, but he has given me clothes, a stereo, a VCR, and jewelry. My gifts to him have been more modest. Once I sent him a bouquet of roses at work, and when I saw him later that night he just melted all over me. No one had ever sent him flowers before. We both called in sick the next day and had to stay in bed, together of course.

My friends all tell me how lucky I am. Do you think my nagging doubts are valid?

A. Jealous people *will* make bitchy remarks about happy couples. It sounds to me like you and your lover are good together. I hope you won't jeopardize that by letting their catty comments make you insecure.

When two people love each other and there's a big difference in their incomes, it's very hard to strike the right balance. He shouldn't have to pretend he's poor, but you shouldn't start pretending you're rich, either. I think you've done the right thing by accepting some gifts (after all, we all want to give presents to people we love) and refusing to let him encourage you to live beyond your means.

Getting a home together would upset this delicate balance. If you want to live together, you'll have to renegotiate everything. Be cautious about simply letting him buy both of you a new house. This is not just a romantic decision, it's a business decision, so treat it that way. If the house is going to be in both your names, you should contribute something — part of the down payment, some of the mortgage, or work on the property. See an attorney and get all your financial agreements in writing.

There's no dishonor in letting someone who cares about you help you build a better career and a secure future. Instead of just quitting your mediocre job, why not let him help you go to school? Then you could have a career or profession you'd be proud of, and buy *him* a VCR. Most wealthy people have money because somebody who loved them (i.e., their families) shared resources with them and taught them how to protect their capital and increase it. Gay people are entitled to do the same for members of our gay families.

If your lover lost all of his money tomorrow, would you stop loving him? Would you let him starve? If your answer is no, relax and enjoy him.

✍

Q. Four years ago, I met Mr. Right, and we fell in love. After a few months, I moved in with him. We have a good time sexually and as companions and lifemates. When we agreed to live together, we agreed to split rent and utilities proportionally to our income, because he made a lot more money than I did. Before moving in with him, I had a small apartment and was saving up for a starter house. My friend had lots of nice furniture, a very large rental house, likes to eat out and spend money, basically living from paycheck to paycheck. On the other hand, I like to read, cook, and in general take better care of my money. I'm still adding slowly to my savings with the idea of getting a house one day.

About six months ago, my lover lost his job, and although he found work again quickly, he's not earning as much as he was. My share of the rent has thus gone up. I've suggested I buy us a house with my savings. We've even looked at a few, but my lover thinks they're too small. He doesn't want to give up his extra space, nice furniture, or social lifestyle. He's still looking for better work while he's got this "filler" job. Meanwhile, I'm living a little beyond my means, and don't want to keep it up and dip into my savings for more than a year or so. Frankly, I think that although he may find better than he's got now, it is unlikely he'll be making what he once was any time soon.

How do I get my partner to listen to some financial planning?

A. It's foolish to pay rent if you can afford to buy a house, any house. Why not make an appointment with your accountant and your lover specifically for the purpose of doing some financial planning? He might listen to an expert more readily than he listens to you. If he won't see someone for this purpose, talk to him about getting wills drawn up. This is a good opening for a serious conversation about your future.

You're not being selfish. Your thrifty nature and your desire to provide for the two of you are laudable. But buying a house together is a difficult process for most couples. You have to take both people's needs into account and compromise. If your lover really needs to buy a larger house, perhaps there's some way to afford this. You could look at property in a different part of town or consider a house that needs more work before it can be resold. You may not be able to afford something as lavish as his heart's desire, but if it does nothing else, looking at bigger places will demonstrate concretely to him what is possible and what is not. If the price for living in a bigger house is replacing the roof, stripping and refinishing the floors, putting in new plumbing, and doing a lot of other heavy work, he may decide it's easier to sell some of his furniture and cozy up with you.

✍

Q. Five years ago, knowing that I cannot have them both, I chose the man over the woman I promised to marry. He is sincere, affectionate, and very caring. When I made this decision, I only did it for a try (to feel the difference). Now I am the prisoner of his love and devotion, but I have no complaint except sex. He is less aggressive and responsive than he used to be. I am the horny one — a sex maniac, he says. Yet I cannot cheat or hurt this man. How can I make him ask to make love with me again like it used to be? He always does it to himself, all alone, and I get silently angry, jealous, and feel like he doesn't need me any more.

A. The sexual tension often seems to leave long-term relationships. When two people make each other feel very comfortable and safe, perversely enough, they may no longer be turned on to each other. When you're with someone for a while, it's difficult to avoid accumulating resentment. Being quietly angry all the time makes people feel like putting distance between themselves and their lover.

Some couples are happy to leave matters this way because they hate the anxiety of pursuing new partners or introducing their current partner to new techniques and fantasies. They would rather have an orderly life than a life full of sexual frenzy. Perhaps your lover is one of these folks. If so, there's little or nothing you can do to change things. If you want mad, passionate sex, you'll have to take all the responsibility for initiating sex and making it hot. Of course, this is bound to make you feel overworked and unloved. Eventually you'll burn out and stop trying. Both partners need to cooperate if sex is going to remain interesting.

Sit down with your lover and ask him if he's satisfied with the way things are going. It would be helpful if the two of you could calmly exchange your views on the relationship without fighting. If you have trouble discussing this alone, a counselor might help you listen to each other.

Your lover is probably not the only one who is responsible here. It sounds like you are harboring some resentment about the way this relationship began and feeling trapped, even if it is by his "love and devotion." It's also kind of strange that you're jealous because he jerks off. Everybody needs some time alone to pleasure themselves. Masturbation is a reassuring and relaxing activity that most people need in addition to having sex with another person. If he doesn't have enough privacy in this relationship to bring himself off without you getting huffy about it, things must be pretty claustrophobic around your house. That kind of pressure doesn't make anybody feel sexy.

This may be a cultural difference, and perhaps there are other differences that are keeping you apart. He shouldn't be making you feel like a "sex maniac" because you still desire and pursue him.

Obviously the two of you love each other very much. Get butch with this boy and make him take this problem more seriously. If he won't talk to you, a potentially great partnership will go down the drain. It would be so much more fun to start sharing your sexual fantasies, go shopping for some toys or erotic clothes, and rent some porn to give each other new ideas than it would be to pack up and move out.

✍

Q. I'm a 36-year-old gay male. Five years ago, after living the classically gay lifestyle, I decided to get married (to a woman) because of a strong desire to have children — something that always seemed to get in the way of my gay relationships. My wife knew of my sexuality before we were married, but it didn't make a difference. We now have two happy, healthy toddlers.

Two years ago, however, I met Rick. After three years of marriage, I needed male companionship. Publicly, to our friends, both gay and straight, my wife, and our families, we are the best of friends, but privately we share a wonderfully romantic, physical relationship. Rick, like me, has had gay relationships end because he isn't ready to give up the prospect of his own family. In fact, I've been helping him to find someone — a female — to raise a family with. So far it all sounds perfect, right?

Well, to my surprise, I was severely criticized by many of my gay friends for marrying, and when the kids came along, most of them dropped out of sight! Rick is now experiencing the same problem. It seems that we are no longer considered to be part of the gay community because of our choices. We're not "really gay" if we're not hopping in and out of bed. Granted, no one is aware of my relationship with Rick, but that shouldn't matter.

It would seem to me that in this age of AIDS and the search for a monogamous relationship, Rick and I have found a solution — albeit at the expense of criticism from those around us. Are we kidding ourselves, or is it really possible to have the best of both worlds?

A. The type of marriage that you describe was probably much more common fifty years ago. Then, there was nothing remarkable about a gay man getting married and having a family. However, there wasn't much of an organized gay community then, and modern gay liberation hadn't been invented. Society does us a grave injustice by making it so difficult for gay people to sustain their loving partnerships, and by making it well-nigh impossible for us to raise children. It grieves me to know that children are being institutionalized when so many of us are eager and able to provide good homes. Some gay men and lesbians will continue to enter into heterosexual marriages until we can marry our same-sex lovers and raise children with them.

While I don't think what you're doing is wrong or bad, neither does this situation sound "perfect" to me. You're telling yourself (and your wife) a few lies that make me uneasy.

If your wife accepts your homosexuality, why haven't you told her about Rick? Do you really think it's reasonable to expect your gay friends to continue to treat you like a gay man when you are married, have children, and they don't know about your male lover? You aren't being kicked out of the gay community. You left it. And please don't try to tell me you're being monogamous. I doubt that your wife would view your relationship with Rick as "a solution" to AIDS.

It isn't uncommon for straight men to compartmentalize their emotional and sexual lives, dividing their time between a wife and casual sex with a mistress or paid professionals. Maintaining this kind of dishonesty and separation takes a toll. It's tiring, and it means that you are not fully intimate with anyone. I wonder how long Rick will be willing to put up with being your secret lover. The thought of him deceiving another woman the way you're deceiving your wife makes me very angry. Rick's wife would think she was the emotional center of his universe when in fact she'd be just a facade that made it easier for the two of you to remain lovers. Women ought not to be used as breeding machines or windbreaks in the homophobic storm.

I think your wife is entitled to know the truth about Rick. Rick deserves more than a shadow life and stolen moments with you. Your wife may be able to accept the fact that she must share you. Or she may want to end the relationship. But continuing as you are would be wrong.

✍

Q. I have, without really trying, found myself in a situation that must be fairly unique among lesbians. I have two lovers. They're very different women physically and emotionally, but I care about them both equally and cherish my time with each of them. They know about each other (and like each other), and thus far, this threesome has not created any apparent hostility or jealousy.

I feel very lucky but also rather nervous. Can it be fair that I am receiving so much loving and sensual attention when most of my friends bemoan the shortage of eligible gay women? How long can this last? Will it end badly? Is lightning going to strike?

My anxiety has been quickened by a recent proposal from one of my lovers that the three of us spend an erotic evening together. My sexual curiosity is piqued. To think that as recently as a year ago I could not imagine receiving such a suggestion, let alone seriously pondering it! From what I know of both of my sweethearts, I believe we would be compatible in bed. I am not able to envision the aftermath. I love both of them, and of course want them to keep on caring for me. Any unpleasantness would break my heart. Have I gotten myself into trouble by reaching for more than I am entitled to?

A. Even if you turn the invitation to a three-way down, just the fact that it was issued changes things a little. Don't base your answer on a fear of being punished for being too happy. There's nobody up there waiting to dump rain on your parade. If your triangle collapses, it will be because it quit working, not because it was too good to last! Hopefully, if that does happen, everyone involved will congratulate themselves for keeping such a good act together for so long, instead of indulging in a lot of blame or punishment. It *is* possible to have a long-term, triangular relationship if the three parties are kind to one another. It's also imperative for the odd girl out to be mature enough to pull on her boots and go looking for something or somebody else to do when her noncontiguous significant other is busy dating the Other Woman.

Since both of your lovers know about each other and don't seem put off, the stability of this triangle is not based on keeping each of your relationships compartmentalized. That's a sign that a three-way evening in bed might work. Some questions to ask are, How would you feel if after the group sex, your two lovers slept with each other? Would there be any pressure not to see one woman unless the other one was also present? If it turns out to be a bad experience, can you all agree to stay together long enough to talk it out and fix it up?

If you decide to go through with it, try to structure the sex so that your girlfriends don't wind up competing to see who can make the best love to you. You should definitely *not* be the first one in the middle. And it would be nice if you all went your separate ways after the evening, so neither of your friends felt left out.

If it seems too risky to climb into bed with both of your loves, you can always table the idea for further study and discussion without saying, "No, never!"

✍

Q. I have a problem that I'm not sure how to handle. Some of my friends tell me that I'm lucky.

I met this real hot stud about a year and a half ago. We hit it off right away and began having safe but great sex, usually three times a week, Monday, Wednesday, and Friday. We had an understanding that we had no holds on each other. Then about a year ago, I met another guy and things seemed okay, and we got into some pretty wild but safe sex, and I started seeing him more and more often until I was going to his house Tuesday, Thursday, and Saturday. I sleep all day Sunday.

Finally it got to affecting my work so much that my boss told me to go see a doctor and find out what the problem is. Well, I went to my doctor and after numerous tests he told me that I was suffering from extreme exhaustion and asked me to recount an average week. When I did, he asked me how I had survived this long. Then he told me that I'd better slow down or it could kill me.

The thing is, my body seems to go on an instant high when I head for either of their houses. It's just that I'm always tired at work. I don't do drugs or use alcohol. How do I tell them both that I'm burning myself out and I've got to slow down?

A. Part of the reason your body gets high when you're headed out to see one of these guys is that you're in so much physical pain from being tired that you've stopped being conscious of it, and your body craves sex (since you won't give it rest) as a way to make itself feel better.

What's wrong with telling each of your steady dates exactly what you just told me? I don't think there's any other way to say it. Unless they're prepared to support you in the event that you lose your job (and maybe they are, you sound like hot stuff), how can they argue?

I suspect that one of the problems here is that even though you have an agreement about not having holds on each other, you're not real excited about telling each of these men that the other one exists. If I was seeing somebody for three hot nights a week I might think I was the only source of nookie in his life.

If I'm correct, and they don't know about each other, you have two choices. You can plead exhaustion to each of them without explaining that you also have an equal commitment to somebody else. If you're a good actor, you may be able to pull this off. Or you can Tell All and let the buffalo chips fall where they may.

In case you exercise the latter option, I have more advice for you. Keep the one that says, "Honey, I understand. My God, you could get a case of mono. Let me come over and make you some hot tea. We'll go to bed early and just cuddle." Get rid of the one that says, "You tramp! You trashy slut! Do you expect me to see less of you just so you can whore around with somebody else?" If they're *both* nice, then things can go on as before, except you should spend at least every *other* night alone and snug in your wee little bed. Betcha don't even have wet dreams.

✍

Q. I've been in a relationship for one year. We're in love and plan to spend our lives together. Our problem is sexual. My partner has a very promiscuous background. I knew that pattern was going to be hard for him to break. I wasn't so naive as to think we'd "cleave" only to one another for the next forty or fifty years. So we agreed that our sexual explorations would be pursued together *only*. We did that, no problem.

Months later, I found out that he's been "exploring" on his own whenever the opportunity arises. He argues that he has no control over it. My view is that after violating my faith and trust in his promises, he's asking me to accept his promiscuity as an illness. Is it lack of commitment on his part? Is it something I must accept because I love him? Is it something he can't change, or is it that he won't change?

A. Your lover may really feel that he "has no control" over his promiscuity, but has he ever said to you that he *wants* to gain control over it and stop? Since there's no desire on his part to change, counseling would do little good. Everything he's said to you would seem to indicate that if you can't put up with this, you'll have to leave him.

You have to stop worrying about how you can change his behavior, and start thinking about yourself. You don't feel loved unless your partner can give you some degree of sexual exclusivity. Can you ignore his exploring, or will it constantly enrage and threaten you? If you're going to get upset and feel betrayed every time he's late coming home from work, you'd be better off without him.

The other thing you have to think about is your health. Is he practicing safer sex? Can you trust a man who's been lying to you for a whole year to tell the truth about that?

It's very painful to love somebody who can't make you happy. If he had simply made a mistake, I think you'd be prepared to forgive him. But this is not an indiscretion, it's a way of life. The quick pain of a clean break is easier to take than dragging things out and verbally beating each other up. It sounds like the two of you are too different to be happy with each other.

✍

Q. What's the prevailing attitude men have toward three-ways? My lover and I recently decided we would like to experience sex with other men but not separately. Although it's not necessary, it would be nice if a long-term relationship developed. We're both quite attractive but not outgoing, and we find it difficult to approach others with such an offer. The last guy I invited home took off like a spooked horse, and he still avoids me! This compounds my anxiety about propositioning men we both find attractive.

A. Most men find it easier to engage in three-ways if the situation is anonymous and spontaneous. It's hard enough to talk about sex and then actually do it with just one other guy that you're dating or have a crush on — but two of them?!? The third party in such an arrangement often worries about being left out on an emotional limb or caught in the middle because the couple's primary commitment will always be to each other, not to him.

Nevertheless, there are some brave and horny guys out there who are looking for the two of you. They want variety, but they also want some intimacy and security. Be patient and keep looking. Advertising may be easier than screwing up the courage to make propositions in person. As time goes on, word of mouth will start to circulate, and this underground advertisement will alert men who are interested in (small) group sex and point them in your direction.

Work on getting over your shyness. There's nothing bad, wrong, or weird about what you and your lover want. But it *is* up to you to set the ground rules, to make the third man in your triangle feel safe and desired, and to offer any reassurance that may be necessary. The more confidence you project, the less likely he'll be to let his stage fright overcome his titillation.

🖑

Q. My other half and I never really talked about monogamy. But we've both been around (I'm 38, he's 35) and know the score. I've always assumed that if I'm out of town on business and don't get arrested or come home with a case of the crabs, what I do doesn't hurt our relationship. Well, the last time I had to take a trip, it turned out that the sales representative I met with was very attractive *and* gay. We took off after our meeting. He showed me all the night life, I found somebody interesting, so did he, and we all went back to his place for drinks in the hot tub, etc. Meanwhile, Tommy was calling my hotel once every hour. After eight o'clock in the morning he gave up. I came back to the hotel to find a stack of phone messages. Nobody met me at the airport. It turns out Tommy has been faithful for three long years (to hear him tell it) and has turned down offers he now regrets because he thought I was doing the same thing. I'm confused, pissed off, and afraid of losing a guy I really cherish. Did I do something wrong?

A. Yeah, you did something wrong, but Tommy was making the same mistake. Most people assume that their personal morality is (or should be) universal, and also assume that somebody they love automatically shares their code of conduct. This is obviously not true. Hindsight says you and Tommy probably should have talked about fidelity before you became lovers. Some couples counselors recommend that people write up contracts to make their agreements about such matters extra clear. But since the two of you disagree about monogamy, who knows? Maybe if you'd hashed this out, you wouldn't have had three nice years together.

Keep telling Tommy you love him. Let him punish you for a little while, then put your foot down and tell him it's time to decide if your relationship really has a future. You don't sound rampantly promiscuous to me, and he doesn't sound like he's ready to be put on a shelf with the knickknacks, so maybe a compromise is possible. Remind him that he never told you what his expectations were, so while you are sorry you hurt him, you haven't deliberately deceived him, just kept your own rules about tact and discretion. Maybe he'll realize that a man who can inflame perfect strangers is too talented to toss out like moldy leftovers.

✍

Q. Although both of our immediate families know about our being gay, we presently live about ten miles from John's family and several hundred from mine. Every holiday his family invites both of us to come and join in the festivities. I know sometimes this feels awkward for them and for us, but they try their best to make us feel at home, comfortable, and accepted as family. Any advice on how to make it easier? What to bring, what to say, how to make it more relaxing?

A. Did you grow up in a barn? They're treating you like family. Therefore, reciprocate. Wipe your feet before you go in the house. Offer to bring something to help with dinner. Make pleasant conversation about subjects they are interested in. Bring a little thank-you present from time to time, and write thank-you notes after special celebrations so they know you appreciate their extra effort. Take turns helping to clean up after meals. If you stay overnight, make your own bed. For some holidays, insist on returning the favor. Take them out to dinner or invite them to your home.

Your lover should also occasionally see his family without you, just so they know they have a choice about inviting you, and get an opportunity to nag him about those things you don't bug your son about in front of his lover.

If you want to take even more pressure off, once in a while let them know you are entertaining your own friends during a holiday. And try to find time soon to take your lover home to your family. Being in *his* position for a change will give you many useful insights.

✍

Q. Fifteen years ago, I left my family. Whipped like a dog, my tail between my legs, I fled some two thousand miles. I would have gone even further, but not being seaworthy, I stopped at the coast. All this for the "sin" of being gay. I made a life here for myself and my lover. We've been together eleven years. He is my family.

The only relative I've kept in touch with is an aunt in Kansas, my favorite person in all the world. She let my brother know a few years ago how to get in touch with me, and we have since exchanged a few letters.

The problem is, I have a niece getting married in June, and it's being turned into a family get-together. My brother is insisting that I go, and my favorite aunt will be there. I haven't seen her for many years. One day I want to go; the next, I can't stand the thought of it. The question is, should I stay here where I'm loved and love, or should I go to the wedding for what could be another kick in the ass?

A. Your lover is your mate, and as such, he is of course your family. But blood is thicker than bile, my dear, and none of us have any choice about feeling connected to our parents, siblings, and other kin. They've treated you badly, so of course you're reluctant to return. But you won't really feel like an adult until you see their faces again and understand that your relations are only people who have made a bad mistake, not ominous figures from a young man's nightmare.

It sounds to me like you really *are* wanted at the wedding. It can't have been easy for your brother to get in touch with you after you went into exile. Your favorite aunt should not be punished for the rest of the family's misdeeds. Won't you feel awful if she passes away and you never get a chance to see her again? Surely her love can buffer you against the rest of the family's hostility.

If you go, remember that you're the injured party. Whether they'll admit it or not, everybody knows this. People who feel guilty tend to be defensive. So be gracious to them. Any tacky remarks should be corrected firmly but not loudly. It's painful to have to educate the people who should know, better than anybody, that

49

you're a fine person, and there's no cause for shame or rejection. It takes years of talking, quiet confrontation, and compromise to get most families to stop tormenting their gay children. And there's always backsliding. Just when you think they've finally learned to accept you, they have meltdown, and you have to begin again, not quite at the beginning, but depressingly close to it.

You don't have to do this, of course. Many gay people choose to abandon their families and live in the lavender ghetto for the rest of their lives. The price they pay is an unrealistic picture of the world and an irreducible self-hatred. You cannot reject from whence you came without rejecting yourself. Your family abused you because they think homosexuals are not as good as they are. You have a perfect opportunity to demonstrate that they're wrong, just by loving them, no matter what. Which is exactly what you want them to do for you, isn't it?

✍

Q. One of the things I most admire about your column is the direct way you point out the spooks of Higher Authority and urge people to abandon their guilt and be their own selves — or rather to own themselves. Hence my astonishment to read that you accept the family as something sacred.

You suggest to the man who left his family fifteen years earlier that he still has an obligation to love his family "no matter what" and say that people who "choose to abandon their families" pay the price of having an "irreducible self-hatred." I suggest that any self-hatred in this matter can be reduced and even eliminated if a more consistent view is taken, and the sacred cow of Family is seen for the empty spook it really is, that there's nothing behind it except individuals one may or may not want as friends.

You write: "But blood is thicker than bile, my dear, and none of us have any choice about loving/hating our parents, siblings, and other kin." Of course we do, as much as one has a choice about loving/hating anyone. And those of us who accept the motto "equal freedom for all" exercise this choice.

A. We may have to agree to disagree. I don't think emotions can be turned on and off as simply as the hot water faucet in the kitchen sink. There's more to being family than a name on a birth certificate. If you're going to be both gay and sane, you can't let the negative aspects of your background control you, but to be completely divorced from your roots is also a form of insanity. I think it's important to accept the place we came from, the way we grew up, and acknowledge the good and bad traits our adult selves retain from the past. Much of the phony quality of the urban gay ghetto comes from an attempt to pretend we are all upper-middle-class, white city people with no emotional ties or roots outside that ghetto.

Furthermore, I believe that some of the difficulty we have forming long-term ties with one another can be traced to the traumatic, unwilling breaks with our families that many of us are forced to undergo when we come out. Someone who's been through that understandably has trouble trusting any close relationship. It may seem crazy to try to fix this by going back to the people who hurt you. But taking another look at the foibles and limitations of our families can help reduce them from the looming, demonic figures that condemned us completely and abandoned us when we felt helpless and terrified to more human, flawed, manageable proportions. It's also a good index of one's personal growth. The second time around, you won't be the scared kid who didn't even know what it meant to be a homosexual. You'll be stronger, more self-assured, and will probably have had a much happier life than most of your married siblings.

The family certainly isn't sacred. I'm appalled by the amount of violence, persecution, and emotional starvation that is accepted as normal within the nuclear family. I wish gay kids and other young people who are incompatible with their parents had the freedom to divorce them and find a more healthy living situation.

I am *not* suggesting that someone sacrifice their independence or happiness to a family that treats them badly. If your family is unremittingly rude or hostile, or if they are abusive or violent, the only sensible choice is to put yourself beyond their reach, out of harm's way. This kind of separation is painful and alienating, but it may be less damaging than further contact. If you can't decide whether it's worth it to pursue a better relationship with your family, it's often helpful to see a therapist. Victims of incest or child abuse should definitely consult with a professional before they even think about confronting the perpetrators or their apologists.

✍

Q. I've been very active in the gay rights movement for many years, and I've taken the "Silence Equals Death" slogan to heart by coming out whenever and wherever I relate closely to others. My lover of the past ten years fears a loss of livelihood if he were more "out." I would rather not have to hide behind the tomatoes in the supermarket when his clients pop into view. But I oblige him.

His parents know that we're lovers, but George and Ilene don't want me to call them by their first names. At their anniversary party I heard everyone calling them George and Ilene, Uncle George and Aunt Ilene, or Mom and Dad, but *nobody* referred to them as Mr. and Mrs. Spencer. I sat quietly most of the night and avoided calling them anything. In ten years, I've been to every holiday, birthday, anniversary, and wedding that has involved this family. If there is one uncle or cousin who doesn't know the nature of our relationship, I'd be surprised. What do you recommend?

A. I'm sure that by now you no longer wish to call your lover's parents George and Ilene, but something a good deal more earthy and direct. As long as you resist this temptation, you will strike everyone who meets you as a quiet and respectful young man with beautiful, old-fashioned manners. Since you are obviously a member of the family, George and Ilene will look odd (perhaps even ungracious) by contrast.

This would be easier on your ego if you were sure that your lover valued you and your relationship more than he values his business reputation and his familial ties. Ironically, it's always the people we love the most who have the power to keep us closeted. The justification for doing this is that they're protecting themselves or us, but it feels like being rejected, denied, and abandoned.

Does your lover understand all the implications of his parents' rotten attitude? If they don't think of you as their son's life partner, will they recognize your joint property rights with him if he passes away? How about your right to care for him if he's critically ill? Air some of this practical business. When someone's family is being this discourteous, it's important for gay partners to protect themselves by having ironclad wills and medical powers of attorney.

It's generous of you to try to keep your politics and let your lover have his camouflage. I hope he's sweet enough to you to make it worthwhile, because it's an exhausting and frustrating task.

✍

Q. My parents informed me this Christmas that I would not be welcome to visit them because my grandmother's health is failing and they're afraid of "the gay plague." Apparently they don't make a distinction between lesbians and gay men. I know this is my grandmother's doing because she's always sending me clippings about fundamentalist ministers and always mentions "God's latest curse on gays." I've been hearing that her health is failing for as long as I can remember, but I think she'll live to read the Bible over my parents' graves, and possibly over mine as well. I've put up with getting these clippings from her for years, but now that she's actually talked my mom and dad into not letting me visit, I'm furious. I was raised to respect the elderly but isn't there something I can do?

A. My, what an evil old lady you have for a grandma. Seems to me your parents should also come in for a little of your righteous wrath, though. Why are they falling for this claptrap?

Since your grandma has seen fit to put you on the mailing list for her fundamentalist clipping service, why not return the favor? Many excellent publications are available from local groups organized to fight AIDS. Many articles about AIDS have appeared in the gay press, condemning the fire-and-brimstone attitudes of misinformed fundamentalist ministers. This is timely and valuable information, worth cutting out, with the date and source written neatly in the margin. Older people are often lonely and appreciate receiving thoughtful and frequent communication from loved ones who live far away. You should have no trouble getting enough material together to stuff granny's mailbox until it's fatter than the Christmas turkey. After you run out of educational material about AIDS, you might obtain information for her about anti-gay job discrimination, new gay rights laws, or how to join great groups like the National Gay and Lesbian Task Force and Parents and Friends of Lesbians and Gays.

Since your parents are swallowing this born-again buzzard's buzzwords, write them a tearful letter about how lonely you were at Christmas and how unnecessary it all was, given that you're not at risk for AIDS. Be sure to tell them that even if you had the disease, you couldn't give it to somebody by eating dinner with them. A quote about our savior choosing to dine with sinners rather than with scribes and Pharisees might also be appropriate. If you can't make them cry, you've forgotten your roots in the Bible Belt, child.

Of course, if you really *did* sit and brood during the holiday, you wasted a great opportunity to celebrate with your friends. It's fortunate that we're able to include everybody who loves us and wishes us well in our gay families, whether they are related to us or not. Those who don't love us and don't wish us well can go piss up a Christmas tree.

✍

Q. No matter what I do, my lover's family hates me. She's very hurt when they pretend I don't exist or deliberately exclude me from family occasions. Yet she doesn't want to sever all connections with them. And I don't want her to feel torn between me and her family. How can I warm them up?

A. Etiquette was created to ensure that perfect strangers would treat one another decently. So use it. Be on your best Emily Post behavior. Don't give them any excuse to dislike you (no matter how provoked). In-laws are rarely uniformly hostile. Either Mom has a soft spot for her favorite daughter, or Brother Bob puts in a good word for Sis and "her friend," or Dad gets tired of never being able to go fishing with the tomboy he once doted on. It can take years, but as people age, they usually feel a need to get closer to their estranged children.

Your lover (not you) should lodge a calm but firm protest if anybody in her family is actually rude to you. She should say something like this: "Since you taught me not to treat anyone like that, I'm surprised to see you doing it now." If one of her relatives says something nasty about you, she should respond, "That's unkind and untrue, and I would rather not hear you talk that way."

If they can't learn to at least be polite, your lover may decide to tell her family that she'll see them when they can be courteous to her associates. It may take them a while, but if she sticks to her terms, they'll come around. Just remember, if the whole thing is kept low-key and civil, it will be easier to reconcile later on.

✍

Q. I confess with trepidation that I may have been committing a major *faux pas* for over a year now. (That's how long I've been out as a lesbian.) There's only one exclusively lesbian bar here, but I prefer to cruise the mixed bars because the music is better and there's more room for dancing. I seem to find myself naturally drawn to women with short hair and a rough or punk look. I guess you could call them butch, but I'm also attracted to very sexual, feminine women, and have slept with many of them.

This is how I discovered the error of my ways: I was sitting at the bar drinking grasshoppers with a friend while we commented on who we thought was looking really fine that night. She started raving about women with muscles who can fuck her all night long. When she asked me if that didn't drive me crazy too, I stammered that I really don't like to be fucked that much, and what I like about the tough women I cruise is how good they look when I fuck them.

She just about had kittens on her bar stool. You would have thought I'd committed a mortal sin. Is fucking "butch" women disrespectful or blasphemous or hostile? I certainly feel really nice when I'm doing it, and I always cuddle them afterward. Sometimes I even make them breakfast.

I thought there weren't any double standards or rules in lesbian sexuality. What's a girl to do?

A. There are rules everywhere. Just about all of them should be ignored, except that flashing sign that says "Walk" and "Don't Walk."

Your rough trade probably think they've died and gone to heaven. Nobody gets muscles without considerable sweat and pain. You gotta like being worked hard to get a hard body. If they stay for breakfast, they obviously have no complaints. I think it's just fine that your girlfriend likes to sit on it, but if you don't, what's the point? Is Big Sister on TV in the bedroom, keeping tabs on who dares to come which way? Tell your friend she has some odd notions about female sexuality if she thinks it's lipstick and long hair that determines who can have a vaginal orgasm.

What's a girl to do? Other girls, of course. Carry on until they have to be carried out, sweetie, you're doing *fiiiine*.

✍

Q. I want my ass to be as clean as possible for my lover, so I douche before we play. Occasionally, well after douching, a cup of water with some shit in it will come gushing out. It puts a damper on the excitement of the moment. I'm wondering what I can do to make sure I've emptied all of my water.

A. The colon is a very long, continuous tube. As you douche, water wanders higher and higher up into the bowel. Curves in the large intestine will often hold it in place until vigorous sex and abdominal contractions expel it.

There are several ways to prevent this, but none are foolproof. You may be putting too much water in. If you and your lover are having anal intercourse, a simple enema might suffice. If prolonged ass-play moves fecal matter down within reach, adjourn for another enema. You may need to allot more time for douching. Do some exercises to make sure all the water has come out. You can do slow deep-knee bends, masturbate (including anal penetration), walk around, return to the tub for more deep-knee bends and J/O. Some people take three or four hours to do a thorough douche.

Put a plastic sheet on the bed to protect it and have plenty of trick towels handy. If there's a mess, clean it up, then go gaily forward. Have Betadine in the bathroom to wash up (and be especially careful to wash his cock before you suck it). Don't let a little shit ruin your evening. By now, neither of you should be surprised (or upset) to find out where it comes from.

✍

Q. Someone I've been having sex with recently has terribly sensitive nipples, and I just love to suck, tweak, and rub them. After he comes, I can't even touch them because that makes him jump so much. The trouble is, I'm jealous. My nipples just don't react the same way. They don't seem to be very sensitive. I don't mind nipple play, but I obviously don't get the same pleasure out of it as my partner (and others) do. Can I do anything to increase the sensitivity of this area? Will some sort of physical treatment or exercise help? I'm sure others will also be interested in your reply, given the emphasis on safer sex in the community right now.

A. Your nipples are probably just asleep. You should be able to wake them up with a combination of gentle, persistent stimulation and fantasy. If the *idea* of doing something is sexy to you, eroticizing actual performance becomes much easier. So fantasize about playing with your new partner's tits when you jack off, and imagine yourself in his place, getting off on it the way he does.

During masturbation or while foolin' around with another guy, you can try ringing some of these tactile changes on your own tits.

Wet the nipple, then blow warm air across it. Shave the area around the nipple. This will take off a layer of dead skin, removing hair that might screen out sensation, and create a new look that could make the nipple seem more provocative and vulnerable. Take some ordinary wooden clothespins and use a pair of needle-nose pliers to spring them a bit, so they don't close real tight. Put two of them on each side of the nipple (not on it, just beside it, to stretch the skin and make it stand out). Then try gently licking or nibbling or pinching the nipple itself. Remove the clothespins before the area gets cold (five or ten minutes), and repeat stimulation. As blood flows back into the area that the clothespins compressed, it should enhance sensitivity. Try flicking the nipple instead of gripping or rubbing it. Don't forget teeth as well as tongue. You can also use ice cubes, a small vibrator, a fur glove, or a piece of velvet to titillate them.

Another technique that sometimes works is to make sure your nipples are being stimulated while you come, or to postpone orgasm until you have tolerated so many minutes of nipple play. Talking dirty about it never hurts either.

✍

Q. My lover and I are having problems with anal sex. We are "firsts" for each other and have been monogamous for almost three years. But we only have oral sex. My lover is endowed like the "bigger" guys on gay videotapes and I am average. We try anal sex with lube, but we can't get past the tip and it hurts. Do butt plugs or small dildos help open up the anus?

A. First promise your asshole that you will never do anything that hurts it. Our phobia about shit tends to make most people's asses very tense. It's a sensitive part of the body and has an excellent memory. If you give your ass enough pleasurable stimulation, eventually it will probably relax enough to enjoy taking a cock.

Here are some things your lover can do to turn your asshole on. He can use one lubricated finger to stroke only the outside. He should press gently on the sphincter without actually going in. Talk dirty about penetrating it, but don't actually penetrate. If he makes you wait, he'll make you want it. A top who's training a virgin asshole can use a lubricated finger to penetrate his partner while he's sucking him off. The new sensation will enhance the bottom's climax, teach his asshole to participate in orgasm, and make it crave stimulation.

Your first butt plug should be no bigger than two fingers. One that vibrates will probably relax the asshole more than one that does not. You can also get rubber sleeves with pencil-sized extensions that will fit over a vibrator. Anyone can take one of these. Experiment with your new toys during oral sex and masturbation.

Often the angle of anal penetration is as important as the size of the object. Going in at the wrong angle can cause pain, even with a small object. The right angle can vary a lot from person to person, so be especially careful when inserting objects that are not flexible. It's easier for the asshole to tolerate an object or a cock that holds still — motion may make the rectum tense. If you push down with your stomach muscles, as if you were trying to push something out of your ass, it will actually open everything up.

When you start using cocks instead of toys or fingers, use rubbers. And don't stick something that's been in the ass into your mouth or into the other guy's ass without washing it first.

Q. My lover has a fantasy about having wild sex at a porn theater. We often talk dirty to each other during sex, and this has become his favorite theme. He loves for me to describe all the men and what they are doing to each other while explicit gay movies flash on the screen. Recently he asked if I wanted to go to a gay movie theater with him. The idea of having sex in that setting turns me on but also scares me. Public sex is illegal, and this is not a very liberal town.

A. The charged atmosphere of any place men gather to hunt for sex is something you should experience at least once. It will make you realize just how isolated you usually feel in the "real" world. It's hot to be surrounded by the sight, smell, and sound of excited manflesh in various stages of getting there and getting off.

Remember that you don't have to do anything. Maybe you would feel safer about going if your lover would agree that this trip is just to look, not touch. If you're nervous about public sex, find a bookstore that has private movie booths as well as a back room. When you get ready to come with each other, get out of the back room, find a booth, lock the door, and start popping quarters (and whatever feels good) into the appropriate slot.

Yes, public sex is illegal. But the risk you're taking is minimal, and exists all the time. I've known gay men who got busted for public sex because a homophobic cop saw them taking a leak and decided to hassle them. If this was the way you usually found sex, I would get on your case about preventing STDs and finding a good lawyer to call in case you did get busted. But for a one-shot field trip, I think you and your lover should just hold hands, click your heels together three times, and say, "I don't want to be in Kansas any more, I don't want to be in Kansas any more ..." until you smell the poppers.

✍

Q. My girlfriend, hoping to make our sex life steamier, brought over a bunch of straight porn and some lesbian sex magazines for us to look at. I found it pretty upsetting and not at all erotic. She said I probably just needed to get used to it and left most of it here for me to look at alone. Well, I sat down and read every scrap, and I'm still repelled. I don't understand why she responds to this stuff. Or why it is important to her that I enjoy it. I thought our sex life was just fine, thank you, without fantasizing about other women or buying any ugly leather implements. I have a feeling she's going to be upset when I tell her this. Is there a tactful way to explain, or should I just tell her if she brings a fake plastic prick into my bedroom I'm going to scream?

A. You aren't required to like pornography; nor are you required to give an explanation. Simply return your girlfriend's magazines and tell her, "Thank you for going to the trouble of getting these together for me. But they really don't do anything for me. Is there anything else we could do that would be fun and hot?"

As a woman who does enjoy porn, I'm curious about why pictures of women making love would "repel" a lesbian. That's pretty strong language. Could it be the harsh, clear light of hardcore photographs doesn't match up to the softer focus and more romantic candlelight of your fantasies? Traditional porn is not very available to most women; seeing photographs of real women having sex is unsettling for most of us the first time we see it.

Ask your lover why she likes these magazines and what she expected you to do with them. I hope both of you will respect the other's response or lack of it. It's hard not to make sexual preferences a moral issue. It's also hard not to see sexual differences as a partner's attempt to deprive you or make excessive demands.

When you say, "I thought our sex life was just fine," it sounds like your lover may have unintentionally hurt your feelings. I doubt that she was trying to send you a message that there was something wrong with the quality of your lovemaking. It's more likely that she's been having such a good time with you that she thought she could trust you with some of her sexual secrets. There are some erotic adventures that you can't embark upon without a suitable companion, and she is probably so smitten with you that she thought you were The One.

And now the Adviser has a question for you: Where can I get a fake plastic prick? All the dildos I've ever seen were *real* plastic pricks...

✍

Q. My lover and I have lived together for fourteen years and are co-owners of a business for which I am the brains and he is the brawn. We are both in our mid-40s. We have experimented with bondage off and on for variety and mutual enjoyment.

The last several years, though, my lover has moved from occasional bondage to almost exclusive bondage. We now own about every known device for binding and gagging, and although I enjoy my mouth filled with a bandana, rubber ball, etc., lips sealed with tape, you name it, my lover can't seem to understand that there are times when I want tenderness as well.

When I try to talk to him about it, he thinks I'm begging for it. When I've physically tried to stop him from trussing me, he ties me that much tighter. If I say something about it being too tight he gags me with a hood so I can't even move my jaw.

This guy is a terrific lover. He never comes without making sure I come too. Our business lives and joint property bind us together in additional ways that I like. We are monogamous. I don't want to lose him and know he doesn't want to lose me ... but how can I get across to him that he doesn't have to spread-eagle me for intercourse?

A. Gee, if my partner referred to himself as "the brain" and me as "the brawn," I'd be sorely tempted to keep him tied up and gagged, also.

You've got a classic communication problem found among S/M couples who don't clearly separate a scene from the rest of their lives. From your lover's point of view, when you say "stop," you don't really mean it, since you get turned on when he ties you up and you appear to enjoy the sex. If you protest every single time he gets sexy with you, whether you really want him to stop or not, how is he supposed to know the difference? That's why the common device of a "safe word" evolved — the code word a bottom (or a top, for that matter) can use to say "Hey, I'm not fooling around or flirting, I really mean this, stop, get out of role, we have to do something different."

To avoid another conversation that ends up with your limbs trussed and your mouth taped, write him a letter. Tell him what you have just told me, add that you need a safe word, and tell him what it is. (Make it a word you are not going to use accidentally during sex-talk. "Cock" and "help" are bad safe words.) The next time he aggresses and you are not in the mood, use your safe word. If he ignores it, *do not* respond sexually to what he does. Go limp (all over). Turn off.

Have you considered becoming the top during vanilla sex? Since bondage and discipline are his forte, he might be unwilling to assume the additional responsibility of initiating and orchestrating more tender lovemaking.

The other thing you can do is provide him with some other means of communicating his irritation or disagreement with you. This is not going to be easy, since he's the strong, silent type. Be aware that once sexual response gets turned off, it can be hard to turn it back on again. Think long and hard before you upset the balance here. You're getting some deep needs met. So is he. Be sure you're not just dithering around, expressing the ambivalence all bottoms feel before doing a scene. You don't want to lose your top completely.

✍

Q. Every Halloween, one of the local dykes throws a costume party. I always suggest to whoever my girlfriend is that she go dressed as a nun. My friends have gotten so used to this that they tease me about it. Well, last year, my current flame (who is rather aggressive) really got into it. She said if she was going to wear a habit I was going to have to dress like a Catholic schoolgirl, in a little plaid skirt, with knee socks and a matching sweater over a white shirt. She even made me put a bow in my hair and call her "Sister Angela" all night long. When we got home she pounced on me. First she gave me a lecture about being bratty all night, then made me get under her long skirts and go down on her. It was very nice and safe and sexy under there.

This year there will be another party, and she *still* has the same costume. She's told me I should take up the plaid skirt another inch. I am petrified but very turned on. How did this happen to a nice Methodist like me? What is it about nuns that gets me so hot and bothered?

A. Nuns have always fascinated lay people (and other nuns, too, I bet). To the nonreligious, they seem otherworldly, serene, but also authoritative and stern. I'm sure the dykes who made Naiad Press's book *Lesbian Nuns* a best-seller were looking for the same thing the guys who read the excerpts in *Forum* were hoping for — some steamy sex behind convent walls. I wonder if Dignity has thought of utilizing this attraction as a recruitment technique?

Your problem isn't why you like dressing up this way. The problem is why you waited a whole year to do it again. Did Sister Angela give you permission to tattle on her? For your penance you ought to go out and buy her a nice new rosary and hem your skirt high enough to show off the lace on your panties.

Friendship

Q. I'm a 23-year-old gay male. Last evening, I received a shocking letter that has left me very confused and concerned. I'm hoping you can help me understand.

For the past three years, I've had a wonderful pen/phone friendship with a guy my age. We received each other's names through a gay/bi youth pen pal service. During those years, we've shared some of our most intimate tears, fears, hopes, and dreams. I've come to love my friend like a brother even though we've never met.

About nine months ago, his letters suddenly stopped. Finally an explanation arrived. He has "found God" as a Christian and discovered how sinful his "previous gay lifestyle" was. He explained that he has given up everything sinful in his life, including being gay. "I'm not the same person that you have been writing to the past three years," he wrote.

What happened? Where is the strong, warm, caring, level-headed guy I knew? He seemed so self-confident and strong. I can't help but think that someone or some group of people has brainwashed him, much like Jim Jones did to his followers. People can't deny their sexuality and be truly happy, can they?

I don't know how to respond to his letter. I feel like I should do something to save him or say something to help him accept himself. Or maybe it's me that needs to do the accepting. This has really left me confused and disillusioned.

A. A religious conversion is a profound emotional experience that does indeed make a person feel transformed. If you write to your friend now and tell him you think he's brainwashed or try to make him accept his gayness, he'll rebuff you. The only thing you are going to get out of him for a while is preaching. If you can stand it, you would probably be better off writing him a courteous but distant note, telling him that you're glad to hear he's happy. Wait six months to a year before making contact again, then drop him a line asking how he's doing. If he *still* believes he has successfully put his "sinful" homosexual past behind him, you should probably leave him alone to work it out.

I don't believe people can be happy if they repress their sexuality, but I also know that some people can't be happy as out-of-the-closet gay men and women. If being gay is incompatible with your religious values, it can be very tough to make peace with yourself. It's also true that some people think they're gay and discover that's a mistake. If someone is bisexual and uncomfortable with the gay lifestyle, they may refuse to take on a homosexual (or, for that matter, a bisexual) identity.

I'm more concerned about you than I am about your friend. I hope losing him doesn't send you into a tailspin of self-doubt. His good opinion and companionship obviously meant a great deal to you. It sounds like you might have been in love with him. I'm very sorry for the pain this is causing you. It might help you to call a nearby Metropolitan Community Church (listed in the resource guide) and discuss this with a Christian minister who isn't a bigot about gay people. Get a new pen pal as soon as possible, or — better yet — get involved with activities that will allow you to meet other young, gay men face-to-face.

✍

Q. I'm in love with my straight friend. Why have I fallen for a man who will never be able to return my feelings? Cutting through all the crap, it's kind of obvious. Friendship. Which is the one important ingredient usually lacking in most failed gay relationships.

He doesn't judge me as a lover. He doesn't care what I look like, how big my dick is, or what my sexual fantasies are. He accepts me as just another person, a close friend without all the "trimmings," someone to do things with and enjoy life with. There's no judging, jealousy, or dating. He just plain accepts me the way I am. Which is something we're all looking for — someone to appreciate us for just being ourselves.

I've had three friendships like this. I'm still in love with all of these men. Why shouldn't I be? There's no greater love than that shared by true friends. It's something that stands up through both the good and the hard times, something to be treasured.

63

But this whole scenario can lead to great psychological trauma. Mainly due to the fact that it's hard, almost impossible, for me to replace one of these perfect men. I actually feel as though I'm "cheating" on him if I start going out with someone else. I'm really not inclined to look too hard because of this. I'm afraid I'll lose him. And I continue to fantasize that maybe he will "become" gay and be my lover.

It's a very complicated issue. Are there any viable solutions? No. I've attempted suicide because of my desperation.

A. If these friendships with straight men are so full of acceptance and other positive elements, why did you try to kill yourself? It doesn't sound to me like these friendships have made you very happy or given you what you needed. Does a straight friend who "accepts you the way you are" know that you're gay? How can someone be your friend if they don't know about such an important part of your life? You say that your straight friends don't care about your sexual fantasies, but I doubt that would be true if they knew they had starring roles in those fantasies.

Of course there are gay men and straight men who are good buddies and great friends. But unrequited love and friendship are two very different things. That's why you feel guilty if you date somebody else. You know that's not a normal or healthy part of a friendship. If you use the guise of friendship to mask sexual or romantic passion, you're not being honest with yourself or the other person. Eventually you'll come to resent and hate him, but you won't have anyone except yourself to blame.

There's no reason why you can't find someone who can be both your lover and your friend. You need to find out why you've refused to do that and keep yourself stuck pursuing dead ends. What are you getting out of this? Why does the alternative — having a lover — seem more frightening to you than the pain you're already enduring?

See if you can locate some counseling. You sound like such a sweet and giving person, I would just like to know that you were with someone who could make you happy. It sounds to me like you deserve that.

✍

Q. What advice do you have for a couple that's compatible every way but sexually? Bob and I have been dating for a few months, and everything about our relationship is going well except for the sex. Ever since the third or fourth time we slept together I've ceased to stay turned on once the sexual activity becomes heavy. If I force myself to think about something erotic, such as a hot man I saw earlier in the street, I can manage to stay involved, but the results aren't very satisfying. Friends tell me it's natural to fantasize while having sex, but until now I've preferred to turn my awareness on my partner and what we're doing together.

I suppose that part of the problem is a fear of spreading disease. I become anxious if he goes down on me, which he wants to do, and he has herpes on his ass, which he's worried I might get. Of the few things two men can do together freely these days, something will interest one of us but not the other. For example, I get very aroused by kissing, but he is neither good at it nor interested. Is it possible to teach someone how to kiss?

We're emotionally close and quite romantic and spend hours lying in bed, talking, hugging, caressing, kissing lightly. Sometimes something hot and original starts up, but as soon as we proceed onto something routine, the fun and excitement recedes and I get turned off.

A friend suggested I continue to date Bob and look for sex elsewhere. I'm not sure this wouldn't hinder the relationship, even though Bob probably wouldn't mind. He claims he's not as concerned about sex as I am — he yearns for affection, which we've been inundating ourselves with from the beginning.

I sense there's a solution for us and wish that my public schooling had paid more attention to sex education so that we could solve this on our own!

A. I think you and Bob have a solid basis for a good friendship that might occasionally include sex. If it weren't for your fear of disease, I doubt very much that you'd consider Bob "lover material." Couples who find that their honeymoon-phase lust has cooled off can sometimes rekindle the flames of desire; a man who develops a problem with maintaining or getting an erection can often get over it (especially with the help of a committed partner); differing levels of desire or desires for different types of sex can be worked out by compromise if the couple enjoys the sex that they *do* have. But if you're so incompatible with this man that you feel like you'd have to teach him how to *kiss,* then settle for making him one of your best friends. Friendship isn't that easy to find, and it often outlasts any romance.

✍

Q. I'm what you might call a "newlywed." I just moved in with my boyfriend. We get along well but have two problems. These are usually the topics of arguments. (1) Trust: We both say we trust one another, but I know I really don't. I'm still scared he'll cheat. (2) Boredom: I'm not of legal age to go to bars. We make ourselves happy, and neither one of us is a barfly. But I feel I may be in the way of his social life. I want to make this relationship grow. I really do love him, and I'm trying, but thought maybe a little advice will help.

A. Why send your honey out the door to carouse alone in the local bar if you're afraid he'll cheat and you're jealous enough to have fights about it — especially if he doesn't particularly want to go to bars anyway? You two need more of a social life — together, as a couple, and apart, as individuals.

Try advertising in the local gay press for other couples to socialize with. Couples organizations that sponsor social activities are listed in the resource list of this book.

The Green-Eyed Monster is pretty hard to argue with, but it's a wise person who remembers that your other half won't necessarily wait to meet somebody else if they have *another* good reason to leave you. If your lover is worth his salt, he'll understand that you occasionally need reassurance that he still loves you best of all. It's better to ask for a pat on the head (or the rump) now and then than wait until your insecurities boil over and you have a fight about a checkout clerk or a gas station attendant who seemed a little too friendly.

✍

Q. My question is one I'm sure you've heard on numerous occasions. I've been friends with a certain young man since I met him five years ago while I was working at a fast-food restaurant. We met through a mutual friend, and we've managed to have our ups and downs since day one. I had a crush on him then. We've grown close as friends and I want so badly to be more. He knows I'm in love with him. I've never felt this way for anyone in my entire life. Now he won't respond to me because I'm a brown-skinned male. I have a dark complexion and he does as well, but he doesn't want to have another brown-skinned male touch him. He thinks it's disgusting. He voices this opinion verbally every time we're together, not knowing that he's literally destroying me. I'm to the point of suicide, but I'm convinced there is no man on this earth for me but him.

A. One of the most awful things that can happen is to fall in love with somebody who doesn't love you back. Even if the person you're in love with tries hard to be considerate of your feelings and kind when they reject you, it's heartbreaking. But this guy isn't even acting like your friend. You say he knows that you love him, and yet he tells you that it would be "disgusting" for a brown-skinned man to touch him. How much more hostile and nasty could he possibly be? It sounds to me like he must hate himself. And I think he's so wrapped up in this self-hatred that he's very self-absorbed, very selfish, and it doesn't even occur to him to think about how this must make you feel.

Somebody like this can't possibly return your love. I know he seems to need your love a great deal. He's probably somebody that you feel you could help and heal. But he won't let you. This man has to accept himself before he can open his heart to others.

You've got to find people you can talk to, people who can support you. Check the resource guide for organizations that serve gay people of color. If you can love somebody who causes you this much pain, you can love somebody who will treat you right. Don't give way to despair. There's nothing wrong with *you*, he's the one who has the problem. Stop focusing so much energy on him, and try to meet some other men who can bring joy instead of bitterness into your life.

✍

Q. I'm very disturbed about something that happened recently. Some old friends of mine got together for the first time in ages for a party. There were drinks and dinner, and we were enjoying ourselves very much. Then the host put a cassette into the video. It turned out to be a pornie. At first, I thought this was just for more laughs, but that wasn't the case.

The other guys took out their cocks and began to beat off. I was shocked. I got up as quietly as I could and walked into the bedroom. I sat on the bed, so upset I trembled. When I thought it was all over I went back into the living room. Everybody acted as though nothing had happened, but they knew I hadn't been with them for that episode. As soon as I could, I courteously said goodbye and left.

Please understand that I'm no prude. I know that there are actual clubs at which guys do exactly as my friends did, and I don't object to them. But there was something about this that was too much for me. I believe that the gang wants to continue exchanging parties. I'd like to stay with them, but I can't while this kind of "entertainment" is going on. I haven't had the guts to talk about this with any of them.

A. It's obvious that you and your friends have different attitudes about what constitutes appropriate sexual behavior. Considering how upset you were, you behaved very well. However, what happened doesn't sound that off-the-wall to me. After a day spent reaffirming old friendships, in a happy, warm, and intimate atmosphere, (almost) everybody was susceptible to getting turned on and getting closer to each other. A J/O circle can be a bonding ritual.

It's more traditional to announce that a social event is going to be a J/O party so guests who aren't interested won't attend, but sometimes these things happen spontaneously, and in these somewhat grim and straitlaced times, it makes me feel good to know people are not relinquishing their right to pleasure.

Your friends probably care less about whether or not you joined them than they do about whether you still care about them. By all means, host one of the parties. You need not play any porn or otherwise encourage sex, and I doubt it will happen again.

This might upset you less if you went to one of the jack-off clubs you've heard about. I bet it'll put a smile on your face to experience this new kind of safer public sex.

✍

Q. I've lived in a large sunbelt area state for three years. The problem? I have no friends. I have dates, but no friends. The ones I've made are either in relationships or have moved. I try to meet people. I attend gay-sponsored functions, fundraisers, clubs, etc. Most people I meet want the same old things. Help!

A. I'm not sure what you mean when you say they "want the same old things." Do you mean that Louie and Larry from the Old Gay Folks' Home are getting awfully tired of servicing such a big crowd? Maybe you'll have to wait until you're an old thing yourself. Or do you mean "the same old things" as in "some men want only *one thing* from a girl," i.e., testing the shock absorbers in Daddy's Caddy?

Meeting people is not enough. You have to find a way to see them again and get to know them. Offer your phone number. Ask for theirs. Call them when you want to see a movie, go shopping, try a new restaurant, work out at the gym, go roller-skating, feed the ducks in the park, or get some sun at the beach. If you can't talk to somebody one to one, you'll never know if the rare spark of genuine friendship is there.

Don't give up on an old friend just because they're in a relationship. For the first six months or so, most new lovers are incommunicado. It's called "going on a honeymoon." The new couple wants time to bill and coo, rearrange the furniture, kiss each other behind the ear, call each other silly pet names, and fight about who loves whom the most. Believe me, it's better if they do this alone.

Call them up once a month to see if they're still blinded by young love. Tell them you want to have them both over for dinner as soon as they can stand to get that far away from the bed. Dinner should be designed to convince your friend's new lover that you're not a romantic or sexual threat. Making it a foursome (even if your relationship with the fourth man is only casual) can make it less threatening to the new boyfriend.

It's tricky, drawing our friends from the same pool of people where we look for lovers. Some gay men solve this problem by making friends with women or straight men. Have you tried casting your bread on these waters?

✍

Q. I know that lesbians are supposed to build a nest with Ms. Right while sex-crazed gay men bounce off each other like subatomic particles in unstable elements, never having two orgasms with the same person. I tried being in love and living together once, years ago, and recalling the experience still gives me chicken skin. I was never so glad to be out of something. I live alone now, and I do not want somebody else's furniture crowding mine or somebody else messing around in my kitchen.

That's not to say I don't enjoy some company in bed on a pretty regular basis. I do. Finding sex has not been a problem. My problem is two old friends who knew me when I had just come out. They've been together for years and think I'm still pining away from a broken heart, traumatized and paralyzed. They keep matching me up with nice girls. If I want a nice girl, I'll have lunch with my secretary. If I want intimacy, I'll entice a saleslady into the dressing room.

These two are loves, really. I know they have my best interests at heart. I can laugh about what they try to do, but a couple of the women they've introduced me to were genuinely disappointed and upset when they found out I wasn't looking for my "other half" (half of what?). Is there a gracious way to get out of this?

A. If you've told these two old friends everything you've just told me, I'd say they have chosen to ignore your attempts to evade matrimony graciously. The time has come to be blunt. The next time they invite you over, ask them if they're also inviting a fourth woman. If they say yes, decline the invitation and tell them if you want a date, you'll bring your own.

Coming out to oneself and others

Q. The gay lifestyle, at least for me, is extremely lonely. I was married for three and a half years, but it ended in divorce. We're still friends, but I didn't feel the desire to have sex with her, and when we did I could never have an orgasm. I've been divorced for nine months and have been trying to cope with my homosexual feelings, but I still feel unhappy.

I'm too shy to meet gay men in a bar. I'm petrified of being rejected. I don't think I'm attractive to the men who are sexy to me. I will stare at them to make eye contact, but I don't receive eye contact back.

I would definitely rather be straight, but I know that I'm only sexually turned on by good-looking males. I'm going to therapy, but it hasn't helped me any yet. I've been depressed and somewhat suicidal. I have some gay friends but don't feel like anyone has helped me. I've called the gay and lesbian hotline here, and they told me about all of the gay-oriented groups. I've been to several.

I feel that gay men are more "sleazy" than most straight men, or at least gay relationships are short-lived. I'm overwhelmed with AIDS fears and personally think that having anal sex is repulsive. To me, this attraction I have to males is repulsive, scary, and sad. Maybe the therapy will help, but it's so expensive. I thought that coming out and accepting my homosexual feelings would be easier, but it has been hell. I feel like a second-class citizen, not recognized by society and rejected by the church. I'm looking into some religious organizations for gay people, but they seem to have only old men attending.

The fact of growing old with a man instead of a woman scares me. It just doesn't seem natural. Neither does gay sex. Is it possible that my homosexual feelings will go away? They're making me miserable, lonely, and helpless. I haven't been able to have an orgasm with men either by being orally or physically stimulated by hand.

A. You're probably still feeling the aftereffects of your divorce. Anyone would mourn the death of a relationship that lasted three and a half years, even if it wasn't perfect. Simply being aware that you're sexually attracted to other men isn't enough to make you happy about being gay. Because you're depressed and your knowledge of the gay community is still superficial, I'm sure that you mostly notice gay men whose personalities or relationships confirm your worst stereotypes.

Tell your therapist that you don't think you're making any progress. Ask him or her if there's anything they can do to make the therapy more helpful. Be truthful about how bad you're feeling. If a counselor doesn't know that you're depressed enough to feel suicidal, they can't give you the level of help you need. If your therapy doesn't get better, change counselors. Sometimes clients and therapists just aren't compatible. You might also need some specialized sex therapy. The fact that you don't respond at all to both male and female partners tells me that you've got some physical problems that inhibit functioning or some intense conflicts about sex itself, regardless of whether it's gay or straight.

Attend gay religious services and make friends with "the old men" you meet there. Believe me, they know something you don't know — how to survive in a hostile world with dignity and humor. If you believe in God, pray. This can only bring you consolation.

You say your friends haven't helped you. You sound so bitter and down that I'm surprised you have friends. Try to do something to express your appreciation for their loyalty. Nobody else can tell you how to be happy, but these folks are hanging in there with you. If your own life is full of pain, try to do something to make someone else's life easier. It's better than feeling sorry for yourself, and it will cheer you up immensely.

Do some more reading. You need more information about gay sex, culture, and lifestyles. Get a copy of one of the gay guides listed in the resources and find the nearest gay bookstore.

Not everybody who is attracted to members of their own sex is gay. Maybe you are not homosexual. There are a lot more bisexual people than gay *or* straight society wants to acknowledge. And there are also a lot of straight men (those guys that you think are less "sleazy" than faggots) who get their dicks sucked or get fucked on a regular basis. From the outside, they look like respectable married men, but they're actually having plenty of casual, anonymous gay sex.

You *can* be in control. This is your life. You don't have to do anything that you find repulsive. If you were taught as a child that sex is a frightening or disgusting thing, you're going to have to work hard to undo that damage. This is especially true if you were sexually abused as a child. Be patient with yourself. It can take a long time for a heterosexual to figure out how to meet and keep friends, find sexual partners, enjoy lovemaking, and have a lasting romantic relationship. If society labels your desires perverse, it makes that learning process even more difficult.

Gay sex *is* natural. People have been making love with members of their own sex since the dawn of human history. Homosexual behavior isn't even restricted to humans; it has been observed in many other mammals. Our bodies fit together, we're capable of pleasuring each other, and our hearts reach out to one another, so no minister or shrink can convince me that there's anything wrong with what we do. There isn't enough love or pleasure in the world. We bring more warmth and joy into each other's lives. It's foolish to think of that as evil or unnatural.

I haven't encountered real evil very often. But I do see deliberate, corrosive wickedness in the faces of the people who hate us. You need to start getting pissed off at these sanctimonious, authoritarian homophobes because they've obviously made you hate yourself.

✍

Q. I'm about 25 years old, soon to be 26. I'm six feet even and weigh 175 pounds, I'm good-looking, and for about six months now I've found myself becoming more attracted to my own sex. But don't get me wrong, I'm not ashamed. I care about women the same. Now this is the tricky situation. I'm still a virgin. My buddies say I'm the oldest male virgin they know.

For the past couple of months I've been passing by this gay bar. There are a lot of good-looking men who go in there, and I'm afraid to go in. I don't know why. I've never been afraid of anything before. What should I do?

My best friend is the only one who knows that I care for men as though I do for women. He understands and knew or expected that I had these feelings. I don't know how my other friends will react. Should I tell them? Should I try it with both sexes first?

A. It would be a mistake to tell your friends that you're interested in other men. You don't have enough experience

73

to know if you're gay, bisexual, or a heterosexual who for some reason is temporarily attracted to his own sex. You need to get a lot more information about human sexuality in general, the gay community, and your own feelings.

You're scared to go into the bar because anything that might happen there is scary. It would be frightening to meet a man that you wanted and to have sex with him. It would be awful to walk into a roomful of strangers and have nobody talk to you. In fact, this bar may not be the best place to begin your quest for self-knowledge. Call your local gay community center and see if they have any support groups for people who are coming out.

Since this decision will affect your whole life, give yourself enough time (and privacy) to make it wisely. If you meet a woman and there's some mutual attraction, I don't see anything wrong with exploring straight sex, as long as you use birth control. Just remember that being gay or straight is more than a simple matter of who gets your dick hard. There are plenty of gay men and lesbians who are capable of functioning during heterosexual sex. But that's not what makes us happy. We need physical and emotional intimacy with members of our own sex to feel complete.

If you're gay or bisexual, it's something you can be proud of, but you'll encounter other people who don't feel the same way. It'll be easier to answer their questions or counter their hostility if you have no doubt that you're doing what's right for you.

✍

Q. I remember reading somewhere that you have a Mormon background. I just completed my mission, and I'm currently attending Brigham Young University. During the two years I spent living constantly with another man in a foreign country, it became pretty clear to me that I am homosexual. (Even though my mission partner was definitely not my type.) But I can't imagine ever acting on these feelings. Right now, my family is proud of me. I'm close to them and love them even though I resent their lack of understanding and am always afraid of losing their approval. My question is, how did you ever abandon your family? The thought of disgracing them makes me cringe. But they're already asking me when I'm going to get married and telling me how many grandchildren they want. The pressure is becoming unreal.

A. Like many conservative Christian faiths, the Mormon Church encourages a person who has doubts about his or her heterosexuality to pray, fast, and get married as soon as possible. For the sake of your own happiness and that of your wife, don't do this. A divorce is painful enough in a more secular environment. For Mormons, who believe in marriage for time and all eternity, the pain and social disapproval a divorced woman (and her children) experiences is very cruel. In some ways it's easier to be a gay Catholic since the more liberal clergy feel that a celibate homosexual can still be a good Catholic. Celibacy is frowned upon among Mormons.

You've been raised in a unique community that has effective methods of social control. Your hometown, family, church, friends, education, and career are all inseparable from the church. When you violate the church's basic teachings, you don't just lose your religion, you usually lose everything else, too. The publicity that accompanies a formal excommunication makes this even tougher on the nonconforming member and everyone close to them. That's why so many gay Mormons have nervous breakdowns, attempt suicide, or become alcoholics.

Right now, you need to postpone making any decision that commits you permanently to a gay lifestyle or Mormonism. Get more information about what it means to be gay, how other gay Mormons coped, and the nature of your own feelings for other men. Contact Affirmation, a support group for gay Mormons listed in the resources at the end of this book.

Once you begin this journey of self-exploration, you'll probably be surprised to find your Mormon background has given you qualities that will actually help you. You've been taught to stand by the truth, no matter how preposterous it may seem, no matter how much people may despise you for it. The only way you really have of knowing what God wants you to do is to ask, with humility and without preconceptions, in prayer. Why not try it?

If your family loves you now, they will love you whether you are gay or straight. They'll be hurt and upset and treat you badly if you tell them you're gay. They won't act very loving in the beginning. But if you're patient and keep in touch with them, they'll eventually express their love again — if not their approval.

I wish I could make it sound easier. But I would be doing you a disservice if I encouraged you to come out before you were sure you were making the right decision or before you have contacts within the gay community that can help you when it gets especially tough. Just remember, Utah is a pretty small part of the world. A lot of ex-Mormons seem trapped in Salt Lake City, unable to leave their favorite bar and their least favorite religion. If it gets too heavy for you in Utah, you can always leave. Even the Marines are combing the countryside, looking for a few good men, m'dear.

Q. As a non-Mormon who escaped Salt Lake City, Utah not so long ago, I was very interested by your advice to the returned missionary from Brigham Young University. You really took time to tell him what he needs to know if he's going to survive coming out there. I know because I went to BYU myself.

A. I was surprised by how much mail I got about the letter from the returned missionary. I guess conservative religious values continue to damage our self-esteem and peace of mind despite all the progress we've made in the political arena. We can debate with and lobby politicians, but it's much more difficult to argue with somebody who claims to speak for God.

I'm amazed by the distance Christianity has strayed from its simple origins — Christ's injunction, "Thou shalt love the Lord thy God with all thy heart, and with all thy soul, and with all thy mind. This is the first and great commandment. And the second is like unto it, Thou shalt love thy neighbor as thyself. On these two commandments hang all the law and the prophets." (Matt. 22:37–40) If all these right-wing TV ministers were to drag an adulterous woman before Jesus today, most of them would probably feel qualified to cast the first stone, despite His warning, "Judge not, that ye be not judged, For with what judgment ye judge, ye shall be judged: and with what measure ye mete, it shall be measured to you again." (Matt. 7:1–2)

Christ was more concerned about feeding the hungry, curing the sick, and comforting poor people who had to work very hard just to survive than he was with any campaign for moral purity. Rather than advocating guerrilla warfare against Rome or adding to the burdens of the common people by interpreting their religious obligations even more strictly, he taught people that they could make their daily lives better if they would treat their neighbors the way they wanted to be treated themselves. Born-again types never remember that the first miracle their "personal savior" performed was turning water into wine so that a marriage feast could be celebrated with a proper amount of joy. Nor do they recall that he was rebuked by the fundamentalists of his own time for feasting with "publicans and sinners," for rubbing husks from grain to eat on the Sabbath, for curing a Canaanite woman's daughter and even the servant of a Roman centurion, for not fasting, for allowing his disciples to eat without washing their hands, and for healing people on the Sabbath!

I wish just one of these self-styled "reverends," "ministers," and "elders" would remember that Jesus instructed his followers not to be like the scribes and the Pharisees who "bind heavy burdens and grievous to be borne, and lay them on men's shoulders; but they themselves will not move them with one of their fingers. But all their works they do for to be seen of men: ... and love the uppermost rooms at feasts, and the chief seats in the synagogues, And greetings in the markets, and to be called of men, Rabbi, Rabbi. But be not ye called Rabbi: for one is your Master, even Christ; and all ye are brethren. ... But he that is greatest among you, shall be your servant. And whosoever shall exalt himself shall be abased; and he that shall humble himself shall be exalted. But woe unto you, scribes and Pharisees, hypocrites! for ye shut up the kingdom of heaven against men: for ye neither go in *yourselves*, neither suffer ye them that are entering to go in." (Matt. 23:4–13)

Here's a little warning I'd like to hear broadcast from the Crystal Cathedral: "Not every one that saith unto me, Lord, Lord, shall enter into the Kingdom of heaven; but he that doeth the will of my Father which is in heaven. Many will say to me that day, Lord, Lord, have we not prophesied in thy name? and in thy name have cast out devils? and in thy name done many wonderful works? And then will I profess unto them, I never knew you: depart from me, ye that work iniquity." (Matt. 7:21–25)

Well — enough of this. Every now and then, reading the Bible is a pleasant change from sex research and medical journals. I'll just close by saying that some of the most important work in our community is done by gay religious workers who try to get us to stop engaging in pointless remorse and self-torture and get on with the more difficult and important work of loving and helping one another.

✍

Q. I'm almost 40. And I must face the fact that I've wasted five years at a dead-end job because I was in love with my supervisor, a married woman who is obviously never going to realize how I feel about her, much less fall in love with me. I must also face the fact that even if she doesn't care for me, I need another woman's love, not marriage and a family. But I'm terrified. Is there any point in coming out so late in life? Frankly, I wonder if other women will find me attractive. I have a lot of love and loyalty to offer, but I'm certainly no movie star. I don't think I've ever met another lesbian. What should I expect? Where can I go? What should I do? My life has been defined by my job and this unrequited love for so long that I'm having a very hard time imagining alternatives.

A. Whew. I don't know what made you decide to cut your losses, but I empathize. I often wonder how many "single" people are really nursing a hopeless passion for a member of the same sex, waiting bravely for the day when he or she will come to their senses and turn to the long-suffering person who has cared for them for so long. I approve of your decision to change your life. And yes, it *is* worth it. There are lots of women who do not realize they are lesbians until they are in their thirties or forties, or even later in life.

Check the resource list for the titles of books you can read to get more information about what it means to be a lesbian and what kind of a life you can make for yourself. You also need to know where you can go to meet other women. Get some lesbian guides and check out your local community. There are also some reputable publications listed that carry ads for gay women. This is a method that many women use to find pen pals or partners, especially if they live in areas where there isn't a big lesbian community.

The lesbian community is diverse. It includes women of all ages, races, and political and religious beliefs. You are sure to find women who are compatible with you. Don't worry about being attractive; you'll do just fine. There are a lot of women your age who are sincerely seeking sex and companionship. There's a long-standing tradition in the lesbian community of reluctance to bring somebody out. But in most small towns and cities there are also a lot of single lesbians who are eager to meet new women, and I'm sure you'll find somebody who won't be intimidated by your lack of experience. Good luck. And don't waste any more time!

✍

Q. I'm 18, and my brother is 23. He's been out of the closet for four years, and my parents basically accept him and his life. For the last two years, I've been experimenting with gay sex, and in the last six months have really come to feel that's what I want. All my life when I did something they didn't approve of, my parents would blame it on my older brother's influence. I'm worried about telling my family because I'm afraid they'll blame it on my brother and maybe even think he and I have had some sexual contact. What should I do?

A. Talk this over with your older brother. If the two of you can present a united front, you can help your parents get over any problems they may have. You don't want them to drive a wedge between the two of you by blaming him for your sexual choices.

Coming out is easier to deal with if you're living away from home. It's also important to feel completely clear about your identity and as guilt-free as possible. If you feel good about yourself, you can view any upset feelings your parents have as a temporary bad situation that will eventually get better. After all, they've already been through this with your brother. This time it should be easier.

They are more likely to believe it is *their* fault you are gay than to blame your brother. After all, they did raise two of you! If they'd contact a local group for parents of gays, it would help them a lot. I'm sure they have a lot of questions that only other parents in the same situation can answer.

✍

Q. I'm a 24-year-old gay black male who grew up in a small city in California. Growing up in this town was not extremely hard on me being gay, although I was shy and a little overweight.

Well, it came to my attention recently that the other gay youths in the neighborhood are not having it so good. My sister told me about a friend of my family (not my friend any more) who hit a man on the bus just because he believed he was gay. And another neighbor bragged to me about beating up the gay guy ("faggot" was his word) around the corner. And just today a boy about 15 years old was walking down the street (he lives on this street) and was called the "f" word in front of me and chased home.

I questioned the neighbor on how he knew the boy was gay. He said he had seen him in the field behind our house with other guys. I asked this neighbor why he chased him. The only answer I got was because he is a faggot.

At that moment I thought maybe I should tell them the truth about me. I can live without these people in my life, even though my brother is their best friend. I think my brother knows about me anyway. I'm 24 years old, not overweight any more, with no girlfriend so far.

I would like to make a difference. But I don't know where to start. Should I come completely out of the closet? Most of the neighbors look up to me because I got a good job (through school) and am making something of myself. Very few have in this neighborhood. And if I lose this so-called friend or even some or all of my family, I wouldn't be losing much.

A. Coming out is a difficult process. Some people are going to accept the news that you are gay. They may even tell you

you they knew already. Other people are going to feel that they were deceived, that you're not the responsible, successful person they thought you were, and will be very negative.

It's probably a bad idea to start coming out by telling somebody who beats gay people up that you're gay too unless you're prepared to defend yourself. Most of us start coming out by talking to family members or straight friends that we're very close to and expect will be sympathetic. It's easiest to come out to one person at a time. Tell them you have something important to discuss — don't just blurt the news out when you've got to leave the house in fifteen minutes to go to a movie. Explain that you don't want to upset or shock them, but you are afraid that if you deceive them it will damage your relationship. Be prepared to answer some very basic and even silly questions. Coming out is not a single event. As time goes on, you'll need to keep on talking about this with your straight friends and family members. They won't be able to organize their emotional response or their questions in one discussion.

It's easy to say you can do without your family and friends when you still have their love and care. Develop more of a relationship with the gay community in your area before you alienate people who are already a big part of your life. Coming out can be exhausting. If you want to get involved, see if there's a gay youth group that you can do volunteer work for. Or you may be able to make personal contact with gay youth in the neighborhood and help them on a one-to-one basis.

You don't have to take out an ad in the newspaper or otherwise come out of the closet completely to have an impact on the people in your life. It can be a more gradual process. In my opinion, everybody should speak out against violence, especially when it's directed against people simply because they are different. You don't have to be gay to think anti-gay violence is horrible.

✍

Q. This question may be naive of me, but as a single man of 25 who has never had a relationship or a boyfriend, and has experienced exactly one (blind) date in his life, I find myself questioning both my sexual identity and my abilities to interact with other gay people. I am of average appearance, but have very long black hair and a short beard that lends exoticness to my half-white, half-Oriental self.

I belong to several gay organizations where I meet very sweet, decent people all the time and discover to my frustration that they are either married or attracted to my other friends but not me. I try very hard not to demand a perfect physical appearance from the men I meet, and I'm willing to be sociable if the guy is sweet, open, and honest (as well as free of tobacco, drugs, or excessive booze) and at least marginally attractive.

But I'm very, very intimidated about meeting new people. It's been impossible for me to initiate a conversation or even approach someone new on my own. I'm rooted to the spot, and I stumble over my words even with an introduction from a good friend. Sometimes the anxiety becomes so great that I begin feeling chills and trembling. My recalcitrance has been interpreted as insufferable stand-offishness, and much to my horror on several occasions when someone wanted to give me a hug, I've actually flinched.

I've had a few awful one-night stands where the anxiety of my inexperience coupled with fright over a stranger in bed with me has caused impotence. My potency returned generally within minutes of the person's departure. This makes me wonder if I'm asexual rather than being gay or straight. (I've been asked that question twice.) I find myself becoming obsessed not just with masturbation and sexual acts but with simple physical intimacy among my coupled gay friends, and I even felt like crying with loneliness once when I saw my *parents* hug each other. That can't be normal.

I don't know whether to seek therapy for this or simply accept that I'm just not meant to have a boyfriend or lover.

A. There's a lot more going on here than the shyness one would expect to experience when meeting new people or going to bed with someone for the first time. If someone who is simply reaching out for a hug makes you flinch, of course sex is out of the question! You aren't just experiencing a beginner's anxiety about making love, you are terrified of any physical contact.

No, you shouldn't simply accept this. You're not destined or fated to be alone your whole life. The fact that you crave intimacy means you're capable of someday having a satisfying relationship with another man.

Is it possible that you were sexually abused as a child? Are either of your parents an alcoholic, or was your family dysfunctional for another reason? The feelings you describe resemble some of the stories I've heard from incest survivors and the adult children of alcoholics about their problems with sex and relationships.

If you want to be able to have a lover — or even just meet and talk to men you find attractive — you need to get some more insight into your feelings and make some changes. This would probably be much easier to do if you had the help of a supportive, well-trained therapist.

Q. Now that I'm in college and have put some miles between myself and my family, I find myself re-examining a lot of the values and assumptions I grew up with. There's a lot less peer pressure here, so I just kind of stopped dating girls. I have a couple of "straight" friends who come over when they feel horny. We've done mutual J/O, and I sometimes give one of them head. I really like it. I don't think it's going to go any further with these two guys, but it's easier to play around with them than it is to admit to myself that I don't really care that much about the opposite sex, and I'd like to be with a gay man who cared about pleasing me. Maybe even loving me.

Only one thing really stops me. I'm afraid of AIDS. It seems like it's mentioned in the papers every day, and all the news is bad. I'm not even 21. Sex with my buddies is big fun, but I sure don't want to give it up to the Grim Reaper. Is it worth it for a young guy to come out in the age of AIDS?

A. Yes. Absolutely and unequivocally, yes. Gay people who don't come out lead miserable, frustrating, duplicitous lives. I know because I've gotten letters from men in their sixties who bitterly regret being in the closet, despite the horrendous amount of persecution gay people suffered when they were young. Don't do this to yourself. You'll always wonder what you missed. You'll never feel really close to anybody because they won't know your secret. Even if you have a good marriage and wonderful children, you won't be able to enjoy them. And you'll make a lot of other people unhappy.

The precautions that gay men must take today to avoid getting AIDS are no more difficult or inconvenient than the precautions straight men take to avoid getting somebody pregnant. Even before AIDS came along, I encouraged my gay male friends and straight women friends to use condoms because they prevent transmission of herpes, chlamydia, syphilis, gonorrhea, hepatitis, warts, and a host of other diseases that are messy, painful, and expensive to treat.

Besides, it's not just gay people who have to worry about AIDS. These days, being a responsible sexual being of any orientation means using condoms or other latex barriers and following safer sex guidelines. Don't trip over a rubber and miss the rest of your life!

Ceremonies and holy unions

Q. My boyfriend and I have been in our relationship for a year and a half, and we are deeply in love. We are planning a holy union ceremony for next fall. We're both devout Catholics despite the position of the Vatican on homosexuality. Our problem is multifaceted. We live in a small, terminally homophobic town in upstate New York where my lover is well-known in business and politics. We don't know where to find a priest or church to unite us. There are no traditions to guide us. We don't know what to wear. We don't want to use words like "wedding" or "engagement," but we don't know what else to use. The list goes on. We want to keep it simple and fairly inexpensive.

I might add that it pisses me off every time I see a breeder's picture in the paper because she got engaged and I think about how she has a family to help plan and pay for a big, beautiful wedding. But that's my problem. We only have each other, and I know that's more than enough. I thank God every day for my lover. I really would appreciate help in planning this ceremony, and I don't know where to turn. What should we do?

A. I suggest that you contact Dignity, a support group for gay and lesbian Catholics listed in the resource guide. They should be able to help you arrange a ceremony to commemorate your commitment to one another.

The term "holy union" seems a very adequate substitute to me for the term "wedding." The period of time you and your lover spent dating, prior to living together, is the equivalent of heterosexual courtship. And your term as live-in partners seems to me to be consistent with an engagement, since that's how heterosexual couples label the period of their relationship in which they intend to make the ultimate commitment and are preparing for it.

Since this is such an important day for both of you, I would suggest formal attire that's consistent with the time of day at which the ceremony takes place. Since you want to preserve your privacy, you need not invite anyone except your close friends and possibly any family members who have been understanding and supportive. Handwritten invitations are the most correct and formal. Engraved ones are a widely accepted substitute.

Events like this can be held in large private homes as well as a church or hall. Perhaps one of your friends has a suitable space if you do not. It is legitimate to locate a safe, supportive space like a gay church for the ceremony even if it's out of town. As long as you aren't asking them to travel thousands of miles, I'm sure your guests will for the most part be happy to travel to share this occasion with you.

You'll probably want to hold a reception after you and your lover exchange vows and provide some refreshment for your guests to thank them for sharing this happy moment. But there need not be a huge crowd in attendance, and you need not bankrupt yourselves to make it a memorable occasion. For a very small wedding party, dinner at a good restaurant is more enjoyable than a formal reception.

Congratulations to you, and my best wishes to you both.

✍

Q. My lover and I are serious in our desire to legally confirm our relationship by marriage just as straight couples can. Are there any states, cities, or counties in the U.S. that permit legal marriages between members of the same sex, and if so, where? What about other nations?

A. There is no such thing as a legal marriage between same-sex couples in this country. Local ordinances that would give some rights to "domestic partners" have been proposed in some cities. But such laws would not constitute a legal marriage for gay couples.

Marriage between same-sex couples is legal in Denmark. On October 1, 1989, as this law took effect, eleven couples took advantage of its provisions. But even in this liberal Scandinavian country, married same-sex couples do not have all the privileges that straight couples enjoy. For example, the law does not allow gay couples to adopt children. I called the Danish Consulate and was informed that the law applies only to Danish citizens. Gay American tourists cannot be married.

This is frustrating, I know. But it will probably take many more years of activism and education before the public is ready to acknowledge that our relationships are at least as important and sacred to us as heterosexual unions. In the meantime, see an attorney to safeguard any business relationships or property you and your lover hold in common. You can become joint tenants, hold each other's power of attorney, and make other contracts with one another. This is perhaps not as meaningful and certainly not as romantic as marriage, but there is no reason you and your spouse should not take advantage of every opportunity to take care of one another, plan for the future, and safeguard the material things you may accumulate together. Many heterosexual couples don't seem to realize that getting married is more than a statement of mutual love, it's also a state-mandated business contract.

If you like, you and your partner can create your own ceremony to express how you feel about each other and hold your own wedding.

✍

Q. I am divorced with a 9-year-old son. I have visitation rights, and he spends time with my lover of four years and me whenever we can. We all get along very well, but I have never made it clear to him that I am gay. We want him to be a part of our wedding next summer, if only to attend, but first I need to tell him about us. I simply do not know how to open such a conversation. I most certainly do not want to lose him. I anticipate no help from his mother. She is homophobic and would be just as happy if I never got to see him again, as long as she continued to see my weekly support checks.

A. If you had custody of your son, I would advise you to answer all of his questions about sex as honestly and as simply as possible. I would also advise you to tell him that your lover is like a second father to him, and that two men or two women can love each other and want to spend the rest of their lives together, the same way a man and a woman feel when they get married. Any child who gets nontraditional sex education should also be told that your ideas about what is right and wrong are not shared by many other people. Your son would need to be warned about how silly and angry adults can be about sexuality so he could use the information you gave him with a minimum of fuss and embarrassment. Hopefully, by the time a child asks about sex, he or she is old enough to grasp the concept that people don't always agree, and it doesn't mean he or she has to take sides.

Since you do not have custody, you should probably be more cautious. Chances are good that if you start discussing your sexuality with your son, he will be confused by this information. The only person he'll have to ask for clarification is your former wife. And she will then have an excellent excuse to go to court and try to cut off your visitation rights. Only you can say if she's hostile enough to do something this mean.

Under the circumstances, I think that inviting your son to your wedding is inadvisable. Instead of being able to concentrate on creating a joyous occasion for you and your lover, you'll be embroiled in a great deal of turmoil and conflict. Think about what that will do to your son, who is probably already having problems coping with the divorce. It's not fair to expect a 9-year-old to cope well with this situation on his own. You'll be busy participating in the ritual. Who's going to look after him? Certainly not his mother! Your son has no context in which to place such an event or understand it. Surely you do not need the approval of a child to validate your relationship.

Incidentally, this advice does *not* apply to grown children, who should certainly be invited to share happy occasions in the lives of their parents. And I can think of no happier occasion than the public celebration of true love.

✍

Q. My fiancé and I live in Orlando, Florida. We want to get married but are having problems finding someone who will marry us. No one will do gay weddings. Would you possibly have information on anyone in this area that would marry us? Also, could you tell me what we have to do to get married?

A. Any ceremony performed to celebrate your relationship will not be legally binding. It's a purely personal way of commemorating your affection. Gay and lesbian couples have chosen many different kinds of marriages, depending on their values and the type of relationship they have.

If you want a service with a religious element, get involved with a group of gay worshippers of similar faith. Check the resource guide. You should be able to find a gay minister, rabbi, priest, or other member of the clergy to marry you and your lover. If neither of you are religious, perhaps you don't need the assistance of a third person to feel that you've affirmed your relationship.

A gay clergyman or rabbi will have a marriage service that you can use. If this doesn't suit you, you can write a service of your own and recite these vows in front of friends or privately, perhaps with a celebration afterward. I would just caution you to avoid inflicting your personal tastes in poetry upon your guests. You don't want the audience cringing and rolling their eyes. For example, anything by Kahlil Gibran or Rod McKuen should not be read in front of other adults, however much you might enjoy perusing their works in private. Vows that include the words "as long as we both shall love" are much more sensible than the more traditional "as long as we both shall live."

Since your marriage will be extralegal, you don't need blood tests or a license. The minimum requirement is to love and trust each other enough to want to confirm that publicly. If a third party marries you, he or she may have their own rules, so talk to them. Some ministers, priests, or rabbis feel that same-sex couples should live together a certain amount of time before getting married, and others may simply want to interview you. The purpose of this is to make sure that you understand what you're contemplating and don't embark upon this serious undertaking without adequate forethought.

☝

Q. Having very few straight friends or close relatives, I never learned the usual wedding etiquette. Now I've been invited to a "celebration of union" by a reasonably good friend. I know that it's usual to give wedding presents to heterosexual couples and would like to show my friend that I respect his union as much as a straight marriage. But I'm stumped. What's a customary wedding gift? When and how is it transmitted from me to him?

A. Several factors might influence your choice of a wedding present. Are your friends just now setting up housekeeping with one another? If so, some discreet inquiries about what they need might be in order. Ask the member of the couple who is *not* your friend for some suggestions. This is a good way for the two of you to start, at the very least, a pleasant acquaintanceship. If your friends have been living together for a while, consider their lifestyle. Do they have hobbies in common? Sports? Are they gourmet cooks, great readers, or opera buffs? Is china or silver an appropriate gift (and within your budget)? Ideally, you want to give them a present that they can use together.

If I'm not sure that my gift will be appropriate or unique, I sometimes enclose a note that says, "Everyone is always telling jokes about getting six toasters for their wedding. If this happens to you, please let me know. I've kept the receipt for this so you can exchange it for something else if you'd like."

Gifts should be sent to the joint home of your friends or to the home of your friend's lover *before* the ceremony and reception. The happy couple is going to be too busy on the day they exchange vows to open presents. I know a lot of people love to display their gifts at a reception, but this is in terrible taste.

✍

Q. It's me again. I bought a nice wedding gift for my friend, as you suggested. That was two years ago. Six months later, they broke up, and now Matthew is having another holy union ceremony. I can see this is going to add up to big bucks over the years. What do you suggest?

A. Special occasions are not held for the purpose of soliciting gifts. If someone is so overjoyed by the news that it's your birthday or you're in love or it's Christmas, and they just can't resist getting you something, that's wonderful of them. But it is not the prerogative of the birthday boy, groom, or friend at Yuletide to haul in the loot. A friend would be very distressed if you strained your own finances to buy them a gift. It would probably grieve them to think you might be suffering from anxiety about money on a day when everyone should be merry.

You should RSVP the invitation you presumably received to Matthew's wedding with a handwritten note expressing your warmest congratulations and your intention to attend or be absent. Beyond that, you need do nothing.

✍

Q. I'm about to be joined in a holy union ceremony at our Metropolitan Community Church. If my in-laws are invited, I have a feeling they'll come, but I know they will be so stiff and uncomfortable that they'll spoil the atmosphere. My lover, of course, thinks we have to invite them anyway. We've agreed to do whatever you say.

A. It is your lover's right to decide whether he wants his parents to be present. Notice I said *wants* them to be present, not *feels it would be incorrect* to omit inviting them. If he issues them an invitation, it is your job to kill them with kindness, lavish them with love and courtesy, and introduce them to simply everyone with great enthusiasm. This is the only way to prevent their stiffness and discomfort from spreading to the entire crowd.

When I give this kind of advice to people, I'm often told that I'm asking them to be dishonest. But I know of no other way to remain morally and socially blameless while simultaneously making it clear to everyone what you really think of a difficult or troublesome person.

Don't let your wedding day become a tragedy. It's not unheard of for lovers to decide they can't stomach each other because they can't handle the stress of creating a big party to tell everyone how beautifully they get along. Anything that would cause a scene between you and your beloved should be avoided at all costs. You are on the same side here. He has no choice about who his parents are. But he does have a choice about who he goes home with, even after his own wedding.

✍

Q. My lover and I are planning to be married. She's generally pretty butch, and we'd like for her to wear a tux and me to wear a white dress. Do you think this is asking for trouble? Her parents will be flying out from Iowa for the event.

A. I'm sure it's no news to your lover's parents that she's "pretty butch." If they can deal with a lesbian wedding, they can deal with the tux. Some straight people actually find butch–femme lesbian relationships easier to cope with because old-fashioned etiquette specifies slightly different treatment for men and women. With a butch–femme couple, these rules need only slight modifications to work.

A white dress signifies that the bride has never been married before. I'm sure you'll look lovely in it, but don't expect people to refrain from making jokes. Smutty remarks are a long-standing part of weddings, and you can't eliminate them without taking all the fun out of the occasion for your guests.

✍

Q. Three years ago, my lover and I threw a major party to announce our wedding. Everybody, but everybody, was there, including a few local politicians. Last week, he ran out on me. He left town with the contents of our joint banking account, the Rolls, and the pool boy. I know this sounds like a Gordon Merrick novel, but it really did happen.

Now I'm terrified to be seen in public. Every time I think about holding that bastard's hand, telling him and the minister and all of our friends that I would love and cherish him forever, I hiss and grind my teeth. I was even *crying*, I was so happy. What a sap I was. And now everybody will know I made a fool of myself over a man who used me.

I can't tell you how hurt and humiliated I am. What can I do?

A. See your attorney and your accountant. Get all assets transferred into your own name. Change the locks, including the locks on the cars. Taking care of this business is unpleasant, but if you don't do it now, you'll be in for even more drama when he runs out of money and comes back sans pool boy to beg for forgiveness and a check.

Then call your best friend, tell him or her that you are devastated and have to get out of the house, and let them take care of you. Go cry on somebody's shoulder. Your friends will be on your side. The people who aren't your friends were making catty remarks at your wedding and haven't stopped since. Don't worry about them. A guy who's as well fixed and tenderhearted as you are won't lack for companionship for long.

Divorces are a fact of modern life. You are the injured party, so hold your head up high. By leaving you this way, your lover embarrassed himself, not you.

✍

Q. I'd like to give a wedding shower for my best friend, who's about to get married to another woman. How can I do it without aping the usual heterosexual (and sexist) tradition?

A. A bridal shower is intended to let the bride glow in front of her female friends, who will give her useful household objects that are not grand enough to be wedding presents and lingerie that is too risqué for her to show her mother. It's also a good idea to keep the happy couple separated as much as possible before the wedding, because when they're together, they're probably going to be fighting about how to hold this event and how much it's going to cost.

Please don't worry about "aping heterosexual traditions." If we stopped doing everything heterosexuals do, we wouldn't be able to breathe, much less fall in love. It's her last chance to show off as an (ostensibly) single girl. Throw an afternoon tea party with light refreshments and some silly games. Discuss last-minute wedding plans. Show her how much you love her.

If this still sounds awkward, offer to help sponsor a dinner after the rehearsal for the folks who'll be directly involved in the ceremony.

✍

Q. My lover of only one year's standing recently got the idea that we should get married. Now it seems like this is all I hear about. I'm a shy person and don't like the idea of getting dressed up and standing in front of a bunch of people. It seems like asking for trouble. I love my partner, but I don't think he's very mature, and this seems like his way of asking for attention. He's also not very secure about me, and I frankly feel he wants some emotional blackmail to hold over my head. It would make me happy if we stayed together for the rest of our lives, but it seems to me that a wedding ceremony makes that even less likely than it is already.

A. You are not ready to get married and should tell your partner to stop pressuring you about it. After all the reasons you list for being reluctant to celebrate your commitment (?) to him, I can't think of one good reason why you should succumb to his nagging. Ask him if he wouldn't rather take a nice trip to the mountains or the seashore instead.

✍

Q. How do I withdraw an invitation to a holy union ceremony? My lover broke up with me last evening. He's done this before, but this time I'm sure he means it to be permanent. We had invited about a hundred of our friends. Fortunately, I kept a copy of the mailing list, because I think he's too embarrassed to deal with it at all. I don't think it's right that his friends should be inconvenienced even though it pisses me off to have this unpleasant chore dumped in my lap.

A. The last thing you want to do is telephone a hundred people and have a hundred separate conversations about how and why this happened. Take refuge in old-fashioned etiquette, which tells us that all meaningful social interactions are conducted on

91

paper. If you had invitations printed, you can use them to notify your guests that the wedding is off. Write in the words, "We regret that the ceremony will not take place," sign your name, and mail them out.

I'm sorry to tell you that if you've received any wedding gifts, they must be returned. But it sounds like your prospective mate was not the kind of boy who would have helped you write the thank-you notes anyway. It's better to find these things out now, before you buy a car or a house together. It might console you to think that by dealing with this promptly and with courtesy, you make it very clear to your circle of friends just who is at fault without the need to utter a single word of blame or self-pity.

Raising children

Q. My brother has a 5-year-old daughter and a 9-year-old son. The son has always been fond of me, and I enjoy him very much the few times I see him during the course of a year. This Labor Day I was a guest at their home for chicken barbecue. The little boy loves to sit on my lap and talk with me, and I also enjoy this as I like children. I am a single 66-year-old and have never come out to my family, but I am sure they all suspect that I am one of the 10 percent.

This Labor Day when I called to the boy to come and talk with me he told me his mother said he could not sit on my lap any more. I just shrugged my shoulders and accepted it. However, I consider this a real slap in my face. I know his redneck, homo-hating mother thinks I will molest him. I am not a pedophile or child molester and never have been. How would you suggest I handle this situation in future? Would you drop them summarily? Or would you continue to associate with them? I think the boy's mother was extremely insulting and callous to do this.

A. It's possible that the boy has reached an age where he finds affectionate physical contact with anybody embarrassing. This doesn't mean he doesn't love you — it just means he's getting more independent and concerned about how other people perceive him. Only babies sit in other people's laps. Even if there's more going on here than that, don't punish the child. Continue to greet him fondly, bring him gifts if that's been your custom, and talk to him without putting him on your lap.

Before dropping your family, why not talk to the boy's mother in private? Tell her that since you have no children of your own, you really love spending time with hers, especially since she has such well-reared offspring. Then tell her you're puzzled by something your nephew said to you, and ask her to explain his statement. If she isn't overtly hostile and nasty, ask for suggestions about how to continue to be close to your nephew. If (as you suspect) this is all her fault because she's homophobic, tell her that you think it's a real shame to make children afraid of adults who are not dangerous.

If you simply disappear from this kid's life, he will lose a friend. Why give his mother the satisfaction? You haven't done anything wrong. She is the one who should have to explain herself. A carefully chosen word in your brother's ear might not be a bad idea.

✍

Q. My lover and I are breaking up, in part because I don't like how she treats her kid. She is a chronic alcoholic and refuses to admit she has a drinking problem even though doctors have told her she is damaging her gallbladder and liver. I don't think she's an abusive parent, just incredibly inconsistent and arbitrary. The poor little guy never knows when Mommy is going to be pissed and smack him one or give him a kiss and tell him, "Never mind." He's not doing well in school and keeps asking why Daddy doesn't visit any more. I think he's a great kid. He's smart, outgoing, and affectionate. I'll really miss playing catch with him and helping him with his homework.

Now that we're separating, I wonder if I didn't stick around this long because of her son. She has told me many, many times that she doesn't care about being a mother but didn't want the boy's dad to have him. If I asked her to let him live with me, I don't think she would care — it would be good riddance to both of us. What are the legal ramifications? I never thought of myself as a parent before, but why should this kid be as messed up as his mother?

A. See an attorney. It may be possible for this child's mother to make you his legal guardian. But be aware that this doesn't necessarily mean you get to have custody of him forever. If she wants to get nasty, she can instigate a court action to take the child away on the grounds that you're a lesbian. Since she is also gay, this would probably just result in the boy's father or one of his grandparents eventually getting custody of him. But drunks aren't always reasonable people. They can be spiteful and shortsighted.

You could ask your former lover to let her son live with you, but this has potential to become quite messy. For one thing, you would need to stay in touch with her to get help registering him for school, giving consent for medical procedures, etc. A homophobic husband or family would have a field day if they heard about it.

A child who already feels abandoned by his daddy is going to have a hard time adjusting to living with his mother's "friend." If you do wind up with him, be prepared to get him some counseling. Young people are pretty sensitive about being handed around like boxes of candy. But it does sound like he'd be better off with you than he is with an adult who is, let's face it, abusive.

Encourage your ex to get into Alcoholics Anonymous. But don't get sucked into supporting her addiction to alcohol. She might use your affection for her son to manipulate you into taking care of her so he won't suffer. Just remember that as awful as being the ward of the state can be, sometimes it's better than life with an incompetent biological parent. If you stay in touch with this family and things deteriorate to the point where the child is threatened, call social services and report the situation.

✍

Q. I've been living happily with my lover for several years. By a previous marriage, I have a son, 11, who now lives with us. (My ex-wife is deceased.) Quite often on weekend mornings, he has come into our bedroom and wanted to crowd in with us. Today, he was naked. He began to make advances toward Jim, my lover. He has also been asking about having a friend over to spend the night.

I'm not really sure how to handle this. My lover gently steered him away this time, but I wonder what might happen if my son continues his advances. Also, should I go ahead and let him have his friend over? I have no doubt about what that would lead to once they were in bed. I just can't accept the notion that an 11-year-old should be having sex. I didn't have my first experience until I was in college — and that was with a female!

What do I say to him? My lover feels we should let the boy do what he wants, but all I need is to have my ex-wife's parents raise a fuss over something like this. And I don't want my lover to be a "child molester" either. I'm afraid that it is all going to be a big scandal if anyone finds out.

A. Insert a bar of soap into your left ear, rotate it six times, then push it out via your right ear. You, sir, have a dirty mind.

If your in-laws want to start a child custody battle, they could just as easily complain that your son is deprived because he can't have friends his own age visit in his own home. Let the boy have overnight visitors. They are not necessarily going to do anything. If they do fool around, so what? Are you a better human being for waiting until you went to college to have any sort of sexual experience? Are you 100 percent sure you *never* played doctor with kids your own age, or is it possible you are editing some of your childhood memories?

Next time your son wants to climb into bed, send him back to his room for his pajamas. Then let him sit and have breakfast in bed and read the Sunday comics with you and your lover. There's nothing wrong with him wanting to get a hug and some adult company. If he initiates anything more than that, you or your lover should ask him (calmly and politely) to please cut it out.

You will raise a happier, healthier kid if you realize that human beings are capable of experiencing physical pleasure even as infants, and that it is natural for us to seek out other warm bodies. A good parent doesn't forbid his son to be sexual. You can't stop him anyway. If you try, you'll only teach him to be ashamed and furtive. Instead, try to teach him what the majority's values are, encourage him to form values of his own that respect other people's freedom and privacy, and help him figure out how to express his sexuality without incurring the wrath of the big outside world. He needs to know what your values are about sex and just how negatively most people view it, so he doesn't embarrass himself or get you into trouble. If you haven't had an explicit talk with him about masturbation, the names for all the parts of the body, where babies come from, and why people have sex, it's long overdue.

There are some good books available to help parents talk to their kids about sex. Check the resource guide. Most of these books are available at the public library or any large bookstore. I know you're nervous about dealing with this subject because you're a gay father. But you still have a responsibility to teach your son about sex, and it's every bit as important as teaching him how to cross the street without getting run over. Don't let paranoia about a child custody battle stop you, or you will wind up raising your son even more conservatively than your wife's parents would!

You also need to have a long, private talk with your lover. Your fantasies about him engaging erotically with your son need to be expressed and dealt with. It could be that the person who is most attracted to this child is you. Many parents have a sensual response to their offspring. But because of the taboo against incest and because of the difficulties involved in combining the role of parent with the role of lover, most parents do not (and should not) act directly on those feelings. Instead, they enhance the tenderness and protectiveness you feel toward your child.

✍

Q. Five years ago, my son and I found out about each other when we ran into each other at a local gay bar. Both of us were delighted. A gay father/gay son combination is not common. (I'm now 51 and he's 23. There is absolutely no sex between us.) At any rate, communication between us opened up as never before. We made an unstated pact: I would hear him out completely whenever he had a problem or some news. I would only interrupt if I failed to understand something. Isn't that what dads are for?

For several years, he bewailed the fact that he didn't have a lover. I encouraged him to find a good man. After some time, he did. I was pleased. He tells me how great it is to have a lover. And he tells me about their good times and their bad times. And he tells me and he tells me.

I don't want to complain about my son communicating, but I don't need to hear every minute detail of their love life. I can tell you how many times they had sex last week and who was on top. I really don't need to know all the private stuff.

But when he calls to tell me all the details (and the calls take at least two hours every day), and I tell him that I'm busy or give him some other excuse, he gets his nose bent out of joint. Essentially what I get from him is: "You don't love me any more because you won't listen." Jeez, listening is one thing. Two hours' worth of pornographic descriptions is something else. I think his lover knows what's going on and is reluctant to visit my place out of embarrassment. I'm reluctant to visit them for the same reason.

On the other hand, I do not want, in any way, to break our newly found father-son communication.

A. Wise up, Dad. Kids use that "You don't love me any more" schtick to get anything they want, whether it's six ice cream cones, a pony, or an Ivy League education. And any good parent knows that nine times out of ten, the kid should *not* get what he's whining for.

The lad is not confiding in you because he needs your advice. He's gloating. This is an unattractive habit that is not likely to win him any friends or influence any people in the rest of his career as an adult. Next time he starts to bend your ear with a hard-core description of his love life, tell him, "Son, I have a feeling you are about to give me two hours of hard-core descriptions of your love life. I could make some excuse to get off the phone, but instead, I will be honest and tell you that I am just not interested. I think information like that should be kept between you and your lover."

"You don't love meeeeeeee!"

"Of course I do, Son. And because I love you, I want to give you an opportunity to have a man-to-man relationship with me. It isn't appropriate to expect a 10-year-old to listen to his father's problems or hear all about his sex life. But we both know you aren't 10 any more. And because you are not a selfish, spoiled little boy, I know you will welcome the opportunity to put our relationship on a more equal basis."

What's he going to say — "I am too a spoiled, selfish little boy"?

✍

Q. My girlfriend and I find that going out on weekends is a lot more fun if we double-date with other couples. This could mean dinner, a movie, or dancing. One couple we've been out with a few times has two children. Maybe I'm just not used to kids or I'm too old-fashioned, but I think they are a pair of brats. They are never clean. They fight and argue with each other constantly. If the adults in the room ignore them or try to hold a separate conversation for even a few minutes, they whine and complain until they get everyone's attention. They are always demanding food — crackers, apples, cheese, candy — until I wonder if their mothers ever feed them at home. The last time they were here, they broke one of my favorite vases. It was a present from my favorite high school teacher. I was (and am) furious. How can we tell our friends that we don't mind seeing them, but we'd rather they left their children at home?

A. What you just said wasn't a bad start. Tell them you'd like to go someplace (like a bar with a good dance floor) where you can't take children. Incidentally, did your friends give you a new vase and say something apologetic like, "I know this can't possibly replace the sentimental value of the item that my child so carelessly broke, but I wanted to try to make amends"? If not, why are you trying to preserve your friendship? You might need new friends even more than these kids need new mommies.

✍

Q. I'm a lesbian mother. My ex-husband and I are on fairly good terms, so my 7-year-old son sees his dad regularly and has a pretty close relationship with him. I recently met somebody new, and I think we have a chance to develop something special. Unfortunately, she hates my son. She admits there's nothing wrong with Danny's manners or his attitude toward her, but she says being a lesbian means she doesn't want to have anything to do with men. Since his father loves Danny, she thinks I should talk to him about sending my son to live with him. I think this is a terrible idea. My ex-husband travels on business a lot, and he would have to leave Danny with a baby-sitter. Our son has gone through enough insecurity and anxiety with the divorce. I don't think he should have to cope with what will seem like a rejection from me. Do I have to choose between being a mother and being a lesbian?

A. Your new girlfriend is one of those highly principled people who see nothing wrong with cutting off somebody's arms or legs to make them fit into their bed. Tell this female Procrustes to keep her separatist politics separated from your relationship. Having a child is not like getting too many waffle irons for wedding presents. You can't just give them away or take them back to Macy's. If she can't see that treating your son this way would guarantee his growing up with hostile feelings toward women and lesbians, maybe you should think about another kind of separation.

✍

Q. My lover is twelve years my junior. We've been living together for nearly six years with my two sons, ages 14 and 16. For a few months now, she has been talking about having a baby of our own through "alternative insemination." Although I love her very much and feel our relationship has a long future, I'm really glad to be done with raising babies and don't want to be saddled with the responsibility of a third little life.

We have had some very heated discussions about it with her getting very upset over my unwillingness. She seems to feel I'm being selfish and not thinking of her desire to carry and raise a child. My sons have been very understanding of my relationship, but they aren't too happy with the idea of a baby, either.

A. If you didn't live with your lover and she was able to assume complete financial responsibility for raising a child, she would have more justification for accusing you of being selfish. As matters stand now, this should be a joint decision. Of course, your lover has the right to have a baby if she wants to, but you also have the right to refuse to make raising her child a part of your life.

Several practical questions need to be answered. Is your lover physically healthy enough to have a child? Can you afford to have her taking care of an infant and not working for at least a year — probably more? Do you have enough room in your house for another child? Is artificial insemination going to be easy to obtain from a donor who is definitely not HIV-positive? Do you have medical insurance to cover the costs? Has she ever been around very young children? Does she know how labor-intensive a baby is, or is her notion of motherhood very romantic and unrealistic? Suggest that your lover do some volunteer work with a day-care center. Baby-sitting is often a cure for would-be mothers.

This sounds like an ideal conflict to take to a couples counselor. When two people have opposing positions, they often have trouble hearing one another. If there is a compromise here, neither one of you is going to be able to see it. Get some short-term professional help.

✍

Q. My lover and I are planning to have a baby. For various reasons we would like to do this via artificial insemination. My lover has expressed a firm preference for a female child, but I have heard that most of the children conceived with AI are male. This makes no sense to me. Can this be true?

A. I have heard that a relatively high proportion of children conceived via artificial insemination are male, but I'm not able to locate any research that would verify or disprove this piece of folklore. There are some things you can do that might up the odds of having a female child (see the resource guide), but there's no guarantee. I have to admit that women who insist they want only a daughter bother me almost as much as new fathers who are downcast if they don't have a son. If you and your lover couldn't love a baby boy and raise him well, perhaps you should postpone having children.

✍

Q. At 30, I feel I'm a happy, reasonably well-adjusted gay male. I've been involved in a live-in, monogamous relationship for several years, and I'm well established in my career. The one thing I'd very much like to become is a parent. I love kids, and I'm sure I'd make a great father. I don't believe being gay is a reason to automatically forfeit one of the best experiences life has to offer.

Ideally, I'd like to find a lesbian of like mind. Even though I live in Manhattan I don't know any gay women. I've considered classified ads, but the gay publications I'm familiar with seem to be very male-oriented in their classifieds. Could you suggest an appropriate publication?

A. Your first assignment, should you choose to accept it, is to track down a copy of the local lesbian newspaper. If you can't do this, you have no hope at all of developing the social skills you will need to negotiate with a real, live lesbian and convince her that you'd make a good daddy, and she should spend nine months of her life incubating a child for you. If you want to coparent a child with a lesbian mother, you'll need to be good friends first.

You can place an ad for a surrogate mother. But consult with your attorney first. This is such a hot issue, with a potential to impact other controversial areas like prostitution, that many state legislatures have not dealt with it. However, it may be illegal where you live. If you hire a woman to have a child for you, she might change her mind once the baby is born and involve you in a lengthy and expensive custody battle. Even surrogate mother agreements that go well are usually very expensive. You're asking a woman to risk her health and life for you, and some of the physical changes that take place during pregnancy are irreversible. Giving up a child can be a horrendous emotional experience.

The best way to prevent these problems is to get to know the woman personally. You can't just walk into a lesbian bar, cut a fertile lesbian out of the herd, and take her home to be inseminated. If you're serious about doing this, you need to put some time into this project (let's be honest, years), and develop a social life that is not so rigidly separatist.

Any coparenting situation has to be discussed thoroughly in advance, and it might not be a bad idea to have a written agreement covering several specific points. Who will pay for the mother's medical expenses during pregnancy and childbirth? Who will pay the child's doctor bills? Are other expenses (food, clothing, day care, recreation) going to be split equally? Will the two of you live together? If not, how many days a week do you expect to be able to see the child? Or will the child live with you? What values do you think it's important for the child to learn? How do you feel about the child receiving religious instruction? Do you want the child to attend a private or a public school? How do you feel about corporal punishment? To what extent will her lover or your lover be involved in the child's life? If you don't like each other any more, what happens to the child? It would be wise to have an attorney review any such agreement.

How much direct experience have you had with children? It takes more than a lucrative career and a decent personality to be a good parent. You need lots of time, ingenuity, and patience. You and your lover should do some volunteer time for a day-care center or baby-sit for friends. Otherwise, you may find that once you've paid off the surrogate mother, you need to hire a nanny.

Consider taking in a foster child. Many social workers won't place a child with a gay couple. But a few will, especially if it's going to be difficult to find a home for one of their charges. You may not want a child who is disabled or otherwise at disadvantage. Just remember that your own child could have a birth defect. What are you going to do then, leave it at the hospital?

Adoption is also a possibility. I doubt a state-run adoption agency will agree to let you take a child, but private adoption (although it's very expensive) is more liberal.

✍

Q. What do you think about spanking? My lover's got three kids, and they're all at an age when they have a lot of energy and get into a lot of trouble. They get on my nerves too, but it really upsets me when she smacks them on the fanny. We've had a couple of fights about this. She tells me to stop making her feel like a child-beater and mind my own business. I don't want to raise a trio of monsters, but isn't there a more humane way to communicate one's displeasure?

A. The adults who are responsible for raising children should not have arguments about child-rearing methods in front of the objects of that discipline. This only teaches the little darlings that there's a big, red button to push whenever they'd like to be entertained. One parent is almost always a little stricter than the other, but it makes life easier if you can present a united front.

I don't think it's abusive to swat a child *once* on the bottom, without using full force, if the child is (a) not a teenager, and (b) has done something that might endanger his or her life. The purpose of this treatment is to impress upon a young human whose capacity for reason and logic is not yet fully developed that he or she must do as Mother says, whether they like or understand the rules or not.

This doesn't sound at all democratic, but for some reason children who are reared democratically tend to become tyrants.

Spoiled and unruly children are unlovable, and this causes them a great deal of pain. A tap or two on the butt can spare them a lot of misery later in life.

No effective method of punishment is pleasant for the person who suffers it. However, I personally find prolonged spankings of children, face-slapping, use of anything other than the open hand, and a blow struck in anger to be disturbing.

But, then, I've never raised children of my own, just repaired some of the bad training adults received in their youth, so what do I really know?

Breaking up

Q. After over ten years of being lovers with a wonderful man, I'm sure now, though I still love him, that I'm no longer in love. Over the years our lives have become tightly entwined, needless to say, first emotionally but also with our families, his children, some real estate, money, etc. I need some advice on how to begin and hopefully facilitate this difficult separation without causing any extra pain or complications. For it is the fear of the latter (and an enormous sense of guilt) that has kept me in this relationship a year or so longer than I truly wished to be.

A. If you still feel that your partner is "a wonderful man" and you really feel enormous guilt about leaving him, I think the ten-year investment you have in this relationship merits a few visits to a couples counselor to see if there's any way to salvage it. Even if the only solution is a separation, a trained therapist or mediator can help you and your lover communicate more clearly about your differences and make this process less agonizing.

But before you can do that, you must tell your lover that you've been thinking about breaking up with him for the past year. This is going to be very painful for him to hear, so please pick a time to tell him when the two of you are not due at some family event in half an hour. Even if he simply accepts the news and the two of you decide not to go for counseling, you are going to need some time to cry together and accept this enormous change.

If you have joint property and other financial interests, you will need to see your attorney and your accountant to make sure that the material goods you've acquired together are not lost in the process of separating. You may be able to continue to own property together if you can work out agreements about how it will be managed. An immediate sale could be devastating for your taxes.

I've known couples who ruined each other financially by being vengeful about a breakup. I doubt this ever makes anybody feel better, but some people find it almost impossible to control the urge to lash out at somebody who's hurt them. This is another good reason to have a qualified, compassionate counselor on tap. Your financial advisers won't be able to save you if your lover is determined to be difficult.

Whenever couples mingle their debts and assets, I think they should have a clear, written agreement about how much money is involved, what's going to be done with it, and what will happen in the event that they separate. Some people feel that doing this will jinx the relationship. But if you really care about somebody and want to be fair, you have to plan for all the possibilities.

✍

Q. Five years ago my lover and I broke up. Sex had stopped and both of us thought we could do better. Not so.

He moved away, but his work brings him back regularly. We get together during those visits and have a good time, as old friends who know each other better than anyone else. We do have many good years invested in our original relationship.

He wants to put it together again. While a big part of me wants that too, the truth is we are both immature and will probably remain that way.

I am so fucking lonely I talk to myself. But I don't want to take a chance on going through another gut-wrenching separation if I am being crazy. Based on what I've said here, do we have sufficient reason to get together on a best-friends-living-together basis?

A. Before you and your ex look for a place to live together, you need to sit down with a counselor and discuss your feelings about each other, the breakup, what went wrong in that relationship, what you expect from a living-together situation now, and how you could prevent some of the old problems from recurring. It doesn't really matter if the two of you are trying to be lovers again or just roommates, but it is *very* important that you both want the same thing. Incompatibility or a misunderstanding on this point would be a disaster.

Many ex-lovers live together with great contentment. But problems may occur if either of them becomes intensely involved with a third party, threatening the security and stability of their living arrangements. There's also the potential for resentment if either roommate does *not* have a romance going and blames his ex-lover for chasing new boyfriends away.

Realizing that one is "immature," or whatever you want to call being less than perfect, is a good place to start growing. People really *can* change. You recognize that you are still very fond of your ex-lover, and you're willing to try something new and different to ease your loneliness. This sounds very mature and positive to me.

✍

Q. I don't need advice. I have a very emotional experience to share. Four years ago, I met a wonderful man. I was 22 at the time. He was 45. After four months, I moved in with him in his condo. Everything was fine. Six months later, he suggested that we buy a house. After two months of looking, we found the home that we wanted. The afternoon that the contract was to be signed, to prove my love, I gave him $8,500 — almost all my life savings — to apply to the down payment.

After moving, things started to change for the worse. Arguing was a daily thing. My job requires me to travel occasionally. He didn't trust me at all. The hotel room phone would ring every thirty minutes to see if I was there. Returning home two days early without phoning him, I walked in and found him sucking off our next-door neighbor! He did a 360-degree turn after that. Everything was fine for about a year.

We decided to try our own business. I again went to my savings for $19,000 to put in the business. After eight months and many hours behind the counter, the store was a success. I never once asked to have anything in my name. I loved and trusted him.

Suddenly he changed again, accusing me of having flings with other people. I wasn't. A family crisis came up that forced me to be out of town for three weeks. My family doesn't know I'm gay. He would call morning, noon, and night. Half the time, I wouldn't be there. My family was getting suspicious. I asked him not to call, that I would call him. He got furious, saying that he would throw me out on the street. I didn't believe him. How could a man I love do that?

Returning home four days later, it was pouring down rain. I had to take a cab. He didn't pick me up at the airport. Pulling in the drive, my heart sank. All my belongings were on the lawn. What the rain didn't ruin was broken. My whole life was on the lawn in the rain. He had sold my car, which was in his name.

After six months of depression, my life savings gone, and still $14,000 in debt, I took a room in a flophouse and got a lawyer, trying to get my money back. I lost the case in court. I'm not trying to say don't trust your lover. But make sure your name is on paper if you have an interest in a home, business, etc.

A. It's usually a mistake for lovers to go into business with one another. It's hard to be sweet on each other if you spend a lot of time during the day doing drudge-work. And the pressure of having your finances depend on the success of the business easily becomes too much. Very few small businesses can survive losing one of the owners — especially if they part on hostile, vindictive terms. However, I agree with you that any business agreement should be drawn up by attorneys, properly witnessed, and signed — no matter how much you love the person you are dealing with. Any property that both parties help pay for should be in both parties' names. Someone who deserves your trust will not object to keeping financial obligations and assets clearly (and legally) defined.

This man sounds like he was trouble from the get-go. The first time he took your money without offering to put your name on a bill of sale, or the first time he accused you of being unfaithful and refused to be reassured, a little red warning light should have gone off in your head and not stopped blinking until you left him. Why did you spend so many years as the emotional and financial hostage of this abusive, jealous, violent, irrational, selfish individual? You don't just need to recover financially, you need some help to build up your self-esteem and learn to set some limits so you don't get taken again.

✍

Q. My lover and I have been together for four years. Three out of the four years have been difficult. We date other people and have *very* separate lives. The word "lover" is an inaccurate description.

Two years ago I met this guy Jim. I was going through the "growing up" stage, from adolescence to adulthood, and we got off to a bad start. But he possesses many qualities I admire.

I'm tired of dating, bars, and the games. I've grown up in more ways than one. All I think of, day after day, is Jim. I *really* love and care for this guy! He has made an impression on me. How do I tell him the way I feel?

A. What's a "bad start"? Did you say or do something unforgivable, or were you just a little tacky? Have you seen this guy at all in the two years since you met him? Has he had a chance to see how much you've grown up, or will you have to prove it to him? I'd have to know the answers to these questions before I gave you detailed advice about how to approach Jim. But the tried-and-true method that works in nearly any situation is to take somebody out to dinner, fidget through the main course, stutter and stammer over coffee and desert, drive them home, and at the last possible moment (usually when they are putting their key in the front door) lean out your car window and cry, "I think I'm in love with you!"

I'm not making fun of you. Honest. The only way to tell him you love him is, well, to tell him. But timing could be crucial here. You don't want your offer of romance to sound onerous. If he thinks of you as a troublesome brat, give him some time to see you in another light before you declare your affections.

Your Adviser has got to warn you, though, that *nobody* is going to take an offer of love very seriously if you are living with somebody else. The presence of a live-in lover (no matter how distant) makes it clear you can't really commit yourself to another man. You need to clean up the messy situation with your present lover even if Jim never notices you again. I can't predict how that will go. It could be that you've idealized Jim and used him as an unrealistic fantasy object because you needed to escape from the reality of your unhappy relationship. But once you're out on your own, even if Jim turns you down, you'll be free to pursue the kind of relationship you want with somebody else.

✑

Q. I was dating a very attractive woman and thought things were going great. The sex was fabulous, we laughed a lot, and I was looking forward to getting to know her better and becoming even more close. Then she stopped returning my phone calls. I finally got her to talk to me, and she admitted that she doesn't want to see me any more. But she refuses to give me any kind of explanation. Not knowing why this happened is driving me crazy! I've offered to apologize, go for counseling, do anything to get her back. And all she does is say, "I think it's better if you don't call me again." Is this fair?

A. No. But since when does love have anything to do with justice?
I realize that what you've just experienced is not the way most people break up. It's typical for one party to give the other a long, personal, and extremely pointed explanation that often sounds

108

more like a laundry list of the formerly cherished one's character flaws. Whether this list is delivered in person, by telephone or mail, or in the presence of a couples counselor does not make it any less painful to hear.

As I've often found myself explaining to a former playmate, there's no nice, nurturing way to break up with somebody. You can't sever a close relationship without inflicting pain. And the older I get, the more I believe that the less you talk about it, the faster you get over it. It's true that by the time I break up with somebody I have a list of grievances as long as my forearm, but there are usually many items on that list that would also have appeared on a list of "Reasons Why I Will Love This Woman Forever."

As I've often repeated to myself, with gritted teeth, no one has an obligation to love you. One kiss or embrace does not imply that another will take place in the future. People have a right to come and go as they please. Being left is bad enough. It's always a mistake to make it worse by running after the fickle beauty, crying, "Are you sure there isn't some mistake?"

Keep your dignity. Take your lumps. Call a couple of friends and tell them your tale of woe. Get them to buy you a good dinner. Curse fate, and keep your eyes open for the next temptress who promises to heal your wounded heart. Enjoy every minute with her because you never know if you're going to have another minute or not.

Anatomy and physiology

Q. I've been taking antidepressants and blood pressure pills for several years. I find that they make me impotent, and even at the times when I am able to masturbate, I have a premature ejaculation. My doctor has tried me on various drugs, and the results have always been the same. Is any damage done when one doesn't have an ejaculation (voluntary or involuntary) over the course of a month or more? I'm only concerned about the medical aspects of this problem since I am passive in nature and would assume this role with any potential sexual partner.

A. No, it will not harm you physically if you don't ejaculate. However, the emotional stress of not being able to function sexually — if you want to be sexually active — can't be pleasant. Even if you're sexually "passive," it must not be very satisfying to service your partners if you can't get aroused and eventually have an orgasm of your own.

From time to time, new medications for depression and high blood pressure are put on the market, so check with your physician frequently to see if anything can be done to regulate these conditions without impairing your sexual performance. However, if sex is not important to you, it is not going to damage your health to do without it. For some of us, abstinence causes less tension than the hassles of cruising, tricking, and romance.

✍

Q. I was born with one testicle and have been called One Meat Ball by my brothers and even my sisters for most of my life. I had hopes of someday filling the other part of the sack so that when I go swimming at least it would look even. I have been laughed at by lovers (women). I have felt like half a man despite fathering five children. It doesn't affect my sex life. I ejaculate a large amount. The right testicle is a good-sized egg, and when I sit down a lot of times I sit on it. Oh, how I would like to reach down there and feel a pair of them. Even if they were unmated or someone else's, the thrill would still be there. I always wondered if they could put a plastic egg in there. I asked the doctor. He said, "What for?" I said, "For my self-esteem." He said there was nothing he could do for me. What kind of doctor will do this for me?

A. I'm sorry that the doctor you spoke with was so insensitive, not to mention your relatives and sex partners. You've had to deal with a lot of rude behavior. Some of this was probably just an excuse to handle your equipment and get excited about it being different, but people should have been more considerate.

You couldn't get a transplant of somebody else's testicle, but you could have an artificial one implanted simply for cosmetic purposes. This is not a difficult procedure. Any urologist should be competent to perform it. If not, he or she should be able to refer you to another doctor. As long as you are willing to pay for this service, it is your right to have it done, so don't hesitate to look for a physician who can help you. If you have an undescended testicle in your abdomen or groin, it may need to be removed so it doesn't become cancerous. A urologist can tell you if you need this surgery.

In the meantime, *please* start wearing a jockstrap. The thought of you squashing your testicle every time you sit down makes *me* hurt.

✍

Q. While standing around the sales counter, a friend and I were debating about a point of decorum. I claim that, as a bottom, it is the height of bad taste to go to bed with and act as a bottom to anyone who has a smaller penis than me. My friend claims that it doesn't matter and that the bottom can have a larger penis. We're interested in your opinion.

A. I think anybody who is planning to top you should put your head in one of the brown paper bags you wrote your letter on and keep it there for the duration of the session. If it were up to me, this would take place on the kitchen floor, not in bed. Courteous treatment is only going to encourage a guttersnipe like you to become even more forward. I'm sure you can be put to better uses than imitating a measuring tape. If you haven't learned yet that good taste and good sex are mutually exclusive, you should be forced to do many, many things that will leave an extremely bad taste in your prissy little mouth.

The only rule about cock size is this: The bottom should have a dick that is big enough for him to hang on to, and the top should have a dick that is big enough for him to be able to come. As long as there are dildos and strong right arms in this world, even your level of appetite should not be a problem. If the marital aids industry of Hong Kong can't take care of you, darlin', write again, and we'll have a cozy little chat about the salutary effects of suturing upon size queens.

✍

Q. I'm basically top when my lover and I have sex, but I do enjoy being on bottom. My biggest concern is things being, shall we say, untidy. Can you give some advice on the male douche? I'm not interested in enema clubs or organizations, just the how-tos of good housecleaning.

A. Don't use commercial enemas full of harsh chemicals. All you need is one of those rubber hot water bottles that are sold with enema and douche nozzles. Most good-sized pharmacies have them.

Squeeze the metal or plastic clip on the hose shut. Fill the bag with tepid water. (Tepid water will feel warm to your asshole. Cold water makes you cramp, and hot water — even if it isn't hot enough to burn you — can be painful.) Hang the bag a little higher than your waist, and sit on the toilet or squat in the tub. Open the clip on the tube to let a little water run out. You don't want air bubbles in your colon; it doesn't feel pleasant. Lubricate the nozzle and insert it. (If more than one nozzle came with your bag, use the one that's a smooth, tapered cone with a single hole, not the one that has all those fluted curves and multiple holes.) Let water in slowly. If you feel cramping, stop taking in more water and rest. When you feel like you really have to shit, take out the nozzle and empty your bowels. Spend about ten minutes walking around or doing deep-knee bends to make sure all the water comes out. It can take two or three tries to get rid of an enema.

That's all there is to it. You should be clean enough for regular dick-fucking if you run a whole bag of water in and out of your tush. But then, if you've simply had a decent shit that day, you shouldn't have to worry. Since the top will be wearing a condom, nothing unseemly will touch his dick. I mention this because a few people find that a preliminary enema makes their colon tense, and actually reduces the pleasure of anal sex. If you don't need one to be clean enough to please your lover, why bother?

✍

Q. I've seen many ads for penis enlargers. Do any of these work? The cost is too high to experiment. What are the alternatives for penis enlargement? Please don't tell me to just accept myself the way I am.

A. The standard line that you will find in sex education texts is that penis enlargers don't work, and you should just accept yourself the way you are. The representative of one manufacturer of vacuum pumps told me that he feels the device is basically a masturbation aid anyway, and that most men who buy it understand this to be true.

Despite all this, I have received one letter from a gentleman who reported that by using vacuum pumps to masturbate, hanging a series of small weights from his cock, and wearing a thick metallic ring that fit around the base of his cock head, he added an inch or so to the length of his penis. This took a while — years — and certainly didn't turn four inches into ten. However, he felt it still made a significant difference in his sex life. And he enjoyed the way his "stretching exercises" felt.

I would just caution anyone who wants to design a similar "home exercise" program to avoid dropping a weight that is attached to your genitals from any height. This can tear ligaments within the penis. You should also avoid using weights that are heavy enough to bruise or injure the penis. Anything worn around the balls or the shaft of the penis that makes it feel cold, tingle, or turn a little blue is cutting off circulation and should be removed immediately.

If you can't wait that long, why not buy one of the penis extenders sold in adult bookshops? This is basically just a hollow dildo, although some of them resemble a very thick condom with a solid head. Some of them have built-in vibrators. It can be tricky to use a device like this without your partner knowing. You should probably have the prosthetic on before sex, and not disrobe completely. Dim lighting would help, and you will probably want to enter him from behind while he is on all fours. If your partner is into gadgets, you may still want to use the penis extender rather than a regular solid dildo because it allows you to hold your partner, use your hands to stimulate him, and gives you the feeling of being inside him and coming during penetration. It's also "safer sex."

☜

Q. While the foreskin of my penis can be pulled back easily enough when the organ is in a flaccid state, this is impossible to do when it is engorged. Since I have never experienced anal sex in the active position, I can't assume that sex will be particularly difficult or painful. Should I be circumcised? I can masturbate easily enough but will this still be possible if I go "under the knife"?

A. You should be able to retract your foreskin completely when you have an erection. If you can't do this, it would probably be painful for you to fuck somebody. And it makes wearing a condom problematic.

However, it shouldn't be necessary to have your foreskin removed. That's what circumcision is. This operation would not affect your ability to masturbate, but it does leave a scar, and recovering from it is fairly painful.

Many men have foreskins that are too tight for them to retract completely. A doctor can stretch the foreskin enough to remedy this problem. In the United States, doctors sometimes recommend circumcision to any adult man who still has his foreskin — perhaps because this surgery is routinely performed on male infants, so they are not used to the concept of an intact penis. You certainly don't have to do this to solve your problem.

☜

Q. I've noticed that sometimes after sex, especially rough sex with dildos, I have some bleeding from my anus. What precautions should one use to prevent the skin breaks in the rectum from becoming infected? Is there a medicated anal douche or can one use a diluted version of an antiseptic such as Betadine or Neosporin?

A. You can stop the bleeding by applying an ice pack. Don't put anything up there for a few weeks. It's especially important to avoid dick-fucking since the injured rectal lining makes disease transmission very easy. Eat extra fiber or take artificial bulk to keep your stools soft. Take lots of warm baths. If the skin breaks get infected, don't use over-the-counter medication. See your doctor. Consider using a smaller dildo, sticking it in at a different angle, or just using it with less vigor. You aren't polishing the silver, hon. Torment yourself by postponing orgasm and getting banged firmly but slowly. Your asshole is not a silo for small tactical nuclear weapons. It's got to last for the rest of your life, so take better care of that thang.

✍

Q. I am only 25 years old, and I have developed an age-old problem. I have a hemorrhoid. Thank heavens there's only one, but it is still a problem. I have a few questions about this delightful condition. Do they ever go away? If so, what can I do to aid the process? Any hints on how to enjoy some form of a sex life while suffering from this condition?

A. Yes, hemorrhoids can heal. But they tend to recur if you don't correct the conditions that made them appear. Hemorrhoids can be caused by chronic constipation or diarrhea, both of which cause straining, and will be aggravated by being overweight or by excessive intake of coffee or alcohol. Friends of mine have gotten good results by using a hemorrhoid cream such as Preparation H at least twice a day for about a month. This is messy but seems to soothe the irritation and help them shrink. It's also necessary to use Metamucil or some other form of bulk to keep your stools soft. A high fiber diet with less red meat, cheese, and fat will help your hemorrhoids to heal. Do not sit on the toilet for long periods of time. It's better to sit down, let go of whatever is going to come out immediately, then get up again — even if this means you have to return to the toilet soon. Frequent warm baths help healing. Once bleeding stops, you can try gentle external massage of the anal area. But you should abstain from penetration for at least a month to allow adequate healing time.

If your hemorrhoids are severe, see your doctor. He or she will probably have additional advice.

✍

Q. Is there such a thing as cumulative impotence? By that I mean, can one incident of sexual non-performance lead to another? Not long ago I was having sex (all very safe) with a great guy when I just plain lost my erection. It was quite embarrassing.

Now when I think I want to have a good make-out, I feel reluctant because I am afraid the same thing will happen again. So I do nothing. I don't awaken in the morning with an erection as much as I used to. Of course that might be because now I am a "gentleman of a certain age."

I have heard of some stuff called Ex-Sativa, which is supposed to restore potency. I am reluctant to go for psychotherapy, but I am also unwilling to give up my sex life.

A. While it is common for men to experience fewer morning erections as they age, you should remember that men of *all* ages are sometimes (for no good reason) plagued by a disappearing hard-on. If you want to retain your potency, you should continue to be sexually active. Masturbating every morning (when you are most likely to have a hard-on and high energy) is a good way to keep your ability to perform.

The same thing probably won't happen again, but if it does, just tell your partner, "Well, that's a nuisance, but I'm not going to let it stop me from having a good time, you're too hot." Concentrate on pleasing him. Your erection will probably return, especially if you stimulate yourself.

Some men find that various creams help them to maintain erections. Sex therapists say the benefit is mostly psychological. I think you can do all the psychotherapy you need on yourself. Relax. It will save you money and give you more time to cruise hunky guys and make it.

If this self-help program doesn't work, see if you can locate a clinic that specializes in treating impotence. Many medical schools have such a clinic affiliated with them. Impotence is often caused by physical problems that are treatable.

✍

Q. It's a turn-on to look in the shaving mirror the morning after a hot date and see a few hickeys or other signs of a night well spent. But I was a little horrified when I got into the shower today and had to jump right out when the hot water hit my back. Upon investigation, I discovered *deep* and *very long* scratches down my back that were very tender to the touch and even bleeding a little. I remember getting very hot fucking this guy, and I remember him running his nails down my back, but how did this happen? Frankly, I'm a little pissed about it. I was planning on seeing him again but now I don't know.

A. Call your partner in erotic adventure and tell him (with a light laugh) that he almost raked the flesh from your shoulder blades. You really can't be too hard on the guy. If you were so turned on that you didn't really feel it, he was probably too turned on to know how deep his claws were sunk in your back. It's not uncommon for passion to leave traces that seem a bit excessive in the cold light of Monday a.m.

If you want to see this tiger again, make a date. Before you throw him on his back, clip the kitty's claws and file them down. But watch out — a person who scratches when they are excited may bite instead if you declaw them.

Have you ever considered purchasing a leather jacket? There are more reasons than one for wearing one to bed...

✍

Q. Me and my lover have been together for five years. My problem is for the past ten years I have fantasized either with a dildo or with my fingers up my anus. I'm not worried much about the dildos I've played with before; it's playing with my fingers up my anus that worries me.

When I play with myself (I'm usually by myself), I get on top of my bathroom sink and let lukewarm water run. I let my fingers get wet and put them inside my asshole (two or three at a time). As I'm doing this I might have a photograph of a hot, hung guy in front of me.

This usually lasts twenty to forty minutes. As I play with my fingers I take turns with the dildo. There are times when I don't climax.

What concerns me is AIDS or cancer in the colon and other diseases. The only symptoms I get after I've played with myself is that I receive a lot of gas in my system. (My stomach was treated last year with antacid.) I have talked to my lover about this, but he thinks this is like masturbating with yourself when you fantasize. I used to do this once or twice a month, now it's twice a week.

A. You're probably masturbating more often because you feel anxious about it, and masturbating is a classic way to relieve tension. However, since you worry about getting sick because of the way you masturbate, this increases your anxiety instead of making you feel better.

There's nothing wrong with what you are doing. If you're still taking antacid, that could be giving you gas. Or it could be the result of the position you are in when you put your fingers or a dildo into your ass. Your asshole could be "gulping" air. This is not unusual. It's natural for pelvic muscles to contract rhythmically when you become aroused.

117

Use a water-based lubricant like KY or ForPlay instead of just water. Water actually dries out mucous membranes. Frequent penetration using only water to lubricate your fingers or dildo could make you sore. You should always wash your dildo between uses, and don't share it with anybody.

You get AIDS by being exposed to somebody else's infected blood or semen. Putting your fingers or a dildo up your ass while you jerk off is not going to give you AIDS, and it won't cause cancer, either.

✍

Q. A recent operation for a persistent bladder condition has left me incontinent. For example, I sometimes lose control of my bladder when I laugh. I cannot run or jump. This is especially problematic during sex. I lost my regular partner during the financial problems and emotional stress of that recent period of poor health. Now I'm not sure another woman, even if I should meet someone attractive, would understand. Should I, at age 52, resign myself to a single life?

A. No! Consciousness about health problems and sex is improving in the lesbian community all the time. Since you don't mention a catheter, I assume you cope with your problem by wearing adult-sized diapers. Fortunately, some new brands are on the market that are less bulky than the old-fashioned kind. Don't hesitate to dress up and go out just as you used to, to your favorite bars or clubs. If you were not active in an organization before your operation, become active now. If face-to-face socializing is difficult or there are insufficient opportunities, place an ad in one of the contact publications for lesbians listed in the resource guide. If you want to be sure you will receive mail only from women who are ready to cope with a health problem, mention it in your ad.

The first time you have sex with someone, put a plastic or rubber sheet on your bed. It would be nice to buy some pretty fitted sheets, especially for lovemaking, that can be tossed in the washing machine afterward. Have a stack of towels handy and ask your lover to tuck one under your tushie. Once your partner knows you're not in pain, she should relax and not worry about your bladder control. It may actually become a stimulating part of the sexual experience, a signal of arousal or orgasm.

I hope your doctor gave you Kegels or other exercises to do to keep as much muscle tone in the area as possible. (Kegels are exercises that involve voluntarily flexing the pelvic muscles.) If not, you may wish to see another doctor and ask about physical therapy.

It may be that this problem is only a temporary one or will improve over time.

✍

Q. What are the dangers of cock-and-ball torture, particularly beating and whipping the cock? Some say none; some say any damage is only temporary; others that — yes — because blood vessels are broken, getting a hard-on can be jeopardized; others simply don't know. What are the facts?

A. The genitals are very sensitive. They don't need a lot of stimulation to respond strongly. Any activity called "cock-and-ball torture" should, in my opinion, be "torture" in a fantasy sense only. Clothespins or any clamp that does not crush tissue can be applied to loose folds of the scrotum. The testicles themselves should not be compressed enough to bruise or flatten them. Light whipping with a short flail can be done on the thighs, testicles, and penis. Whipping heavy enough to leave marks should be reserved for padded areas like the buttocks. Ice cubes or hot wax (*not* from a beeswax candle — use "plumber's candles," which melt at a lower temperature) can provide lots of sensations with no tissue damage. Cock-and-ball bondage should not be tight enough to cut or abrade the skin, and it should not be left on long enough to make the penis or scrotum swell or turn blue. The amount of time bondage can be left in place varies, but if your balls are cold to the touch, it's time to untie them. Yanking the testicles can cause tearing inside the scrotum, and a sharp blow to the penis can make it impossible for you to get an erection, or cause an erection to bend at a strange angle.

Can you hurt your cock and balls during sex? Hell, yes. You can hurt them badly enough to require surgery, even removal of a testicle, or lose your ability to function sexually. Remember, S/M stands for sensuality and mutuality — if it isn't sensual and the pleasure isn't mutual, it isn't S/M. Beating something to a pulp is tedious as well as dangerous. Play only with tops who know how to give you maximum sensation with little or no tissue damage.

✍

Q. I recently saw a short news clip about bulimia on television. I thought I was the only person in the world who would force themselves to vomit after an out-of-control episode of gobbling down every kind of food imaginable. But this program seemed to imply that only women have this problem, and I'm a gay man. Guys at the gym frequently ask me how I keep my weight down, and I never know what to tell them. Lately I've been having problems with horrible stomach pains. I think I may be injuring myself, but I don't seem to be able to stop.

A. The majority of people with eating disorders are women. However, a significant number of gay men also experience bulimia, anorexia, or other types of "food abuse." See your doctor *immediately* and get a referral to a physician who specializes in eating disorders. There are also some groups listed in the resource guide.

☞

Q. I am gay, monogamous, and have had a lover for one and a half years. Having no lover before, I masturbated quite often, nearly every day. My right testicle has atrophied and is much smaller than my left one, which I think is my normal size. I had given up masturbation for about six months while I was under medication for the atrophied testicle. Unfortunately, it has not improved. My lover does not want me to be celibate as my physical problem does not affect our relationship. I feel that I should do something to get my right testicle back in shape.

A. Call the closest gay hotline and get a referral to another doctor, preferably one who you can talk to about your sexuality.

Many people believe that frequent masturbation or sex with a partner will drain your vitality or weaken the genitals. The opposite is true. The best way to promote sexual health is to stay sexually active. Masturbation does *not* cause the testicles to atrophy. You can continue to masturbate as much as you like, and it will not have any ill effects on your health. In fact, I'm not sure that your testicle has atrophied at all. Most men have one ball that's noticeably larger than the other one. I don't know what kind of medication you were taking or why your doctor told you you needed it, but I think you should get a second opinion from another doctor. I hope you weren't treating yourself! That would be a terrible idea.

If, in fact, you did have a medical problem that made one of your testicles become smaller, there probably isn't anything a doctor can do to make it get bigger again. Treatment would probably just prevent further damage and shrinkage.

As long as your testicles are working okay — in other words, you want to have sex, your balls don't hurt you during sex, you have erections, and you are producing semen — your lover is correct and you can resume having sex with him without further anxiety.

✍

Q. I have to face the painful fact that I am impotent. About three years ago I began to experience problems getting an erection. I blamed it on too much to drink, tension, etc. I've tried all kinds of relaxation, even some therapy, and told myself it would go away, but the truth is I've simply been avoiding having sex because my cock won't function.

This is really humiliating and unnerving. What's wrong with me? Do I have to resign myself to making love to my partners and making excuses for myself?

A. At least 10 million American men have problems with impotence. Sex therapists used to preach that 90 percent of all cases of impotence were caused by psychological factors. Now, experts believe faltering erections are often caused by physical problems that can be treated.

Some of the common physical causes of impotence are: diabetes, low blood pressure, taking medication for high blood pressure, arteriosclerosis, hormonal imbalances, and prostate operations.

New treatments for impotence include changing medication for men with high blood pressure, hormone treatments, use of yohimbine (a drug that constricts the veins that carry blood to the penis), injections of papaverine (a drug that increases blood flow to the penis), operations to correct blood flow problems, and penile implants. Medical insurance sometimes covers such treatments.

For more information, contact the groups listed in the resource guide.

Of course, your head can also have an impact on what happens between your legs. But a clinic that specializes in treating impotence can help you regardless of the source of your problem.

✍

Q. About one year ago I noticed a change in my erections. My once straight, fat penis bent when erect, and the erections were incomplete. I asked my urologist about what was happening to me, and he called the condition Peyronie's disease. He has had me take large doses of Vitamin E and thinks that in time my penis will get back to normal.

I also have small, painful testicles. Another urologist told me the pain comes from a varicose vein in the scrotum. I have had overly sensitive testicles for at least thirty years and the pain for five to ten years. The pain occasionally becomes so severe for short periods that I find it difficult to handle my scrotum myself, such as bathing it in the shower. At those times the pain extends to the entire right area of my pubic region and into the thigh.

I'm in my mid-60s and have had a diminishing sexual desire for about three years. My present urologist thinks that I will eventually regain my sexual desire and be able to enjoy sex again. So far I can see no improvement. It isn't that I lack partners. I just don't feel like doing anything. I rarely even feel like masturbating.

A. Well, I'm not surprised. If your penis rarely becomes fully erect and your testicles hurt, masturbation can't be much fun.

Peyronie's is a "systemic disease of unproved etiology" (in other words, nobody knows what causes it), a fibrous tissue process that causes scarring in the penis. There is a localized hardening of material between the corpora cavernosa, which results in the penis being unable to straighten out. People who suffer from this condition may be genetically predisposed. It is associated with taking beta blockers (a high blood pressure medication), but no one knows if this connection means the medication causes Peyronie's. You certainly should not stop taking beta blockers if your doctor feels they're necessary.

Sometimes Peyronie's spontaneously disappears. Vitamin E is a recommended treatment. Steroids and surgery have not been very successful. If the material is removed, it tends to grow back. Radiation therapy has also been tried.

A good doctor would have more recommendations for treating your painful testicles. Can't that varicose vein be removed? That would probably make you feel a lot better. If your present urologist can't help you, find another one.

Here's hoping the Peyronie's spontaneously disappears. I am sure everyone else reading this column also sends their best wishes for your recovery. Someone in his mid-60s who has no lack of partners shouldn't be forced to forego those opportunities!

Q. Do you have any knowledge or experience with colon cleansing by using a bulking agent drunk with water and then douching? I should add that I'm HIV-positive and concerned about jeopardizing my immune system. Instead I want to protect or improve my immune system, which is normal at present. What can you tell me about colon cleansing? What risks are involved?

A. There are many kinds of programs that claim to "cleanse" the colon. I'm assuming that the one you mention includes a high colonic — that is, an intensive series of enemas that remove all fecal matter from the entire large intestine.

Some people have told me that high colonics made them feel better — cleared up their skin, improved their digestion, gave them more energy. The theory is that the bowel is full of "putrefying matter," "poisons," and "mucus" that should be flushed out.

There is no traditional medical evidence or research to back this up. My personal opinion is that since the large intestine's function is to remove water from partially digested food and eliminate waste, as long as it's doing that job, you should probably just leave it alone. In most cases, a properly administered high colonic does no harm, but having too many of them will dehydrate your tissues, remove lubricating mucus that your body needs to eliminate feces without tissue trauma, and move lots of money from your wallet into somebody else's.

I empathize with your desire to keep your immune system in peak condition. But if it's already in good shape, why meddle with it? Don't fix what isn't broken. It's too bad that so many holistic practitioners reject Western science since it provides a reliable method (perhaps the *only* method) of documenting the value or worth of a treatment regimen. Without that kind of evidence, all we have is "vibes" and testimonials. You'll have to do your own research and make your own decision about this; my opinion may or may not be accurate.

✑

Q. Whenever my lover vaginally penetrates me, I feel as if I need to urinate. The fear that I will lose control makes it very difficult for me to relax and enjoy the feeling of having her inside me. Sometimes the anxiety is so great that I cannot have an orgasm, but I don't think she realizes this, so it's just very frustrating. I have asked her to describe her sensations to me when I have my fingers inside her, and what she tells me is very titillating, but it doesn't sound like she has the same problem. Is there something wrong with my bladder? Perhaps it's too large. I have a tilted uterus. Could my vagina also be tilted at the wrong angle?

A: Many women feel as if they need to pee when something is filling the vagina. Unless you have experienced damage to the pelvic muscles during childbirth, surgery, or an accident, it's very unlikely that you will actually urinate. It's safe to relax and just enjoy penetration. Trying to control your bladder will, as you have seen, halt the contractions that cause orgasm.

Instead of second-guessing your lover, why not tell her about this problem? If you could tell her when you begin to feel the urge to urinate, she could tell you exactly what she was doing inside your vagina. Maybe she's pressing up a little too hard or moving your cervix. Fucking is, after all, a kind of internal caress, and there are as many ways to stroke the inside of the vagina as there are to manipulate the clitoris. There's nothing wrong with asking her to avoid pressing on areas inside your body that make you feel uncomfortable.

I've never been able to figure out exactly what a "tilted uterus" is. There is absolutely no evidence that there's one right angle for the uterus and no evidence that "tilting" causes medical problems.

Sexual problems

Q. My lover has a little dick. I do not mean, as he sometimes claims, a dick that is at the graceful end of huge. This dick is *little*. The first time he let me touch it, I couldn't find it. (Noting the expression on my face, he declared defensively, "It gets bigger when it's hard.") Soft, it's roughly the size of my thumb.

This is not a problem. I *love* his dick. I love to call it my little pal or my favorite tasty morsel. I love it even more when he holds his head up and demands that I call it his massive love-log or his huge throbbing member.

No, the problem isn't between us. It's the condom manufacturers! We are both HIV-negative and basically monogamous. But that cute little tramp has strayed from time to time, and we hold to the general principle that men are tramps, so we are religious about safer sex.

For us, a regular condom acts more like a diaphragm. (I suppose I should add that my receptacle is reputed to be as generous as his intrusion is tiny, though I say that's a vicious fabrication.) The condom stays still, and he thrusts in and out of it. It's about as tight a seal as a tent on a mouse.

For years, we have been using Sheik Feather-Lite Snug-Fits. But they have been getting harder and harder to find. Recently, when our pharmacy was unable to provide them, we wrote the manufacturer. Imagine our dismay when the reply came back! To paraphrase them, the market had shriveled. Our brand is discontinued! Where can we find a condom that will fit?

A. It's good to hear from a couple who have a sense of humor about sex. It would be a real shame if the two of you couldn't keep doing all the delicious and nasty things your

125

lusty minds can conjure up. I have a few suggestions about your condom dilemma.

Have you tried Mentor condoms? They're only 2.0 inches in width when lying flat, and they have an adhesive ring at the base that can help hold the condom in place even if it's too large. Yamabuki Huggers are only a little bigger than Sheik Feather-Lite (1.88 inches instead of 1.81 inches). There are also Sensuals and Arouse brand condoms (1.69 inches and 1.75 inches in width respectively), ManForm (1.75 inches), and Zero-O (1.75 inches).

✍

Q. My lover and I have been together for five months. We are completely monogamous, have a deep love for each other, but we have one problem that I don't know how to cope with. My penis is rather large, and my lover is having a great deal of difficulty letting me enter him. It took me several weeks before I could enter him, even though we were both well lubricated. I had to bend my penis so that it would get soft before I could penetrate him. I'm very sensitive about hurting him, so if he cries out, I get soft. He can only allow me to stay in him for a short period of time. I take a long time to come, so I've only been able to come in him once.

We considered getting a dildo for him to use to get used to my size, but he is fearful this will hurt him. Now, I enter him and lie perfectly still and let him use my penis as a dildo. This is quite satisfactory for him, but since he cannot allow me to stay inside him long enough for me to come it drives me up the wall.

Even if I'm never able to fuck him, I'll stay with him, but it sure would make life a lot easier if I could romp in bed with him.

A. Does your lover realize that if you leaned out the window and announced how big your dick was, within five minutes you'd have a line of men at your front door that would wrap around the block? They wouldn't be lining up to wince and insist you bend your erection, either. They'd be there prepared to throw their feet over their shoulders and take what you have with gusto!

He should quit being such a princess and get with the program. The best thing he could do is to practice with a dildo. Get some that range in size from small to large. Since he's able to accommodate your penis as long as you aren't actively thrusting, he won't hurt himself with a dildo that he can control — especially if it's smaller than your cock. Until the day when you can vigorously fuck him with your own meat, you can use the dildo together to teach him how to enjoy the sensation of friction and motion.

There's nothing that makes me madder than a bottom who treats their top like a sexual accessory. Nobody expects him to go from zero to ten inches in sixty seconds. You're being more than considerate. Now he has to demonstrate that he's willing to do more for you than whimper and get done. If he doesn't shape up, I think he should have his orifices sealed with plaster of Paris and get locked up in a large box with nobody but other bottoms to keep him company.

🖎

Q. I'm a college student in New York City. Being in shape and rather attractive, I have no trouble getting dates. I'm attracted to older men, but the fact that men 35 to 50 years of age turn me on is not my deep, dark secret.

When flaccid, my cock is less than one inch long, and when totally erect it's almost but not quite three inches. I've gone to bed with guys who called me names like "Peewee," which humiliated me. I haven't dated anyone for almost a year because I fear that other men will not be happy with my size. In personal ads, I notice guys only ask for well-hung men. What is it that drives so many men to want bigger and thicker cocks and not focus on me? Am I so abnormal that nobody would ever consider me as a lover, but will drop me when we hit the sheets?

I really pray you can give me some sound advice. I find the thought of suicide more appealing every day. Don't tell me to get counseling since I do not feel that I need it. Besides, they wouldn't be able to give me a magic pill to allow me to feel good about my size. Is it possible that women would not mind my small penis? Would intensive therapy change my sexual orientation?

A. I'm surprised that someone who feels suicidal would vehemently reject the idea of doing some therapy to bolster his self-esteem but seems willing to embark upon treatment to change his sexual orientation. I hate to disappoint you, but women are every bit as likely as men to be size queens. I doubt you could switch from one sex to the other anyway.

Of course, there's no "magic pill" that will solve your problem. You're going to have to do some hard work to accept your body as it is. You need to develop some social skills that will allow you to survive as a sexual person and meet your needs for pleasure and companionship. Some help from a qualified professional would make this much easier.

I won't lie to you. Having such a small penis does put you in a minority. It means that many gay men will not consider you a potential sex partner or lover. You need to look for someone who doesn't care about penis size or prefers men with a small endowment. But men like this do exist. I know they do because some of them have written to me. You just need to find the self-confidence to seek them out. There's a support group listed in the resources that may be able to help you with this.

✍

Q. A few weeks ago I made a mistake that I'll be regretting for a long time. I got arrested for masturbating in a public restroom. I wasn't charged with soliciting, only with "lewd conduct" in public. I went to court. The judge (who, I swear, winked at me when reading the sentence) gave me a fine and two years of probation.

After I spend two years (plus) being a good boy, how do I go about an "expungement"? I'm too embarrassed to bring it up with an attorney and relive the whole ordeal by going over it with him/her. I just want to know what the process would be and what it means to be on probation for the next two years. It was a stupid mistake, and I just want to clear it up as best I can. Someone told me that even after going through an expungement one's record is never really totally clear. If this is so, should I waste any more time, money, and undergo any further humiliation by even attempting to expunge my record?

A. Contact the public defenders' office. One of their clerks should be able to explain the terms of probation to you and also tell you if your record can be expunged. This is done on a case-by-case basis, and you may not be eligible. Unfortunately, there's no guarantee that the expunged information will disappear completely. Government agencies like to try to hang on to incriminating records.

It may be too late for a gay attorney to do you much good. Anyone who is charged with an offense of this nature should refrain from speaking to the police, admitting to any guilt, or making a statement until they have obtained an attorney. But please don't let embarrassment stop you from taking steps to protect your future now. I'm sure the police and the judicial process made you feel awful, but don't let them paralyze you. It's not at all uncommon for men, gay or straight, to jack off or have sex in tearooms. You were just unlucky enough to get caught. If you don't want this conviction to follow you around for the rest of your life, bite the bullet and see if anything can be done to repair the damage.

✍

Q. No matter how hard I try, I cannot seem to get my lover off when I go down on her. I haven't slept with that many women, but this has never been a problem before. Now I'm wondering if all my previous partners were faking orgasm! She isn't experienced enough to offer any helpful suggestions, but I know she's disappointed and frustrated when lovemaking doesn't work.

A. Can your lover masturbate to orgasm? If she cannot, then there's very little chance that she will be able to have an orgasm with you. There are some good self-help books for pre-orgasmic women listed in the resource guide.

If she can masturbate to orgasm, she can use this ability to teach herself how to come with a partner during oral sex. You should temporarily view oral sex as a method of foreplay. Let her direct you. She should feel free to tell you to change the position of your tongue, the speed or amount of pressure, etc. Remember that the clitoris has a lot of nerve endings in a very small area, so an eighth of an inch can make the difference between just getting excited and getting off. When she's too excited to stand it any more, she should tell you she needs to come, and masturbate.

You need not feel left out while she's doing this. You can masturbate, too. Or you can stimulate her nipples, talk dirty to her, or just hold her. She might want you to kneel above her face so she can eat you while she's masturbating.

Eventually (sooner than you might think), she will probably surprise both of you and come spontaneously, without touching herself, while you are going down on her. There are a few women who don't have orgasms from oral sex. If this is true for her, experiment with other techniques like fucking, manual stimulation, or tribadism. Even couples who really enjoy making love with each other sometimes like to end a hot sex session by making themselves come. You can learn a lot about each other's bodies by sharing this private information.

This will take the pressure to perform off both of you. She won't have to worry about her inability to produce an orgasm, and you won't have to worry about your adequacy as a lover. It isn't your responsibility to "make" her come. There are *two* people in that bed!

Q. My lover was raped while walking to her car in the university parking lot. Luckily, they caught the guy and put him away. Immediately after the attack, while she was dealing with identifying and testifying against this maniac, it seemed as if my role should simply be to support her and take care of her. There wasn't much time, and we were both too tense to think about sex. Now things are back to normal, except that we have not resumed lovemaking. I feel awkward about approaching her with my selfish needs. I guess I am afraid of reminding her at all, even vaguely, of what happened. How much more time should I give her?

A. Not one more minute. I wonder who you're really protecting here. If she hasn't told you she's unwilling to have sex, don't make assumptions — especially not one that could put a permanent bolster down the middle of your bed! Draw a bubble-bath, put her in it, plant yourself next to her, get your arms around her, and start kissing everything you can see. By now, she may be wondering if you think she was sullied or ruined by being the victim of a brutal assault. Bad memories may interfere with her pleasure, but the physical evidence that you want her will be a lot more reassuring than anything you say, however nice. I'm sure the two of you will need to talk about this (after all, you need some reassurance too and some praise for being brave, nurturing, and protective). You might want to see a counselor at a rape crisis center. But do it after you've given your lover concrete proof that your passion is as strong as your compassion.

Q. I'm a gay man who likes heterosexual pornography. Well, I guess it's really more than a case of just *liking* it, or I wouldn't be writing you this letter. I've bought dozens of magazines of male nudes and more hard-core gay material, and it doesn't inspire erections or anything other than mild curiosity about what's on the next page. But when I see movies or photos of men and women screwing it gets me instantly hot, and I have no trouble coming while staring at these images.

I was recently embarrassed by a request from my roommate to borrow a magazine since all of his were "tired." He offered to swap some of his old stuff for mine. I told him he was welcome to take anything that interested him. After going through a stack of my used porn rags he asked (with a funny look on his face), "Where did these come from? Did you inherit them from your father or what? I'm not into pussy."

Well, I'm not either. Am I? I managed to find two or three male magazines that hadn't done anything for me, and this seemed to placate him. A big stack of dog-eared porn from his collection is sitting by my bed, and I don't know how to tell him I don't want or like any of it. Why am I so confused?

A. You're not confused, you're just honest, and that's bound to confuse other people.

I've known several gay men (and lesbians) who liked straight porn and did not respond to same-sex material, just as I've known straight women who go nuts over gay male porn and straight men who read nothing but dirty books about lesbian lust.

One gay male acquaintance of mine swears he watches straight porn films just because they are technically better, and that the production values of, say, *Debbie Does Dallas,* have yet to be equaled in gay hard-core cinema. Another acquaintance with a large collection of straight videos says he keeps them around to put his hustlers (who insist they are heterosexual) at ease. Since he rarely sees the same hustler twice, you'd think a small assortment of boy/girl flicks would suffice. Nevertheless, he's always previewing new movies and has many more straight X-rated videos than gay ones.

Maybe you like straight porn because it was the first kind of sexually explicit imagery you saw, and these images have been associated with masturbation so often that you've developed a habitual, dependable, and exclusive response. If you have a history of cruising adult movie theaters that play straight porn, you could associate het blue movies with tricking with men. Or you may simply be one of those not-uncommon people whose masturbation fantasies and preferences in porn are the direct opposite of what they do with their real-life partners.

It doesn't mean you are a latent heterosexual. There's a big difference between enjoying looking at pictures of men and women fucking and pursuing the actual experience. Besides, who says you are looking at the *woman* in these scenes? It may be the straight *man* you've eroticized.

Your roommate's comment was rude. It takes a lot of nerve for somebody who is borrowing something to complain about what you have generously offered to share. Next time he needs some new stimulation, send him down to the corner newsstand for the latest issue of *Playgirl* and keep your own collection intact. Don't cast your pearls before swine.

131

Q. My lover is very masculine and is often called "sir" or "mister" when we go shopping, get gas for the car, or see a movie. I am turned on to her butchness and enjoy being a bit of a femme flirt and a tease. But lately she has taken this too far. She is cross-dressing, deliberately attempting to pass for a man, which is very different from just acting or looking butch. I'm embarrassed to be out in public with her. I'm afraid that people will think I'm with a man. I don't want to be mistaken for a straight woman. Lately my nightmare has been that we will go to a lesbian bar and be asked to leave on the assumption that we don't belong there.

A. If you happen to run into anyone you both know when you are out together and your lover is cross-dressed, they will know you are a lesbian. As for people who don't know you, who gives a flying fuck what they think? Believe me, their picture of what it means for you to be a lesbian is no more accurate than their perception that you are part of a heterosexual couple. Isn't it nice to know you can safely hold hands with another woman in public because no one knows what's really going on?

Tell your lover about your anxieties and find out why this is so important to her. Maybe she's just testing out her drag to see how good it is and will eventually want to confine this activity to the bedroom. Maybe she's hoping to turn you on even more than she did before by being "merely" very butch. It's also possible that she's having some conflict about her gender and needs some more information or counseling about transsexuality. If this is true, I hope you can be supportive. Rejecting someone in that vulnerable a position is not unlike trashing a gay person for coming out.

This is not to say that if your lover decides to start taking male hormones or have sex reassignment surgery, you're obliged to remain with her when she becomes a he. Given how you feel about being mistaken for a straight woman, I doubt you'd be able to stay in a relationship with a man, even a man who started life in a female body. But a lot of butch women feel the need to think about sex reassignment at least once in their lives. Most of them eventually decide it's not for them. I'm just saying you shouldn't freak out if she's just asking herself hard questions about her own gender.

You might also be having some problems with this because you are feeling a little too passive. If she's paying extra attention to her grooming in order to cross-dress and you are just doing what you usually do, you probably feel left out. Talk to your lover about what kind of male image she's trying to project and see if you have a complementary "femme flirt" character that you can also develop.

Then go buy yourself a corset or a leather miniskirt and some extra-high heels, and buy her a mustache and some spirit gum. Happy gender-fucking.

✍

Q. My mate and I have a good sex life as long as I follow the rules. Number one is we only make love in the morning. I would like to make love at night at times, but as soon as I start anything, he says he's tired and it's time to go to sleep, and he does. This at times upsets me a lot.

I'm the one who has to get up early enough to make time, and I always have to get things started. He just lays there and enjoys himself. I have asked him to be more aggressive, and at times he makes a half-hearted attempt, but he soon goes back to not doing much for me. I sometimes want to feel as good as I try to make him feel.

We have discussed this, and he knows how I feel but makes no real attempt to do anything about what I want. What can I do to make him more receptive to my wants and needs, or have I catered to his wants too long to change him?

A. There isn't much you can do that you haven't tried already, Reader Dear. It takes two to tango, two to talk on the telephone, and two to save this marriage. I think you've already done more than your share by always taking the initiative, accepting his timetable for nookie, and gently reminding him that "do unto as often as you would be done by" is the Golden Rule for connubial bliss. Unless his hands were welded to his sides at puberty, your lover hasn't got any excuse at all.

I won't advise you to do what many people would have done already, which is to stop providing any crumb of sexual gratification to someone who doesn't have the strength to lift his head from the pillow and open his mouth for something other than a yawn. You already know that it isn't much fun to have someone pleasure you reluctantly after they've been nagged into it. It's even less fun to have them make love to you in a towering rage because their balls will drop off if they get any bluer.

This isn't your problem, it's his problem.

133

$\mathbb{A}$

Q. I don't know if you'll even want to respond to this problem. My lover and I have been together since '72. We're in our late 50s and have had a great relationship, business and sexual. Last October, we went to a Halloween party — me as W. C. Fields and James as Mae West. He'd never done drag before and looked hysterical with his white beard and crimson lips.

For Christmas, he asked me for a makeup kit. I thought he was kidding and didn't get it. He was upset and bought himself a kit.

We hosted a New Year's Eve party for eight, and when he came down for dinner, he was dressed in his dinner jacket and his face was made up beautifully except for the bright red lipsticked mouth. Our guests were a bit disconcerted. He told them that he liked the feel of it on his lips, the taste of it, how it looked on his mouth, and loved seeing it on my mouth after he'd kissed me.

That night, when I came to bed, James made love to me like a tiger. In the morning, my body looked like a casualty of war — his lipstick on my lips, chin, neck, ears, nipples, and cock. I complained, and it pissed him off. For several weeks, we didn't have sex (a record). In the meantime, he added a new fetish — women's panties. I gave in and have put up with both.

No matter what I say, this beautiful guy feels he needs lipstick. I don't mind the panties, they come off before sex. Any suggestions?

A. If you knew how many people write to me complaining that after a few years, there's no more lust in their conjugal bed, you would be kissing your lover's pillow in gratitude instead of bitching about the lipstick stains. Do you have any idea how lucky you are to have a partner who has discovered something new about his sexuality and is excited about sharing it with you instead of using it as an excuse to break up?

Obviously, drag is something that hasn't appealed to you in the past. You may get short-circuited by the garish contrast between a masculine beard and red lipstick. Your comment that James was "beautifully" made up except for the excessive lip-gloss is interesting. Could you get it up for this if he went all the way and did better, more complete drag?

If you want to get semiotic about it, sluts (like studs) have no intrinsic gender. But if a big dick is the sign that identifies a stud, everybody — male or female — who wants to be a hot fuck will want a big dick. And since a big, pouty, red, juicy mouth is the sign for slut, ditto. In other words — don't look a gift tiger in the mouth.

Q. I'm a straight woman who is writing to you because of something that happened to a very close, gay male friend of mine. I was awakened one Saturday night by a panicky phone call. He was stranded in the parking lot of a nearby supermarket. Could I come and get him? Of course I could. When I saw the condition he was in — clothes torn, two black eyes, obviously severely beaten — I was nearly as hysterical as he was. But I kept calm enough to take him immediately to a hospital. On the way, he told me that a group of men had forced him into a car. While we were waiting at the emergency room, he began to cry and begged me to take him home. I didn't understand why until he whispered that he could not face the doctor because he had been raped.

I'm afraid I was nonplussed, even though I consider myself a feminist and have read the literature about sexual assault and spoken with other women friends about their experiences and fears. I couldn't imagine how it happened, whether or not he might be hurt, or what kind of help he would need. So I took him home.

I spent the rest of the weekend at his house and took care of him as best I could. I spent much of the time just listening to him pour out his fear and shame and tried to comfort him. But after that weekend, we never spoke of this again. I wonder now if I did enough.

A. Your friend is very lucky that you're a compassionate and resourceful person. You can't force someone who rejects medical treatment to see a doctor. If your friend had been willing, the doctor should have ascertained exactly how your friend was assaulted and checked him for life-threatening damage. A doctor should also have tested him for venereal diseases. Sometimes rape victims are given prophylactic doses of antibiotics. It's hard to say whether your friend was right to insist on going home. A homophobic or ignorant doctor wouldn't have been much help. But a good physician could have reassured him that his physical and emotional injuries would eventually heal.

Injury during rape (whether the victim is male or female) can take many forms. This is a crime of violence, not of passion. The victim can be beaten, stabbed, choked, or shot. Repeated anal intercourse or forced oral sex can bruise or tear the lining of the rectum or throat. Sometimes foreign objects are forced into a victim's orifices and tear or block them. The humiliation of being helpless and the fear of being in danger again can cause trauma that plagues the victims long after their bodies are whole.

Nobody knows how common rape is. It's an underreported crime for several reasons. The victim is almost always ashamed. A rape is more terrifying than other kinds of assault, which makes it difficult for victims to speak out. There may be no visible, serious injuries to support the victim's claim that he or she was abused. Often the victim knows the assailant and is afraid of retaliation or is afraid no one will believe them. Your letter is not the only one I've received that describes gay men being raped. There's a need for more extensive social services to deal with this problem.

You can help your friend by refusing to let this matter drop. Don't let him try to macho his way out of this. Call the rape crisis line in your area. They probably deal with many more women than men. However, they'll be able to tell you if special services for male rape victims exist in your area and will do their best to help male as well as female victims. Local agencies that help victims of anti-gay violence or violent crimes in general are another useful resource.

These crisis centers often have advocates who will help the victim get to a safe place, go with them to seek medical treatment, talk with them about filing a police complaint, and help them deal with police if they want to report the crime.

It's too late for your friend to avail himself of these services, but you should encourage him to talk to a trained professional or the members of a support group about what happened to him. He should also go and get a complete physical and tests for STDs.

Sexual specialties

Q. I am a chubby-chaser, and I am not ashamed! Not of me, and not of them! (Actually, I prefer the hefty look of a man dressed casually for the outdoors, like a lumberjack or a cowboy — "chubby" always reminds me of Santa Claus.) Anyway, what I want to know is, *Where are all the big guys?* Why don't more of you go out more often? Here I am, scanning the crowd, desperate to find a huge man I can't get my arms around, but eager to try — and all I see are these skimpy little asses and skinny little waistlines and pinched-up, hungry faces. I want a mountain of a man, a big man, I mean we are talking *humongous* here. So where are you keeping yourselves? Is Richard Simmons keeping you all captive on a Fat Farm? Send word, I'll send rescue!

A. The big men (hefty, hulking, fat, chunky, chubby, obese, heavy, plump, pot-gutted, call it what you will) are not out there because when they go out all they see are asses the size of cupcakes and waists that two hands could span and lips that never touch sour cream. From where they're sitting, guys like you look just like all those refugees from Reducin' Richard's Camp Concentrate on Slenderization.

Maybe your letter will get some of them to turn off the TV or leave Burger King and hie their big but sluggish butts into the nearest hot spot for insomniac homos. Maybe it will even persuade some of them to believe that you are cruising them, not smirking at them. Or allow them to accept an invitation to get it on without wondering if it's really a put-on.

If all else fails, pick up one of those skinny little dudes, throw him over your shoulder, carry him kicking and screaming into Marie Callendar's Pies, and stuff his face. Once you get some meat onto their bones, some of those cadaverous bartenders get kinda handsome.

If this sounds too much like a 4-H project, you might want to contact one of clubs for big men and their admirers listed in the resources and see about lassoing somebody hot and hefty who's done his own beefing up.

✍

Q. I'm a normally developed gay adult male with a secret. I find baby paraphernalia to be extremely arousing. When I go grocery shopping I always imagine that I will buy some baby food, and a little dish and a spoon, a baby bottle, a bib, etc. But when I walk past these items I can never bring myself to put them in my shopping cart. How would I ever explain them if somebody saw them? Do you know where I can get adult-sized diapers? Is there any reading material or a club for people like me? I enjoy normal sex but often have a fantasy that I am wearing diapers or sucking on a pacifier. I wish I could find someone who would put powder on me, diaper me, put me in a crib, give me baby toys to play with, and otherwise treat me like an infant. Is this something you have encountered often? These fantasies are very powerful and often I masturbate to get rid of them, but I'm also confused about them and don't want anybody else to know.

A. Your fantasies are common enough for people to start newsletters, clubs, and businesses that cater to them. For what it's worth, the clinical term used to describe your fetish is "infantilism." If you want to go to the library and look for "case histories" (i.e., dirty stories told by psychiatrists), that's what you should look for in the index. Most shrinks will attribute your turn-on to not completing the phase of being a real baby and say that you are trying to go back to that time in your life so you can evade adult responsibilities.

My personal opinion is that the attraction of *any* sexual experience has a lot in common with being an infant — the absence of inhibiting fear, the spontaneity of physical reactions, the sense of every sensation being new and overpowering, loss of control, selfish pursuit of pleasurable physical feelings, being fed, nurtured, and held, etc. A fetish is just a sex object that most people don't respond to. If your turn-on was big dicks or washboard stomachs, other gay men would not think you were weird at all (and heterosexuals would think you were strange).

I've listed resources for people who share your fantasy, but they won't do you much good if you can't even buy a baby bottle of your very own. How could you ever tolerate the anxiety of placing an ad to share fantasies with someone, even if he likes to play baby too?

Your first task should be to allow yourself to acquire all the items you need to enjoy this fantasy during masturbation. Go to a big grocery store far away from your own neighborhood. You never have to visit that store again, so who cares what they think? Men buy bottles or baby food for their own kids quite often. You don't have to make any excuses or explanations. The very worst thing that could happen is somebody might ask you how old "your child" is. By all means, buy your baby food, a no-spill bowl with Donald Duck on the bottom, a matching bib, tiny silverware, and a teething ring.

Adult-sized diapers are available at most pharmacies or surgical supply houses. Measure your waist before you go, and make a note of this and how much you weigh, in case they need it for the size. People are usually embarrassed when they buy these things, so don't worry about the pharmacist thinking you are strange. Nobody's going to ask you why you want to purchase this item. You'd be surprised if you knew how many people don't have complete bladder control and are discreetly wearing diapers under their normal clothing.

If you need to feel that your secret is safe, buy a locking chest you can keep your baby clothes and accessories in. Of course, baby food looks a lot more natural on the pantry shelf than it does in a locked box — you can always say you keep some on hand for a lesbian friend who has a baby. And anybody who is rude enough to inquire why you have adult diapers stashed in your linen closet is too rude to be invited in for tea ever again. You have my permission to snub them.

If you're ever ready to look for a partner to play baby games with, you can try answering some ads. At least subscribe to one of the magazines. Just knowing you're not alone will make you feel much better.

✍

Q. Your answer concerning infantilism was good but incomplete. Men into the diaper scene tend to fall into three general categories: (1) guys into watersports who have discovered the warm convenience of diapers and plastic pants over cold, clammy, and visibly wet jeans; (2) men who desire complete regression to an infantile or baby state; and (3) daddies and diaper boys who are into the diaper scene as a form of dominance and submission (a mild form of S&M).

So beware! That attractive basket you are ogling may be a diaper in need of changing!

✍

Q. I'm a middle-aged gay male with a latent interest in zoophilism from childhood. Since I've never had the occasion to really experience it, it becomes increasingly frustrating with thoughts of dogs, horses, bulls, and monkeys — especially their masturbation habits. There used to be ads for books and movies on the straight side with women but not for gays. Now I don't even see ads for porn that features women with animals. It makes me feel dirty and weird to the point where I've never even confessed to my lover of six years. Am I so unusual?

A. Since most people are reluctant to divulge their fantasies, especially if they differ from the norm, there's no way to tell how many men share your interest in animals. But even if you are unusual (i.e., a minority), that doesn't make you "dirty and weird." Outnumbered, yes. Wrong or bad, no.

I have personally encountered gay men who had a sexual interest in large dogs (including a couple who bred Dobermans) and a horse rancher who carried on with his stallions. I've also met a bisexual man who grew up on a dairy farm who could converse in great detail about attractive versus unattractive cows. And I've seen ads from gay men expressing a range of interest in animal sex — anything from acting the part of an animal to swapping drawings or photos to actually doing it. Every time I go to the zoo there are an awful lot of people of all sexual orientations watching the monkeys jerk off. So you aren't the only guy who gets off on thinking about this.

Since no behavior that affects other people or animals is involved in a fantasy, your Adviser gives you carte blanche to enjoy any erotic thought that crosses your mind and encourages you to embroider it and make it outrageous. Why should Noah be the only one who gets to spend forty days and forty nights with two of every kind of beast on the face of the earth?

However, there are some ethical problems associated with actual sex between humans and other animals. Any kind of compulsion is odious. If the animal finds the contact strange, painful, or silly, it should be free to bite or scratch or stomp on your foot and get away. Inflicting any physical damage on the animal is equally odious. The human penis is obviously the wrong size to be used on certain species (like chickens) or breeds (like Chihuahuas). If you begin a sexual relationship with, say, a dog, gratifying the dog becomes as much your responsibility as feeding him every day. The animal will expect this kind of attention and become upset or angry if it is withdrawn. There is also the possibility, with dogs, that they will become hostile and jealous of any person you have a sexual relationship with.

There are also some technical problems. A stallion or a bull possesses an impressive penis, but it's a rare human being who can do more than simply stare in appreciation. The sex drive in these animals is very powerful, and they are quite difficult to control when they want to fuck. There's a good chance of getting mangled — it happens all the time to handlers who are assisting during breeding. A few infections can travel from one species to another, so use of condoms is mandatory.

It sounds like what you need at this point is to hear from other guys who have similar interests and get some new fantasy material. Why not rent a post office box and place an ad, offering to swap stories? Just be careful not to send or accept pictures through the mail. Right now, the feds are heavily prosecuting any erotic material that features bestiality.

✍

Q. Why is it that I feel attracted to men so much younger than me? I'm in my 30s and feel drawn to men in their teens. I feel guilty about my desires for them and know that any sort of relationship with someone younger entails dealing with many differences in life experiences. Am I crazy for even hoping to have a positive relationship with these beauties? I'd really like to hear what you think about this topic. I broke up with a young lover two years ago and am really reluctant to deal with my latest attractions.

A. Many men are attracted to teenagers. We don't really know why people develop any sexual preference. But this topic has been discussed less and less in the gay press as penalties for intergenerational sex have increased. In this country, it's possible for a gay man to spend more years in prison for having consensual sex with an adolescent boy than he'd get for manslaughter. In contrast, it's uncommon for a father or step-father who rapes his own preadolescent daughters to spend any time in jail.

Our government is not willing to provide alternatives for young people whose families batter them, sexually molest them, or desert them. They wind up in foster homes, the juvenile justice system, or the street. Society *is* willing to expend huge amounts of money and the time of law enforcement personnel to punish men who offer throw-away kids cash, sex, or affection. I don't think that struggling for survival in the red-light district of a strange city is a good way for someone to grow up. But vicious harassment of boy-lovers is no solution.

It sounds like you are aware of the problems that can exist in a relationship between an adult and a teenager, other than the obvious legal ones. Teenage boys are sexual beings who are often very curious about their own bodies and eager to experiment, but they are usually not mature enough to be equal partners in a relationship. They can be grateful to an adult who provides them with pleasure, money, mobility, new information, and other resources, but it's unwise to expect them to "settle down" or give you a commitment.

A sexual affair with a younger partner may turn into a warm friendship. It also has the potential for turning ugly. Young men who have been abandoned by their families because of their same-sex activities or their independence and rebelliousness can have a variety of problems that they take out on the people around them. This can include drugs, a propensity for violence, and general instability. Of course, not all cross-generational relationships are between clients and youthful hustlers. But young men who are still living at home are under the supervision of their families. They rarely have the privacy or freedom to form sexual relationships with their peers, let alone with an adult gay man.

I don't want to tell you that your desires are wrong. But we live in a world where crossing the generation line is dangerous. The North American Man-Boy Love Association (NAMBLA) is the last above-ground group in this country promoting discussion about abolishing age-of-consent laws. Systematic harassment by local vice cops and the federal government has nearly destroyed the group. There's nothing illegal about writing to NAMBLA for more information or ordering their publications. But you can't assume that the police will not gain access to their membership list and use it to attempt to entrap you. Use the resource list to get more information about pedophilia, but beware of anyone who offers to send you erotic or sexually explicit material featuring minors through the mail. "Child" pornography (anything that includes models younger than 18) is no longer commercially available in this country. The material that's advertised is frequently sold by the federal government in an attempt to entrap pedophiles. And, unlike other kinds of pornography, in some states it's a crime to merely *possess* child pornography.

✍

Q. My partner and I enjoyed our eighth anniversary last month. We're very happy and very much in love. We make satisfying love two or three times a month.

Now the down side. I have hidden a personal fetish from him all these years — cigars. Since my earliest moments, cigars have been my one erotic passion. Before we met, I dated numerous cigar smokers but didn't find love. After we met, I never told him because I was certain he wouldn't understand. I still don't think he would.

My partner was a virgin, as pure and naive as an adult could be, when we met. He is still very uncomfortable with unusual sexual or social behavior. I have dropped small "cigar hints" over the years that he has never picked up on. He complains about the smell if we are ever near a cigar smoker. None of this gives me much hope.

So I "cheat" on him. I have cigars custom made: seventy-ring, ten inches. On the evenings my partner comes home late, I spend an hour fucking my ass with these monsters and masturbating. I love it, but I feel guilty and unsatisfied. I have planned dozens of ways to tell him but each year makes it harder. I am so afraid of alienating him. I could keep going as I am, but sooner or later he'll find out.

A. It's interesting that you picked someone as a lover who is so uptight about sex that you dare not share such an important part of your libido. I wonder if your fantasies about him catching you in the act and being punitive are not part of what makes this activity such a turn-on. There's nothing wrong with this. But you might feel less tormented if you could decide that the way you masturbate is your business, and you're never going to tell him about it. Then you could develop some more conscious and elaborate fantasies about being discovered, exposed, and chastised without having all this awful and unnecessary guilt about "cheating" on him.

Everybody jacks off, whether they're in love or not. It's not adultery. Masturbation is a form of self-love and self-nurturing that very few of us could do without and remain physically or mentally healthy. I will bet you that your honeybun finds the need to stroke himself from time to time, and when he does, he probably has a few dirty, secret thoughts of his own.

143

If you really want a lover who is able to view cigar smoking as foreplay and the cigars themselves as sex toys, you are going to have to get this guy to perv up his act. For all you know, there are things that he is dying to have you do with him. Long-term relationships become boring and even asexual if the partners involved don't tell each other the truth about their desires. Why settle for frustration? Life is too short!

It's hard to take the role of a sexual initiator and teacher when you feel vulnerable. The sexual disapproval of a loved one really smarts. But think of the potential rewards. Your lover may kick and scream a bit, but in the end, after he's had his horizons and a few other things broadened, he will be grateful.

Check the resource list for clubs for guys who dig cigars. Get in touch. I'm sure some of them have had similar problems and can give you support.

✍

Q. I am in a very loving situation with my roommate who has been with me for three years now. We are two different personalities, and that produces some clashes. These are always resolved, with one exception. I consider myself to be very conservative, and so I'm sometimes shocked by my lover's craziness. He likes to rim my unwashed butt. Although it's *him* that does it, I'm really grossed out, and he gets offended if he can't "get in a few licks" every night or so.

A. Exactly how much do you hate getting rimmed? Are you really grossed out, or do you just think you should be? When he does this to you, do you get a hard-on, or do you lie there like a dead thing, grit your teeth, and pray for it to end? If rimming is a prelude to hot sex, I can excuse your lover for doing it over your protests. If you detest it, then he's using your body nonconsensually, and you have a right to insist that it stop. If this is enough to make him threaten to leave you, seek couples counseling first. I think your relationship can be salvaged despite your sexual differences. I get so many letters from people who are concerned because they've been together for a while and the sex has gone *out* of their relationship, it would be a shame if yours fell apart because the sex was too wild.

Are you at risk for AIDS, hepatitis, herpes, anal warts, amoebas, or any other STD? Would you feel more comfortable about rimming if your lover used a dental dam? If he puts a gob of water-based lubricant like KY or HR Jelly on the side that goes against your ass, you will be able to feel every swoop of his tongue. He won't be able to taste your ass, but the fragrance will still be there. And you can relax about hygiene. See if he will accept this as a compromise.

There's only one publication I know of for gay men into scat, *Jack's No. 2.* You can find it listed in the resource guide. Even if you're not interested in reading it, get your lover a subscription. This will at least send him the message that you love him and validate his, um, tastes even if you don't share them.

✍

Q. You were right to point out to the man whose lover got turned on by licking his less-than-clean anus that there are the health dangers if monogamy is not involved. But if a couple is monogamous, there really shouldn't be any problem at all.

My guess is that the author of that letter is sufficiently uncomfortable with homosexuality that "normal gay sex" is probably okay for him, but more experimental activities between him and his lover trigger his equivocal feelings — staying away from such things may make him feel "clean" whereas giving way to things like ass licking probably is too much. His self-esteem can't take that. Too bad, because his lover really needs to take him that way, and the rubber dams just won't do the trick.

I know something about this because I have a lover (with whom I have lived happily for almost twelve years). For him, the scent of my anus is the true aphrodisiac, and when presented with that scent, he licks, then fucks me. Invariably, I get off just sniffing and licking him. Without going into details, let's just say that nobody in our house uses toilet paper except guests. I was a little hesitant when he first wanted to enjoy my anal scents, but when I saw how it turned him on, my hesitation vanished. And so I lost my inhibitions and reciprocated.

The curious thing to me is that you really are nonjudgmental about activities such as this since you recommended *Jack's No. 2.* That organization does a lot of good in lifting inhibitions. My lover and I have occasionally run an ad expressing willingness to meet novices who are concerned about safety. We have invited some of them to our house and let them watch us have sex. After they have witnessed that, they understand that guys who like getting into each other's shitty butts can be well adjusted, healthy, and loving.

A. No, I'm not judgmental about people who have eroticized shit. It's not one of my personal favorites. Because I love anal sex, I have managed to become almost shit-neutral, but I am not yet shit-positive.

There are a couple of reasons why I didn't just urge the man to loosen up and let his lover have his way with him. One is that it's important to recognize and respect other people's sexual limits, even if that person happens to be your lover. The other is that there are some serious potential health hazards involved in rimming, whether the anus is clean or not. The letter-writer did not say if he and his boyfriend were monogamous, for starters. It seemed to me that encouraging him to wash beforehand and use a dental dam was a compromise that would help him be more comfortable with this activity and give his partner at least some of what he wanted.

I'm very concerned about this myth that unsafe sex between monogamous partners is risk-free. I wish you could see all the letters I have gotten from men who assumed they were HIV-negative only to discover later that they did indeed have AIDS and had infected someone that they loved. It is heart-breaking, as are the letters from men who exposed themselves and thus their partner to HIV or other diseases because they could not manage to be 100 percent faithful.

Unsafe sex in the context of a monogamous relationship is less risky than having unsafe sex with many partners. But somebody you love *can* give you AIDS, whether you're having kinky sex or vanilla. This disease can have a very long incubation period, and we've recently discovered that a few people can carry the virus in their bodies for several years and still be HIV-negative.

The rare couples who have been active only with each other for ten years or so can of course do whatever they like. If they're healthy, there are no diseases to transmit. Some of us feel that we can't practice safe sex, that being sexually exclusive is the best we can do. It's particularly hard if your jones is actually tasting and ingesting piss or shit or cum. If seeing and smelling it isn't enough, then you may feel that your choice is between no sex and unsafe sex. Even kinky people can be hard-pressed to be creative enough to get their kicks without any germs.

It's an era of hard choices, insufficient information, and paranoia. I don't condemn anyone's sexual practice, but I have to try to give clear information about what is risky and what is not. My message is to avoid exchanging cum and waste products. If you can't do that, restricting it to one partner makes you somewhat safer, but if both of you are not completely healthy and totally monogamous (in the sense of being exposed to blood, semen, or other secretions that can carry disease), you are still taking a chance that one or both of you will get sick.

This doesn't mean that swallowing cum or anything else that comes out of the body is evil, sinful, or bad. STDs are just an unfair, unpleasant fact of life, like income tax, earthquakes, and people who walk their dogs without cleaning up after them. There probably aren't very many people who succeed in having only risk-free sex, but I've gone to so many funerals, I want to encourage as much risk-reduction as is humanly possible.

✍

Q. Ever since I was about five years old, I have had a strong fetish for soft, clear plastic. I would like to wear clothes made of clear plastic, and I like to look at clear plastic shower curtains and furniture covers.

The only way that I publicly display my fetish is to wear a clear plastic raincoat when it rains. Even this modest display has brought some ridicule and criticism which included being asked to leave a gay bar.

I'm very curious whether this is such an unusual fetish. It's the same as being into leather but with a different material. How would I find others into this fetish? Am I going too far to wear clear plastic (over appropriate clothing) into a gay bar?

A. I'm very sorry to hear that you were ejected from a gay bar for wearing a see-through raincoat. The bouncer must have lost the key to his chastity belt that night. I certainly don't think this was inappropriate behavior on your part, especially if it really was raining outside!

I have read more about a fetish for clear plastic or vinyl in British publications like *Skin Two* than I have in American magazines. See the resource guide for more information. There aren't as many people who turn on to plastic as there are men into leather or even rubber. This is partly because leather has become a generic symbol for anybody who wants to feel a little frisky and sexually outrageous. Rubber may not interest you at all, but anyone who shares your fetish will probably be part of the small network of folks into latex.

Place personal ads. Search out publications. If you're handy, buy the kind of plastic you like and make your own private, J/O fantasy clothes. (You can make seams with clear tape.) And don't omit the possibility of talking about *all* of your sexual interests with friends and sex partners. Some of them will get giggly because it's a novel idea or they disapprove, but if you want to have a sex life that includes your fetish, you will have to be persistent, positive about yourself, and ingenious. Someone who is just indulging what they think of as *your* kink isn't as much fun as another enthusiastic fan. But sometimes you will discover that you've been having sex with a fellow "perv" who just needed a nudge to come out. Good luck.

✍

Q. You wrote a lengthy answer on fetishes, but you didn't name the fetish that I have had since I was a child: soft velvet corduroy. Is this fetish an unusual one?

A. Theoretically, it's possible to have a fetish for any substance or material, item or object, or part of the body. The Victorian sexologist Richard von Krafft-Ebing, in his 1886 *Psychopathia Sexualis,* mentions several examples of people who are aroused by fur, velvet, silk, feathers, and so on.

I'm not sure how useful this term is. Most of Krafft-Ebing's fetishists were criminals who stole the things they had eroticized or injured people who possessed or wore them. Krafft-Ebing was fond of portraying sex as a disease. Today, many people find that they are aroused by things other than their partner. But they're much less likely to feel guilty about it. It's easier to incorporate these hobbies into partnered sex, partly because we are better educated about sex and more tolerant, partly because most of us are always looking for ways to have more fun in bed. Someone who might have been a lonely, crazed deviant in 1893 is probably the president of a leather club today or the editor of a newsletter for the devotees of clear plastic raincoats.

All of Krafft-Ebing's fetishists were men. If he were around today and tried to tell a lady corset enthusiast or the lead singer of my favorite punk band that she didn't have a fetish for tight lacing or her leather jacket, he would get strange looks, at the very least, and a punch in the nose if he got too insistent about it.

The passage of time changes the forms that human sexuality takes, just as it changes economics, literature, and every other facet of our existence. There's nothing inherently alienating or immature about having a fetish. It's sometimes difficult to make contact with other people who have similar interests, but even a partner who does not share your response will sometimes help you out, especially if you cooperate with some of their desires and fantasies.

Krafft-Ebing's assumption that fetishists were deranged may have derived from the anti-masturbation bias of the era. Most

Victorians assumed that "self-abuse" was responsible for a great deal of mental illness, disease, and crime. It's certainly true that some fetishes are so rare or specialized that it's difficult to see how a partner could assist with their use or appreciation. A fetish can be just a complex form of masturbation. Nevertheless, a person who has this type of erotic response may still long for the sexual recognition and validation that our culture teaches us to expect only a lover to provide.

You didn't ask for all of this philosophical discussion, but that's what you get when you tell your Adviser that you have something fascinating like a fetish for "soft velvet corduroy," and don't tell her anything else about it!

✍

Q. I'm a transvestite just coming out, at over age 30, at last! I want to start my breast development and all that goes with it. I don't know where and how to get the female hormone pills. I have a very straitlaced doctor who won't approve of my choice. I have been gay for as long as I could remember but was afraid to come out as a female.

A. If you want to be female instead of just dressing up and creating a feminine illusion, most doctors will call you a transsexual instead of a transvestite. In reality these two categories often overlap. Before you start taking expensive hormones that can produce permanent physical changes and have some dangerous side effects, you should visit some drag shows, get to know the queens, make some friends who can support you, and start experimenting with just cross-dressing as female. Being able to fulfill their fantasies temporarily and privately is satisfying for many transgenderists.

No one can be happy if they are not true to themselves. Just doing drag may not satisfy you. In that case, consult the resource guide for sources of information about transsexuality. I don't want to talk you out of doing whatever you need to do to be happy. But the identity you are exploring draws a lot of disapproval. Take the time to learn everything you can from books, experts, and peers before you embark on physical transformation. A sex change is the answer for many people, but it can be a very difficult process, and it will not solve all your problems. Take good care of yourself while you learn and grow, and the right decisions will become clear to you.

$\mathcal{Q}_{\cdot}$ I grew up thinking I was a boy. I still automatically (and unconsciously?) often speak of myself in masculine terms. In most of my dreams I am a man. I've tried therapists, but they all seem very uncomfortable with the subject. I thought I was uninterested in sex until I discovered gay erotica. I feel like I am a gay man trapped in a woman's body. Why am I like this? Is there any support group for people like me?

$\mathcal{A}_{\cdot}$ Ideally, you should be able to talk with a counselor who is experienced with helping people who are uncomfortable with their biological sex. Experiment with some cross-dressing and male role-playing during sex. You may eventually want to live full-time as a man, perhaps even take male hormones and have some surgery that would make that easier. Unfortunately, there aren't a lot of qualified counselors dealing with gender dysphoria, and most of them are more familiar with male-to-female transvestites and transsexuals than with female-to-male.

If you make contact with some of the organizations listed in the resource guide and read their material, it will give you more information and put you in touch with a network of people who share your feelings and concerns. It's difficult and scary to explore your own gender identity, but don't let that discourage you. Finding understanding partners and putting together an image that you feel comfortable with can be hard, but if you don't figure out what you want, you'll never be happy. It's worth the pain and trouble to understand yourself and make your appearance and sexuality consistent with your own needs and self-perceptions.

There are a couple of problems with female-to-male sex reassignment that medical science may never resolve. You should understand before you take male hormones that some of the changes they produce in your body — increased body hair and facial hair, a deeper voice, and an enlarged clitoris — will be permanent. Relatively few surgeries to construct a penis (phalloplasties) have been conducted. All of them are far from perfect. Since these operations basically provide you with a flesh dildo that may not even be usable for intercourse, many female-to-male transsexuals (FTMs) choose to skip genital surgery and use dildos for penetration. A surgically constructed penis will not be able to provide you with an orgasm, so even FTMs who undergo phalloplasty usually opt to keep their female genitals intact.

This means that you have a choice between having a body that is perfectly consistent — but only in a cosmetic sense — with being a man, or having a body that functions sexually but is hermaphroditic. If you opt for the former, you will pass everywhere except in the bedroom. If you opt for the latter, you have to develop at least one relationship with someone who can validate your male identity while seeing and touching a body that still has some female components.

This may sound impossible, but it's not. People who are turned on to transsexuals or transvestites are an underresearched group, but they do exist. I think it's a mistake for FTMs to give up their sexuality. I've given the same advice to male-to-female transsexuals (MTFs) who know that having an artificial vagina constructed will make them look more like women but are afraid it will mean giving up orgasms. The MTF genital surgery has a better track record. Some MTFs report being able to have vaginal orgasms. But no surgeon can predict how your nerve endings will function, how much scar tissue there will be, and so on.

✍

Q. I like being choked. I don't mean that is all it takes to get me off. I like all the regular sex things, but if somebody will just gently squeeze my throat enough to make it difficult to breathe while they are fucking me or giving me a hand job, my erection immediately becomes firmer, and I come with greater intensity. I've been told I have a death wish and once a trick made a joke about hanging me, which does not interest me at all. The only way I can gratify my preferences without feeling odd is when I am sucking somebody off, but I miss the warm feeling of a man's hand around my throat. Is there any way to put partners more at ease with my peculiar needs?

A. There are a few references to erotic interest in choking or strangulation in the literature of deviant psychology. We both know that means your interest is probably not all that rare. (By the time Victorian sexologists invented a word for homosexuality, there were gay bars all over London.)

Accidental death sometimes results from sexual choking if bondage devices restrain a person and cut off the air supply completely. If you pass out before you can release the pressure around your throat, you will choke to death. This is one sex game that's definitely safer to play with a partner!

151

Since your partner is only doing this with his hand or you control the effect yourself while sucking cock, the only way you could get hurt is if you ran into somebody who didn't know when to stop squeezing. If you ever find a partner who isn't uneasy about your "peculiar need," arrange a signal to tell him to stop. Perhaps you could keep your hands in the air as long as the degree of pressure was a turn-on and thump the mattress when he should let go.

In the meantime, why not find a way to ask your partners to do this without using the word "choke," which seems to upset people? After the action gets hot, say, "Please put your hand here," and place his hand on your throat. Then say, "Hold me down that way, please." (For some reason, a request to be held down has a better chance of being perceived as normal than a request to be smothered a little.) Or just say, "Squeeze." If they ask you why, say, "It reminds me of the way it feels to have a cock down my throat."

I doubt you have a death wish. You're having too much fun with all this kinky sex to want to put an end to it all. I think choking is erotic for some people because they associate it with the alterations in heartbeat and breathing that usually take place during the sexual response cycle. Almost everybody gets slightly out of breath during plateau phase, and this intensifies until most of us are wheezing or gasping during orgasm. Light-headedness or dizziness is also associated with arousal.

I wish someone would explain to me why elaborate, pseudo-Freudian explanations for the paraphilias are so beloved by armchair psychologists. Haven't any of these people heard of Occam's razor?

✍

Q. After years of fantasizing about bondage, I finally confessed to my lover of four years that I was just dying to have him tie me up. He was happy to oblige, although we didn't have any rope on hand. He wound up using the cords from our bathrobes and (believe it or not) two fishnet stockings left over from his Halloween drag. It looked pretty funny, but I really didn't care. I don't think I've been that hot for him since our relationship was in the honeymoon phase.

I guess after having that much fun I should have expected to pay for it. When he untied me (we had to cut the stockings to get them off), I couldn't feel the thumb on my right hand, although I could move it normally. After about two weeks, the numbness passed off, but I was more scared than I wanted to admit.

My lover has been asking me when it's going to be *his* turn to get tied up, and I don't know what to tell him. I certainly don't want to damage the man I love.

A. There's a nerve that runs along the base of the thumb, close to the surface of your skin. It's very easy to pinch it. Sometimes you won't even feel a warning prickle or tingle in the hand. This is why experienced bondage enthusiasts use wide (two to three inches), padded leather cuffs on the wrists and ankles. The cuffs have D-rings to which you can attach rope or chain. They protect your joints from nerve damage caused by thrashing around in ecstasy.

Check the S/M section of the resource guide for more information. The leather community has recently started to publish its huge body of folklore about how to play safely. Common sense is enough to get you past most pitfalls, but why reinvent the wheel? Besides, you might get some ideas for other sex games that will keep your second honeymoon going on and on.

Disability

Q. I'm a fairly healthy man, a double amputee. Both legs are off just above the knees, and that makes me only four feet long, not tall. I'm 53 years young and just an average-looking man. My ex-lover and I split thirteen years ago, before my legs were amputated. I can't find anyone to go out with, and my life is a living hell. I've got so much love to give and no one to share it with. I've answered ads and placed many. So far all I've had are kinky replies.

A. Check the resource guide for support groups for disabled gay men and lesbians. It sounds like you have succeeded in making initial contact with other men by advertising, but you have rejected them because they were "kinky."

Please reconsider. I know that you view your amputations as a misfortune. It isn't a fetish for you; it's made your life harder. But think about this. Would you rather have sex with someone who is doing you a favor, trying to overlook a handicap that they actually find upsetting, or would you rather have sex with someone who is attracted to you and finds that handicap exciting?

Of course, you may eventually get lucky and meet someone who feels neutral about your disability because they are more interested in who you are as an individual than in your physical difference. That would be ideal. But in the meantime, why close yourself off from social or sexual interaction with men who have eroticized amputees? Some of them are decent, handsome, interesting guys.

Also consider forming friendships (sexual or nonsexual) with other disabled men. Often there are support groups formed by Vietnam veterans who are disabled or men who have been hurt on the job. These groups aren't gay-specific, but some of them are nonhomophobic. Take advantage of every social opportunity you can find. You need the experience, the practice, and the feedback that you can only get by pushing yourself to interact more with others.

✍

Q. Over the past year and a half I have run ads looking for leg amputees to be friends with, correspond with, and get into a possible relationship. This is a sincere interest, but I have had little or no luck at all. Can you tell me how I might meet this type of person?

A. Check the resource guide. If a support group for disabled gays exists in your area, you might be welcome at meetings. Most men of your generation who are amputees were injured in Vietnam. You might want to make contact with a gay veterans' group. Why not do some volunteer work at a Veterans' Administration hospital? If you've been advertising primarily in the gay press, try running ads in specialty newspapers that cater to kinky people of all sexual orientations. You can find a good selection of these in any adult bookstore.

Be persistent. When you have a rare or unusual sexual preference, it's often very difficult to find partners. Make yourself as visible and available as you can. Some porn magazines will accept reader-written material. You could write a brief story about your interest and offer to let them publish it with your post office box, so interested readers could correspond with you. I know there are gay men who are amputees who are looking for somebody like you. Good luck in your search.

✍

Q. At age 6, I had a rather severe polio attack. I was paralyzed from the neck down. Due to nine years of complete rehabilitation, my muscles are back to normal for a guy my age; even my legs. However, since the nerve endings were attacked, I was left with a very definite limp. Every other part of my body is normal or better. I spend some of the time in my wheelchair and use a cane or crutches when not in the chair.

I'm a good-looking guy with all the physical attributes that go with it. However, I — and guys like me — do have a problem. We get embarrassed very easily when we have to walk. (If we're standing still, we look great!) Therefore, it's difficult for us to meet other guys — even other guys who are handicapped.

Life can be lonely at times, and I have so much to give — a sense of humor that won't quit, a sense of life that dwarfs others that I know, and much more. I'm financially fine and dandy — it's the social aspect of my life that needs correcting.

A. Whether you're dealing with able-bodied folks who are "perceptually impaired" (i.e., prejudiced about the physically different) or with other disabled people who see you as being more privileged, the burden of breaking the ice and educating them will fall on you. This isn't fair — you already have enough problems — but very few people have enough empathy to project themselves into your situation.

The most common fear that able-bodied people have about disabled people is that the disabled person will be too needy. Able-bodied people assume that if you're disabled, you must be living at poverty level, emotionally as well as economically. Everything you can do to create an impression of self-sufficiency will be reassuring.

However, let's not forget that able-bodied people can be inconsistent shits who get pissed off if they can't turn a physically challenged person into an invalid they can hold at emotional arm's length even as they cosset them. An able-bodied friend or lover may resent your attempts to be independent or get impatient if it takes you a little longer to do things for yourself. We all have this Victorian notion that "sick" people (which includes the disabled) ought to be saints like Tiny Tim. This leaves no room for someone who is disabled to get angry or horny, make a mistake, care about money, be ambitious — be *human.*

Another major barrier is the able-bodied person's fear of hurting the disabled person physically or being present during a medical emergency and not being able to help. Then there's the fear of saying or doing something that will hurt the disabled person's feelings. This often keeps well-meaning but ignorant able-bodied people from asking questions that would help them to allay their other fears or leads them to blurt out questions that sound rude and curt. Since disabled people have often been taught to be ashamed of their physical differences and gloss them over, this makes communication even more difficult.

It makes me angry that more gay people aren't concerned about basic civil liberty issues for disabled folks — things like wheelchair accessibility, signing events for the deaf, or having a sliding scale to make activities affordable for people who are living on disability or other state programs. The lesbian community has been much more sensitive about these issues than gay men. The AIDS epidemic

156

should have created more tolerance for physical differences and limitations.

But the average able-bodied gay person still doesn't evaluate a disabled gay man or woman as a potential friend or lover without paranoia or prejudice. This is a shame. I get a lot of letters from lonely gays and lesbians who say they would do anything to find a lover. I wonder how many of them consider looking beyond the able-bodied world.

✍

Q. I am a 35-year-old, hearing gay man. My lover of two years is deaf. I am learning sign language (still!) and find that it's great for communicating during church, on an airplane, in a noisy bar, or just in those moments when one is too breathless from spent passion to speak aloud.

My question is not about any problem we have. How can we raise the consciousness of our [hearing] friends? A lot of times we wind up going to lesbian events like concerts because they are signed. Many of our [hearing] friends won't even use me as an *interpreter* to talk to my better half. They just talk to me about him, as if he wasn't there.

There are half a dozen or so deaf gay men who hang out at one bar in town. I am the only nondeaf person in this crowd. Many is the time I have overheard really rude remarks from men who think I cannot hear them. My typical response is, "And you think you're *not* handicapped?"

A. I can imagine one of your casual acquaintances making polite excuses for not learning sign language, but speaking about someone who is present in the third person if you have a willing interpreter is so rude it takes my breath away. When someone does this, you should immediately go over to *their* partner and ask, "Does he often get this way? Is it hard on you being with someone who's so insensitive?"

It would be very nice if all public events were signed. The usual excuse is that they aren't signed either because hiring an interpreter is too expensive or because there are no deaf people present. But deaf people don't come to an event if they know it isn't in their language. This vicious cycle has to be broken. If the interpreter does nothing but remind hearing people that they have deaf brothers and sisters, they have not signed in vain: That is money well spent.

Do you think you could get some of your closer friends to attend sign language classes if you scheduled a special event a few months from now, stipulating that all conversation at that event *must* be signed? Or you could refuse to speak to them at parties, stand in the corner, look at them and giggle, and sign madly back and forth with your lover until they can't stand it any more and have to be able to understand what you're saying about them.

I wish you luck. Human laziness is more powerful than any other force, with the possible exception of greed.

✍

Q. In my last year of high school, I injured my spinal column during a diving accident. I'm in a wheelchair, and I live with my parents. But I do attend college classes, and I have plans to find my own place to live. The accident interrupted many things in my life, one of which was a process of questioning my sexual orientation. I'm just now starting to feel that I want to enjoy the rest of my life and quit feeling sorry for myself. But is it worth it to even think about coming out as a disabled person? I don't think I'd have much luck sweeping anybody off his feet at the disco.

A. There should be a gay students group on your campus. If so, start attending it. This is a good way to meet people and make some friends who can help you explore your sexuality.

Many gay men are fixated on a stereotype of male beauty that does not include disabled people. But I think there's actually more tolerance and support for differently abled folks in the gay community than there is in the big outside world. Besides, if you're strongly attracted to other men, you're not going to be happy unless you can express this attraction. You can no more decide to remain heterosexual than you can decide to be two feet taller.

I know you're going to feel nervous and self-conscious about meeting new people, but remember, they're going to be nervous too. It takes persistence and courage to get people to see you as an individual rather than a label, but it can be done. One way to make this happen is to refuse to behave according to their assumptions. Never let other people limit you. The accident has limited you enough. For example, who says you can't go to the disco? You can dance in your wheelchair, can't you?

✍

Q. Although I applaud your advice to the young gay man with an injured spinal cord, you did not tell him what his sexual abilities (if any) were liable to be. I think your optimism about his performance was overstated. Since this information is difficult to obtain from doctors, you should give him the truth.

A. Doctors and even family members are often reluctant to give sex education, birth control, or regular tests for sexually transmitted diseases to disabled men and women. Instead, they often assume that if someone is disabled, they have no interest in sex and no ability to do it or enjoy it. This is rarely true. Even the most severely disabled person has a body, some physical sensation and control, and usually a desire to participate in all social activities, including sex.

Disabled people should ask for sexual information from their health-care providers and insist that their families and friends recognize and support their need for erotic expression. Those who are institutionalized still have a right to enjoy sexual pleasure, and attendants should be trained to leave them alone if they are masturbating or provide any physical assistance (positioning in a whirlpool bath or on a bed, putting on a condom, holding a vibrator) that they need to be sexual with others or themselves.

A person with an injured spinal cord can expect to lose sensation and control of the limbs below the level of the injury. However, men will still experience erections and women will still experience vaginal lubrication — although there may be no feeling or control. Most people with spinal cord injuries can enjoy oral sex. If they are passive partners during intercourse, their partners should be careful to check for adequate lubrication and relaxation to prevent injury or infection, since the disabled person will not be able to tell what kind of state their orifices are in.

A partner will also need to help the disabled person arrange any limbs they can't move themselves. A bed can be equipped with rails to make it possible for somebody to get into it from a wheelchair. Spinal cord lesions usually affect bladder control. A disabled person who has some control should empty their bladder before sex. If they are catheterized, they should show the catheter to their partner, explain how it works, and tell them what to do if the catheter is accidentally pulled out. Washing before and after sex becomes very important since a catheter can increase the risk of urinary or vaginal infections.

The paralyzed portions of the body are sometimes subject to involuntary muscle spasms, which look strange but don't hurt. Being turned on can make these spasms happen more frequently. Taking a mild tranquilizer sometimes prevents them, but it is even easier to just wait until they go away. The nondisabled partner should not be alarmed.

159

A spinal cord injury makes genital orgasm impossible. However, above the level of the injury, erogenous zones can become more sensitive. A disabled person can enjoy stimulation of these zones, massage, being held, receiving physical attention, and pleasuring their partner. Some people with injured spinal cords like vibrators since they provide strong, continuous stimulation. Sex is a matter of the heart, mind, and body — not just a genital experience — and is good and necessary for human health even if orgasm is not experienced.

It sounds like a lot of trouble, doesn't it? But able-bodied people should not shy away from disabled partners. Somebody who has the guts to live independently instead of in an institution, cope with pain and discomfort, and insist on living a full life despite the prejudice and inconvenience that's inflicted on them by an able-bodied world is probably tougher than you are. Like racism or sexism, able-bodyism limits your perspective on life and restricts your social circle to people who are exactly like yourself. Disabled people don't want special treatment or coddling — they just want the same chance you give other people you meet, to be looked at, greeted, and evaluated rather than being ignored.

✍

Q. I have a question regarding one type of ad that appears in gay papers — able-bodied men wishing to meet disabled men. As a disabled man (I'm 31, had polio at the age of six months, and am required to wear long-leg braces and crutches to get around) I would like to know if you recommend answering these ads.

It's pretty difficult to meet men who are comfortable with a disabled person, and I was wondering if the advertisers might offer me better opportunities, although it mystifies me why an able-bodied man is interested in a man who has paralyzed and wasted legs and has to wear heavy steel braces just to stand.

A. Well, I can't specifically recommend that you answer any particular ad. But if you see an ad that sounds good to you, why not write the guy and ask him the same questions you've just asked me? If you are nervous about being exploited or victimized, rent a post office box so you can keep your home address confidential. It's generally a good idea to meet the advertiser in a public place for coffee or drinks before getting further involved.

There are men looking for every other kind of man that exists. I can't explain why somebody would be especially drawn to differently abled guys any more than I can explain why some men insist on twelve inches or more, or a beard, or a significant difference in age. Would you feel this ambivalent if, in fact, the attribute in question was a huge cock or a washboard stomach? Believe me, the fetish doesn't work any differently. Your braces may be nothing but a bother to you, but they could be another guy's dream come true. If it's that easy to make him happy, and he makes you happy, don't complain!

The idea of one's partners being turned on to something that is stigmatized can creep people out. For example, fat guys often get angry if a potential partner identifies himself as a chubby-chaser, and a similar spat can ensue with very effeminate guys who don't want to think of themselves as queens. Just between you and me and several thousand readers, I'd rather make it with somebody who thought my body (for better or worse, in sickness and in health) was sexy as hell than get it on with a social worker who did me the favor of ignoring my "flaws." Why settle for a charity fuck if you can be adored? Get your letters out before the rates go up again!

✍

Q. I have asthma. Most of the time I can keep it under control with prescription drugs. I also have to avoid things like heavy perfume, cigarette smoke, and furry animals. During the day I don't have much trouble breathing, but at night it really bothers me. I'd like to be more sexually active, but it seems like the women I date all assume that we'll slip under the covers together when the sun goes down. Getting aroused usually makes me pant, and when you combine that with an asthma attack, it's suffocating. It's impossible for me to be physically close to another person once I get short of breath. I feel like they're crowding me and stealing my air.

A. Conduct your date in a normal fashion until your friend makes it clear that she'd like to spend the night. Then tell her what you just told me. I don't see why she would mind sleeping over if she had a sexy morning (and maybe the rest of the whole day) to look forward to. Have a comfortable place where she can sleep separately if you need some extra space.

Get more assertive. When you ask women to go out with you, schedule brunch or afternoon dates instead of movie-and-dinner dates. After you've eaten or gone to the museum or whatever, pounce on her and ask her if she feels like getting a little frisky. I know it's traditional to wait until the moon comes up to actually put your hand inside somebody's blouse or Levi's, and it's scary to be the one who makes the first move, but if you don't do something different, you're not going to have anything to keep you company at night besides your inhaler.

✍

Q. I have sciatica, apparently as a result of switching to an office job after years of working outdoors. The pain is immobilizing. It feels like I have a hot wire embedded in my butt, and it runs down my leg and into my calf and foot. I've seen a regular doctor and a chiropractor. They both tell me I need to rest, should avoid wearing high heels or sitting, and they've given me some other treatments. Every now and then I have a good day, and then I find myself remembering a former hobby of mine, masturbation. But I find myself unable to masturbate to orgasm. On a really good day, I remember that I used to engage in this strange form of acrobatics I called sex. Is this ever going to change?

A. You should talk to your medical people about sex. In severe cases of sciatica, people are sometimes advised not to come (or to try not to, anyway) because it might inflame the sciatic nerve even more. But a time limit of a couple weeks is usually placed on this prohibition. By the time you really want to masturbate, you'll probably be able to reach orgasm. Right now your body is too fucked up to properly transmit the messages of sexual arousal. You may be able to have sex before your sciatica is completely healed if you lay on your back and keep your legs propped up on pillows so your pelvis is tilted at the correct angle to keep pressure off the nerve.

Sciatica does get better. It can take weeks of bed rest. It's tempting to get up and busy, but that's a big mistake. Remember that nerves heal more slowly than any other type of human tissue. Once you've had sciatica, it tends to recur, so you'll need to make sure you don't wear the wrong shoes or sit in bad chairs that will bring it back.

✍

Q. I'm a lesbian, but that's not what I want to ask you about. My little brother is mildly mentally retarded. He lives at home with my mother and father. They've devoted an amazing amount of time to helping him remain as independent as possible. But I think they see him as a perpetual child. It's pretty clear to me

162

that Bobby has the sexual needs of an adult. Furthermore, he asked me recently what a "queer" was and told me he liked boys better than girls. He has one really good friend that he met at a recreation program for retarded young people, and I think they may be lovers, or at least they've fooled around.

Now that I've said that, I'm not even sure what my questions are. I have a lot of vague fears. Like, what if my mother finds out? Does Bobby need to know about condoms? Who should tell him? What if he falls in love with somebody and wants to live with them?

A. Bobby has already singled out the person he loves and trusts enough to ask about sex. That's you. Your first task is to find out how much he knows. Get some children's books about sex and read them to Bobby. Fill in the gaps in his knowledge and correct any misinformation he's picked up from his friends, teachers, or television. Make sure you tell him that everybody masturbates and it's okay, it won't make you sick. This information is crucial, and it's missing from a lot of "where babies come from" texts. Since you don't want to get him into trouble, make sure you also let Bobby know that masturbation is something people do in private.

Sex education is always repetitive. Children need to ask the same questions over and over again. Bobby will do the same thing even though he's not a child. Be patient. This is going to take a while. He'll be asking the questions not just to make sure he understands what you're telling him, but to make sure it really is okay to talk to you about sex. Every time you answer him clearly and calmly, you build trust and convey the message that sex is not scary, that it's a normal and healthy part of life.

Starting this process will let Bobby know he can ask you about sex. Before you try to tell him about condoms, try to find out what kind of sex he's having. Tell him it's important to make sure he uses condoms if he's having sex with another person. Tell him he has to do this so he doesn't make somebody get pregnant or catch a germ that will make him sick. If you can't find any pictures that show how a condom is put on, show him with a dildo and a rubber. This is not something that he can figure out by listening to you talk about it.

You also need to talk to your mom and dad. If you think they're really going to resist the information that their son has sexual urges, try to enlist the help of a doctor, social worker, or teacher who can back you up. If your parents aren't prepared, they'll be pretty upset if they hear Bobby talking about this neat stuff you're teaching him or he shows off his new box of prophylactics.

The coming-out issue may be even harder for your parents to accept. There's the possibility that they will blame you for "making" Bobby homosexual. It might help to tell them that many adolescent boys go through a phase of having sex with each other, and that's the phase Bobby is experiencing. The truth is that there are gay men and lesbians who are retarded. Since most of them are under the control of their parents or an institution, it's very difficult for them to lead openly gay lives.

But your parents aren't going to live forever. What's going to happen to Bobby when they die? I think it's time to start looking for an environment where Bobby can live, maybe with some assistance and partial supervision, and be a little more independent.

STDs, safer sex, and AIDS*

Q. When a friend was diagnosed with AIDS early last year, we discussed his options to prevent the spread of HIV. He was not receptive to the limitations of safer sex. I believe he continues to have unsafe sex, limited only by his difficulty in finding partners and his physical deterioration. Others have told me of PWAs and those who are HIV-positive and *know* it who continue having unsafe sex, not caring that they are spreading HIV infection.

I've lost too many friends to AIDS and ARC to be complacent and allow this to continue without doing something to stop it. But what can I do?

A. We'd all like to think that everybody is being responsible in the face of this epidemic. But the truth is that there are some angry people who feel that if they are going to die, they don't care how many people they take with them. By acknowledging this, I don't wish to contribute to a panic about "AIDS carriers." The

---

* *Author's note:* At least half of the questions I get pertain to safer sex and AIDS. These include a surprising amount of queries about very basic issues, such as how to put on a condom or whether you can get AIDS from unprotected anal sex. Because there is still a lot of ignorance and misinformation about this crucial topic, I've devoted this chapter to answering some of these questions. However, our knowledge about AIDS and other STDs is changing all the time. It's quite possible that by the time you read this some of the information I've given will be outdated. Please keep yourself informed and protect your health by learning all you can about AIDS from the most current and authoritative sources.

people who falsely assume they are healthy and dispense with safer sex precautions do far more damage.

Anybody who invents an excuse to have unprotected gay, lesbian, or straight sex is being every bit as crazed and irresponsible as the rare PWA who takes out his or her rage on their partners. *Everybody* is responsible for safer sex. It's not the active partner's job, it's not the passive partner's job, it's not your lover's job or your trick's job. The only person who can protect your health is you. You must bring this awkward topic up with potential sex partners and make it clear that you expect total compliance before anybody takes their pants off.

Sometimes that isn't enough. People don't always respect the bargains they make to get sex. If you're flirting with the hottest man in the world and he seems hesitant or hostile about using latex barriers, wave good-bye. Who needs to have the subject brought up again when your willpower is weakened? Who needs to wonder what he's doing with that condom when you can't see his hands?

I don't know if this advice will satisfy you since you seem to be looking for some way to control the behavior of your HIV-infected friend and others like him. I have nothing to suggest because if reason has failed, your only effective options for stopping this person are barbarous. Of course, we could encourage the state to take over this function, but I think it would bring the same light touch to this matter that it wields on the issues of reproductive freedom and the First Amendment.

✍

Q. About a year and a half ago, I met someone who is a registered nurse. We had a short relationship, and one night we had anal sex without a condom. During sex, he did *not* have an orgasm and assured me that everything was okay. He also told me repeatedly that because he was a nurse and worked with blood, he had to be tested for AIDS frequently and was always HIV-negative. I'm sure you can guess the conclusion to this tale. He moved away from here. I have since learned that he has become ill. How great are the chances of transmission in a case such as this?

A. It's possible to become infected with HIV as a result of only one exposure to the virus. You should wait at least six months after you had unprotected sex and then get the HIV-antibody test. If your test results are negative, chances are good that you were not infected. A very tiny percentage of HIV-antibody tests give false results or are not interpreted properly by the lab. If this really worries you, you can always get retested. On rare occasions, someone who has HIV in their system can still test negative. Unfortunately, we don't know why this sometimes happens. And it's extremely unlikely that you'll be one of those people.

If it's true that your partner did not ejaculate during penetration, your chances of becoming infected are greatly reduced but not eliminated. Pre-cum can contain HIV. Everyone should know that *coitus interruptus* (pulling out before you come) is no more reliable for preventing the transmission of disease than it is for preventing pregnancy. There's just no substitute for that silly-looking, pesky condom.

I don't intend to lecture you. I'm just very sorry that this has happened to you. If you need some help to manage the stress, call your local AIDS service organization or gay mental health agency and set up an appointment for one or two sessions of counseling. Some cities also have support groups for the "worried well," and you might find such a group helpful.

✍

Q. I have a rapidly growing collection of dildos of various sizes and shapes. I have used them only on myself. (I realize sharing toys is a no-no.) I have used both water- and petroleum-based lubricants. Is a petroleum-based lubricant harmful to the latex?

After use, I wash the dildo with warm water and a mild dishwashing detergent (especially useful in removing petroleum-based lube), towel dry, and then swab the surface with alcohol and allow it to air-dry. Is this sufficient disinfection and cleaning? So far I have had no problems, but I am relatively new to this, and I don't want to cause myself health problems or inadvertently destroy a toy.

A. Petroleum-based lubes can damage a latex condom enough to make it worthless as a viral barrier. But I doubt that your dildos will be harmed, particularly if you keep on using such a good, thorough cleaning procedure. You can also use hydrogen peroxide, Betadine, boiling water, or bleach. Just make sure the bottle of hydrogen peroxide or rubbing alcohol is freshly opened and not exposed to light — these disinfectants rapidly lose their potency when exposed to oxygen or light.

If you'd like a little more protection, you can prevent rectal bacteria from getting into the porous surface of a dildo where it can be hard to eradicate it by putting a condom on the dildo before you use it.

I should mention that some medical authorities feel that oil-based lubricants are bad for your bowel because they are difficult for your body to eliminate. Data are still being collected regarding this. So, while the Vaseline or Crisco or whatever you're using won't hurt your dildo, it might not be doing your insides much good.

✍

Q. My lover and I have been together for approximately a year and a half. We have developed a relationship that is spiritual, honest, loving, and passionate. Our sex has always been full of surprises and continues to be special every time. We feel blessed that we can share so much together.

About a year ago, my lover found out that he was HIV-positive. He eats well, rests well, and has an open and positive attitude. He has not shown any symptoms of ARC or AIDS although it is clear that his immune system is impaired, given his consistent low T-cell count. I had tested negative several times before my lover and I even met.

We enjoy safe sex, although sometimes I wonder how safe sex is, exactly, for both him and for me. During anal sex, he always uses a condom, although I regularly do not use one when I fuck him. I realize this is "unsafe" for him primarily since his system is impaired, yet in passionate moments we sometimes forget. I wonder exactly how safe it is for me to French-kiss, rim, and fuck him without a condom. For example, if he were to have a thrush infection, would I be susceptible to catching it if we kiss deeply? Is it possible (or likely? or unknown?) that by rimming, I can be exposed to any opportunistic infections my lover may have, and am I likely to develop symptoms of these infections themselves, seeing as I appear to remain virus-free?

I wonder how many other men out there wonder the same things. Have there been any research efforts conducted on partners of HIV-positive men? Is there a trend toward HIV-negatives turning positive? Do the HIV-positive men encounter greater health traumas as a result of the exchange of saliva and other body fluids with the exception of cum and blood?

If I continue to test negative does that mean I am "immune" in some fashion? Have the steps we have taken to have "safer sex" paid off? When would my lover be most infectious during his HIV infection — now that he is healthy and symptomless or later when (and if) symptoms do appear?

A. It's wonderful that you and your lover have such a passionate relationship. But you are not having safe sex. By "forgetting" to use a condom when you fuck him, you are endangering your own health, not just his. During anal sex, HIV may be able to penetrate the lining of your urethra and enter your bloodstream. Bareback fucking is not safe for fucker or fuckee. Lyn Cannon, supervisor of the San Francisco City Clinic cohort study, which has been tracking the health of a group of gay men since they began researching hepatitis B in 1978, told me that they recently had three men seroconvert, apparently as a result of having unprotected anal sex as inserters.

French-kissing is safe, but rimming is not. Both of you should start using dental dams. The sensation of taste is the one that is deprived the most by practicing safer sex. But you can still taste his mouth, armpits, toes, behind his knees, etc.

As long as your own immune system is working well, most opportunistic infections associated with ARC and AIDS (such as thrush) should not be able to flourish in your system. But there are exceptions. Check with his health care provider about specific precautions you should take with any illness he might develop in the future.

Studies of the sexual partners of people who are HIV-positive show that there is a tendency for some of them to become antibody-positive. But much depends on whether or not people use condoms or engage in high-risk behavior such as sharing needles. A study of forty-five heterosexuals who had AIDS and their spouses showed that 58 percent of the spouses were antibody-positive. Spouses who sometimes used condoms and sometimes didn't had the same rate of seroconversion as spouses who didn't use them at all. None of the spouses who used condoms consistently for the two- to five-year period prior to enrollment in the study seroconverted. (Fischl et al., "Contacts of Adults with AIDS," *Journal of the American Medical Association* 257 (1987), no. 5: 640–644.)

I was unable to locate similar research on male couples. But since condoms break more often during anal sex than vaginal intercourse (in their March 1989 issue, *Consumer Reports* found a breakage rate of 1 condom in 105 compared to 1 in 165, respectively), seroconversion rates may be higher for gay male couples.

The research on infectivity is not conclusive. A 1988 study of the spread of AIDS among heterosexuals in Africa, Europe, and the United States suggests that an infected person may be most likely to transmit the virus just before their immune system collapses enough to justify a diagnosis of AIDS. However, this may vary a great deal from one individual to another or from one strain of the virus to another. We do not know enough about AIDS to say with certainty that it is safe to have unprotected sex at any point during the course of the disease.

It's a mistake to use research to justify playing the odds. If you have an HIV-positive partner, it is imperative for you to practice safe sex, and that means using condoms every single time you fuck or do oral sex.

Continued negative testing does *not* mean you are immune or that the precautions you are taking are adequate. As far as we know, there is no immunity to HIV. And as I've stated already, there are some big problems with the way you are having sex with your lover. But it can take a long time — perhaps even years — for someone to test antibody-positive after exposure to the virus.

There are a lot of reasons why people are reluctant to practice safer sex, even when they know they should. You may feel that it is pointless, if you feel you've already been exposed to the virus. You may be reluctant to upset your partner by making changes in your sexual routine when he is already worried about being HIV-positive. Exchanging body fluids can be a way of trying to reassure your partner that you do not feel he is dirty or contaminated. And you may feel guilty about being HIV-negative when he is not, perhaps even guilty about the possibility that he might die and you might survive him. This is very difficult stuff to talk about. I urge both of you to seek counseling to help you sort this out.

✍

Q. I've had a lover for almost ten years. He's 30, still as sexy as when he was 20, and we're compatible and monogamous except for participation in our J/O club.

When he and I get together for sex, he likes to be jerked off in several different positions, a service that I happily provide. I like to fuck; I always have. But for a change one night about six years ago I tried just fucking him between his legs near his asshole (being careful not to enter), and fucking the crack of his ass and between his legs from behind. That first time was incredible; the most recent time a couple of days ago was just as good!

I used to enjoy "real" fucking, but this has been more enjoyable for him (no pain at all, and a nice massage, too), and I have more control over my orgasm and can fuck for an hour and more. (My "record" is about two hours and fifteen minutes without losing a hard-on and without him being even slightly uncomfortable. It's like pure ecstasy.) We pretty much limit ourselves to doggy style, although it's been good face-to-face as well.

Although I don't have that special feeling of being inside my lover and he knows I'm not really "in" him, the delicate feeling of my cock being warmed by him and my ever-increasing sexual excitement as well as knowing that we're both being "safe" is an immensely pleasurable time for me.

Perhaps we don't have to be quite so safe, but we've found we prefer this approach to fucking. Even though we say we're never with anyone else, we only have our words on it and while we'd trust each other with our lives, it's still our personal responsibility to protect each other. Your readers who are concerned about fucking and don't like condoms should try this approach. If your partner really wants to be entered, use a finger or a dildo, and stay alive and keep him around for more loving!

A. Thanks for writing in with this cheerful and lusty suggestion. Is this what the B-52s mean when they urge us to "shake your honey's buns"? Here's hoping you and your lover keep on shaking it and making it for many happy years to come.

✍

Q. Recently I heard a disturbing rumor that some reputable brands of condoms are not reliable. (They leak or break.) And I've also heard that nonoxynol-9 is not, in fact, effective against the AIDS virus. You can't imagine how discouraging this was after I've put so much effort into using both of these things and not allowing myself to make any excuses. I expect that *you* will tell us the truth about this matter!

A. Research conducted by the Mariposa Foundation and the University of California at Los Angeles recently revealed that many condoms produced by major manufacturers do, indeed, perform poorly when subjected to tests that simulate the stress of sex. Some of these failures may be due to the condoms' deteriorating during warehouse storage. Manufacturers should start putting an expiration date on their product and monitor storage conditions more closely since excessive heat, exposure to light, and age will all weaken latex.

The good news is that Ramses, Sheik, Gold Circle, Gold Circle Coin, Pleaser, and Mentor condoms all performed very well. However, Mentor has recently changed manufacturing companies, so this rating may change.

Another interesting tidbit of information is the fact that when the Fourex Natural Skins condom, which is made of lamb membrane, was tested, no viral leakage was detected. There has been some concern that natural "skin" condoms might not be effective viral barriers, since the membranes they are made out of have a slightly uneven thickness. I would still caution you to use latex condoms, but for those of you who are allergic to rubber or just can't adapt to anything except a "skin," this is hopeful news.

Regarding nonoxynol-9, I know of no research that indicates it does *not* kill HIV. However, a study (again by UCLA) found that another spermicide, oxtoxynol-9, which is found only in Ortho-Gynol Contraceptive Jelly, is a superior viricide. Another chemical, benzalkonium chloride, used in spermicides marketed in Europe, is also more effective than nonoxynol-9 against chlamydia, herpes, gonorrhea, and HIV. It is not available in this country.

This study was done in 1987, and the *Los Angeles Times* had to use the Freedom of Information Act to get the results released. This is criminal. The FDA has to recognize that people are using spermicides for disease prevention as well as birth control and start certifying and ranking them for that purpose.

So don't throw away your safe-sex paraphernalia yet, just incorporate this new information. We can never afford to think we know everything about AIDS and its prevention and stop keeping up to date. But it would be ever so nice if our government would cooperate just a wee bit more. If this is an example of President Bush's kinder, gentler AIDS policy, I say, let's turn him loose in his boxer shorts in the Castro with nothing but a five-year-old condom and let him hitchhike home to the White House. And if we can't do that, next time we get a chance, let's throw the rascals out!

✍

Q. Is there anything (comforting, apologetic, helpful) one can say or do if the condom breaks? This has only happened to me a time or two, and I think it might have been easier to live through the bombing of Hiroshima.

A. Well, after you say, "Oh, shit" or "Goddammit," you should say, "How did this happen?" and "I'm sorry." The fact is that no matter what you say it's going to come out in a muddled rush that will sound something like, "Oh, zit, owdithisapenmmsorry."

The trauma of such an event is considerably reduced if you use a condom or a lubricant that contains nonoxynol-9. This chemical does a dandy job of killing HIV in the test tube. Although we don't know for sure that it works the same way in the human body, you'll be glad it's there if a condom breaks.

If you've done everything you can to reduce the possibility of breakage (don't store condoms in direct sunlight or at anything other than room temperature, don't let them get old, put them on with an empty reservoir at the end, hold onto them while you're fucking, stop and change condoms if you're fucking real rough or for a long time, use only water-based lube, don't reuse them), you'll still feel lousy if one fails, but you'll get over it faster.

Using condoms regularly greatly reduces the risk of disease transmission. But they are not perfect. Some of us choose to accept that risk, others only use dildos for penetration, and some of us have given up fucking altogether. I keep oscillating between all three of these choices and writing lots of angry letters to my congressperson.

✍

Q. Is it safe for two people who are *both* either HIV-positive, ARC patients, or even AIDS patients, to engage in unsafe sex practices? Are they at any additional risk? Could unsafe sex accelerate their illness? I know if I tested positive, I'd find someone else who is also positive and try to live a loving, monogamous relationship without the hassle of condoms. Is this improper thinking?

A. Experts are currently saying that couples who are HIV-positive, regardless of whether they have an ARC or an AIDS diagnosis or are still healthy, should be using condoms and following all the safe-sex guidelines.

We simply don't know if this in fact does anything to preserve people's well-being. There may be a relationship between how often you are exposed to the virus that causes AIDS and how quickly you get AIDS (or whether you get sick at all). During the course of the illness, the virus's ability to infect another person may vary a great deal. There are different strains of the virus, some of which seem to be more deadly than others. There's also concern that two partners with compromised immune systems might expose one another to opportunistic infections.

I know many HIV-positive couples who have studied this information who still opt to go ahead and have unsafe sex with each other. And in the absence of better data, I certainly can't condemn them. This is the kind of decision that two people have to make for themselves after obtaining all the available facts and talking them over. I don't think there's a single choice that's right for every couple.

         ✍

Q. I wonder if you could help me realistically evaluate a safe-sex issue. According to the Surgeon General and the CDC, you cannot get AIDS from urine. But according to almost all gay newspaper guidelines, you can. Which is it? Of course to be absolutely certain one should avoid all bodily fluids, but when long-term habits are established what can I realistically tell myself? I already have AIDS, although my opportunistic infections are now at a minimum.

A. Most medical people are prejudiced against "deviant" sexual activities like watersports and have little or no interest in ever finding out whether they are safe to do. A lot of gay agencies and health professionals share this bias.

There are no recorded cases of people getting AIDS from ingesting or being splashed with urine. However, urine can contain HIV. Because your immune system is impaired, I would urge you not to take other people's piss into your mouth or anus. You might be exposed to something like hepatitis that could be deadly to you. If this is the only or primary way you get off, I'd recommend that you use your own piss. Boiling urine will kill any HIV that might be present, but it won't kill other viruses like hepatitis. And, of course, piss is safe for "external use only."

However, if you drink somebody else's piss, the only person you might endanger is yourself. So the decision to do it or not do it is up to you. As sexual activities go, it's certainly safer than getting fucked without a condom or swallowing cum.

         ✍

Q. A year and a half ago, I met and started dating a very nice young man. We've had some very good times, and I've grown to love and care for Ron a lot. But from the start I've felt that this is not a relationship that would make me happy or content in the long term. Ron is eleven years younger than I, and our expectations and goals are worlds apart.

Ten months ago, I asked Ron to take the HIV-antibody test with me. Our sexual behavior was stretching the limits of safe sex. The result was a positive test for Ron and a negative test for me. Ron was really crushed by his test result, and I tried to be very supportive — and continue to be. But I find Ron becoming more dependent, and I don't like it. Added to this is a growing sexual frustration. I'm reluctant and scared. I'd like to turn this relationship into something strictly platonic. But when I bring this up, Ron gets upset and talks about "nothing to live for" and "no future."

I feel guilty for wanting out, but this relationship is more than I can handle. I feel trapped!

A. It's a pity that you apparently didn't share your qualms about the relationship with Ron before you both went for antibody testing. I'm not sure what the test was supposed to do. As I've often told people, you can't stop having safer sex just because you have a negative test result. A negative test may mean you have been exposed to the AIDS virus, but your body has not had enough time to manufacture antibodies that will register on the test. And every time you have unsafe sex, you risk exposing yourself to the virus. It would have made more sense to tell Ron you needed to re-establish your sexual boundaries.

Breaking up with him now is bound to make Ron feel that you are rejecting him because he is HIV-positive. And, in fact, that is what you are doing. Because you know his antibody status, sexual acts that you could deceive yourself into accepting before now seem too dangerous. But these acts were always risky! You were also willing to tolerate his emotional demands and feed his illusions about the future of this relationship (perhaps because he is so young and attractive) as long as no serious obligations were placed upon you.

You must tell Ron that you want to stop having sex with him. But please try to be more honest with him in the future. If you're still going to be his friend, tell him that, but if you've gotten so resentful that you don't want him in your life any more, it would be kinder to say so now than to lead him to expect support he will not receive.

If Ron really feels he has nothing to live for without you, he's going to need some professional counseling to help him get through this breakup. Get some referrals for him before you give him the bad news.

✍

Q. My boyfriend prefers J/O to sex even though we have kept our vow to be monogamous, which we made a year ago. Our doctor says we are both healthy and can do anything we want with each other. Frankly, I'm getting so hungry for sex I could die or get some fast food on my way home, if you know what I mean. We used to look at porn movies together on our VCR and use some oil to rub each other off, but lately he doesn't even want me to give him a hand job. Am I a sexual failure or what?

A. It's really hard to confront a lover about a sexual problem without making him defensive. All too often, any mention of the problem degenerates into hysterical denial, followed by a desperate attempt to change the subject by bringing up everything the two of you have ever had a fight about. But do not be deterred. The longer you wait, the more resentful and anxious you will be, and that will reduce your ability to stay calm and persist in exchanging information and looking for solutions rather than spewing out venomous references to his autoerotic, narcissistic, boring selfishness.

Don't wait until you blurt something out. Pick a time, preferably when neither of you feels especially tense and you don't have to be somewhere else in half an hour. Tell him you're bringing this up because you love him and are afraid you're not making him happy, and because you're unhappy, which makes you fear for the future of your relationship. Describe what you perceive is happening and ask if he has the same perception.

He'll probably deny that the picture you paint is an accurate one. Don't let him make you defensive. The goal here is simply to provide an opening for both of you to express your feelings about the kind of sex you are having and want to have with each other. Instead of defending your "position," ask him what he sees going on and if it is satisfying his needs.

If he wants to pretend everything is okay, you'll have to take all the responsibility for saying, "Well, it's not okay with me, and I want us to agree to a moratorium on solo-sex or see a couples counselor or do something else, if you can make any suggestions." This is a rotten position to be in, but it's better to be the bad guy and push things than to swallow your anger. If you resent him enough, you will subtly sabotage any attempt he makes to kindle your passions and get himself off the hook.

It could be that your lover is simply so terrified of getting sick that he can't enjoy sex with a partner. Maybe it's a combination of anxiety and just getting used to jacking himself off. The unpredictability and uniqueness of another's touch is exciting, but never as faithfully effective as one's own touch. Maybe he's having fantasies he can't verbalize while you are touching him. Maybe he's afraid to have sex with you because he hasn't been able to be monogamous, and he doesn't want to give you a dose of anything he might have caught. Maybe he's waiting for you to take the initiative. Maybe he didn't like the kind of sex you were having before vowing to be monogamous and is reluctant to return to a disagreeable pattern. Maybe he's trying to provoke you into tying his hands behind his back. You'll never know till you ask.

One more suggestion — when you do bring this up, have a list of fun new things to try ready to perk up his imagination. You've got to know what some of his erotic weaknesses are. Make him an offer he can't refuse.

✍

Q. I'm a lesbian who works in a massage parlor. Because of my work, I try to be very health-conscious. Lately AIDS has come up as a topic of conversation at the parlor. I have taken some pamphlets written for gay men in for everybody to read, but I'm not sure how it applies to us. Do you have some specific suggestions for what we can do to stay healthy?

A. Check the resource guide for literature about AIDS published specifically for sex workers, for women in general, and for lesbians.

The primary route of transmission for AIDS among women is IV drug use. (Of course, not all sex workers are IV drug users.) The best way to avoid AIDS (or hepatitis and other blood-borne diseases) is to quit shooting up. People who continue to use needles should *never share their works.* If you have to share your set, draw bleach into it and expel it three times, then rinse it well by drawing water into it and expelling it three times so you don't inject bleach. Taking it apart and soaking it in bleach for half an hour before you rinse it will make it even cleaner. This won't hurt your works. Cookers should also be cleaned, and you should throw away cottons and not reuse them.

Even if you hide your rig, you should clean it before you use it because you never know if another household member or a friend has borrowed it. Needles used for tattooing, piercing, or shooting up steroids can spread disease as easily as needles used to shoot up junk, cocaine, or speed.

The second most common way for women to get AIDS is heterosexual contact with men at risk for the disease. "Safe-sex" guidelines for gay men assume that both partners are willing to negotiate and compromise to protect one another. Prostitutes may have a difficult time persuading their clients to accept safe sex. It will help if everybody in your parlor agrees to demand the same things from their clients. If you can, talk to women who work in other parlors, too. If clients hear the same thing from two or three women, they may start to get the idea and be more cooperative.

Insist on using rubbers. No fucking and no blowjobs without rubbers. The virus that causes AIDS is spread by semen. If a client refuses to use rubbers, try lowering the light or using a position in which he can't see below his own waist. Once he has a hard-on, he may not feel you slipping a rubber on with a lubricated hand. Some prostitutes have become adept at keeping a condom in their mouths that can be rolled over the head of the penis before the john ejaculates. If you have to, "accidentally" let his penis slip out of your mouth when he comes. Don't swallow cum.

A birth-control sponge or spermicide that contains nonoxynol-9 can be inserted prior to tricking. This chemical will kill HIV, but ideally should be used *with* a condom for complete protection. However, some protection is better than none. A spermicide that contains 5 percent nonoxynol-9 will kill HIV in less than sixty seconds in a test tube. Make sure whatever you use contains at least 5 percent nonoxynol-9.

Hand jobs are safe as long as you have no cuts or open sores on your hands. Bedding and trick towels should be boiled or soaked in the bleach solution before laundering.

Talking dirty, watching porn, dressing up, bondage, phone sex, massage, mutual masturbation, sex toys like vibrators and dildos (as long as they are not shared), spanking, cock rings, wrestling, cock-and-ball bondage, fondling, tit-clamps — any sexual activity that does not expose you to his bodily fluids — is safe. A little kink can make you and your trick safer.

Some sex workers have moved into areas of the business where there's little or no contact with customers — for example, stripping, phone sex, or domination.

✍

Q. I've noticed that fisting appears on virtually every set of "safe-sex" guidelines. But usually it appears with no explanation about why this activity puts one at risk for AIDS. Since the virus seems to be carried in blood and semen, wouldn't activities that involve only a hand or a dildo be safer than having somebody's cock come inside you? The guidelines from my city's health project say you should give up fisting because "it isn't worth the risk." Well, I happen to like it a lot, and I don't want to stop unless there's a good reason.

A. In my opinion, anal fisting is included in lists of "dangerous sexual activities" because most health workers assume it always (or nearly always) results in physical injury — not because it necessarily puts you at risk of contracting AIDS. It's especially silly of them to put vaginal fisting on lists of "unsafe sex" for lesbians.

The assumption is that a man (or woman, although relatively few women engage in this practice) who gets anally fisted has a higher risk of having the lining of his bowel abraded or torn. If he then allows someone to come in his ass, any disease-causing organisms in his partner's semen have instant access to his bloodstream. This is certainly true as far as it goes. It is really and truly stupid to allow someone to fuck you if they are not wearing a condom. However, research has shown that HIV can penetrate the intact lining of the rectum. It doesn't need to enter via injured tissue.

Any time you put something big up your ass (including a big dick), you increase the risk of trauma to anal tissues. However, if fisting is performed carefully, in the absence of semen, any risk of disease transmission would be to the top, from the bottom's bloodstream into his via scraped cuticles, assuming he had prepared his hands correctly for fisting by trimming his nails and filing them until they were extremely short and smooth. This is why fisting tops should wear latex gloves.

However, "safe-sex" guidelines do not recommend that you abstain from fucking after you have been fisted or be doubly sure to use condoms. Nor do guidelines specify that tops doing hand-balling (or any kind of anal penetration) should wear rubber gloves. This kind of specific advice would probably be perceived as advocating a stigmatized and potentially dangerous activity.

Not everybody can comfortably accommodate an entire hand. Not everyone is gentle or sensitive enough to dilate their partner's rectum to that extent. But it can be and is being done. To simply label the entire activity as deviant or dangerous and refuse to give practitioners advice about how to do it as safely as possible is irresponsible. It means that people who find that degree of ass-play erotic will continue to engage in it, but without taking proper precautions, unless they are lucky enough to run into a fellow practitioner who is well informed about how to perform fisting safely.

The statement that "it's not worth the risk" assumes that deviant gay sex (as if there could be such a thing) is inherently more dangerous than sucking and fucking, or that it is less important or central to people's lives. Therefore, it's considered fine to recommend that people stop doing kinky sex, under the guise of preventing the spread of AIDS. The fact is that most of us have only a few sexual activities we *really* get off on. Switching to something else isn't that easy, and you certainly can't measure the place any given practice has in somebody's sexual repertoire by counting the numbers of other people who do it. If health workers are willing to recommend oral and anal sex with condoms, despite the fact that semen is known to contain HIV, then they must not discriminate against less mainstream forms of gay sexuality — especially if those activities are actually *less* likely to expose participants to infection.

Please do not take this as carte blanche to put anything of any size or shape up your ass as quickly and as often as possible. The tissues in the rectum are delicate. Nothing should ever be forced into your ass, and nothing should be put up there that is breakable, sharp, or that can't be taken out as easily as it is put in. If you find that part of what you enjoy about maximum anal penetration is the pain it produces, substitute some other painful activity like wearing tit-clamps or a spanking. Mucous membranes are not the appropriate site for erotic pain.

Nontraumatic fisting requires a very relaxed and aroused bottom and a top with well-manicured hands, rubber gloves, and a lot of lube. Any rectal bleeding after fisting should be seen by a doctor *right away*. A high fever, glassy eyes, or a painful abdomen are also signs that you need to see a doctor immediately. If your rectal lining is torn, an infection called peritonitis could result, which is potentially fatal. See the resource guide for more information about how to do fisting safely. And never, never fuck without a condom, not even if he promises to pull out before he comes.

✍

Q. My spirit is willing, but my flesh is weak. After agonizing about the current health crisis, I finally went out and bought a packet of Trojans. Boy, did I feel silly. I was going to be a brave little soldier, but the first time I tried to use the damn things, it was my Waterloo. I couldn't get it up. My trick left in disgust. And the rubbers have gotten lost somewhere underneath my dirty laundry because, frankly, I am afraid to try again.

A. Are you sure it wasn't the dirty laundry that caused your trick to leave in disgust?

Don't throw the rubbers away (if you can find them). Using them during oral and anal sex prevents the spread of most sexually transmitted diseases. It's not unusual for guys who aren't used to condoms to have trouble adjusting to them. They do cut down slightly on the amount of sensation your cock gets during sex. If you're already anxious about AIDS, that can also make it difficult to perform. And rubbers do remind some gay men of unpleasant heterosexual experiences, which is a definite turnoff.

You need to do some (un)dress rehearsal. Wear a rubber the next time you're jacking off. Don't try to come in it — in fact, the first few times you try this, take it off before you come. It might also help to read some porn that includes men using rubbers.

When you can successfully masturbate while wearing a condom, try wearing one at least part of the time you're with a partner. Remember, it takes time to change any sexual pattern, so if you have problems keeping an erection, take the performance pressure off. Either revert to masturbation or just remove the rubber until your erection returns. It might be sexy if your partner was wearing one as well and did some mutual exhibition and J/O.

There seem to be two different strategies for obtaining maximum pleasure from a condom. One strategy is to go with the tightest-fitting and thinnest condom possible, on the grounds that it will transmit more sensation. However, you then run an increased risk of breakage. Other guys prefer to use condoms that fit more loosely, on the theory that if a foreskin sliding up and down your cock is exciting, the condom will mimic that sensation. Putting a little water-based lube in the tip of the condom before you roll it on makes a *big* difference in how good it feels to wear one.

Eventually the rubber won't bother you. Putting one on can be sensual. You're doing the right thing to protect your health, so keep trying — just don't expect instant perfection.

✍

Q. I've been celibate for three years because of my fear of catching AIDS. My hormones can't take this much longer, so I have contacted a man through a personal ad. So far we've just been writing letters, but he wants to meet me right away. He's everything I've dreamed about, good looks, build, etc. My problem is how far can we go sexually? He agreed with me that we would follow any safe guidelines you could suggest.

I really enjoy the old-fashioned, face-to-face type of sex (missionary), but what about our cum? Is it safe to get cum all over ourselves? To mix our cum? Please don't laugh, I'm very serious.

A. I'm glad to hear that you're determined to have healthy sex. Somebody who has enough willpower to be celibate for three years shouldn't have any trouble following safer-sex guidelines — especially if your partner is as attractive and cooperative as the guy you met by advertising!

When you say you like old-fashioned, face-to-face sex and ask if it is okay to mix your cum and get cum all over yourself, I assume you are talking about body-rubbing and inserting the penis between each other's buttocks or thighs without actual anal penetration. This is a *very* low-risk kind of sex, unless you have an open cut or sore that semen might get into. You can get cum all over your body and mix your cum with his as long as none of it gets into your mouth or anus. Using a body lotion or baby oil can make this kind of sex a lot more fun.

The basic idea behind "safe sex" is to avoid getting any of his body fluids in your mouth, anus, or a break in the skin like a cut. Mutual hand jobs are safe. If you use condoms during oral or anal sex, that's usually safe too, although there's some risk the condom may break or tear. Use a condom only with water-based lubricant like KY jelly, and don't use a rubber more than once!

It's also safe to lick your partner's balls and scrotum, and the shaft of the penis. Put a condom on him before putting the head of his penis in your mouth. Putting your tongue in his asshole probably won't transmit AIDS, but can give you other diseases like hepatitis or intestinal parasites. For absolute safety, substitute a lubricated finger.

✍

Q. I'm a male in my late thirties, married, have three kids, 14, 11, and 6. Last summer I was put in the hospital for pneumocystis pneumonia. The doctor reported I had AIDS. Here's my question. The biopsy on my lungs was negative. I have not been fucked in twenty-five years and never used IV drugs. I was always the top. I've been in good health for seven months. Is it possible I don't have AIDS? My antibody test is positive, but I hear it's an iffy test. How can I get another opinion?

My wife thinks I had viral pneumonia. I have had a vasectomy. I am uncut and wear stubs (a rubber that covers the glans) on my dick for sex. They are not too reliable. Can I wear a regular rubber if I had a vasectomy? This way my skin covers the little rubber. Do I need sperm to carry the virus?

A. You need to talk to somebody who will explain more about AIDS to you than the doctor you had while you were in the hospital. Call your local AIDS hotline. You can ask them how to get retested for the HIV antibody. However, you should know that a positive blood test is usually sent back to the lab for double-checking. There's almost no chance that your diagnosis is wrong.

Even if you're always "the top" during sex, you can still be infected with HIV. You can get AIDS from men or women. Having a vasectomy doesn't mean that you can't transmit the virus to your wife or other sex partners. Using a stub is not enough protection because it only covers the head of your cock. You should be using regular condoms. Because you're uncut, you need to pull your foreskin back before rolling a condom on. And you may need to hang on to it while you're fucking. But it'll still work just fine. Your wife should be using spermicidal foam with at least 5 percent nonoxynol-9 in it as a backup in case the condom breaks. This chemical kills the AIDS virus.

It sounds like you are reluctant to tell your wife about your exposure to AIDS. But it's important for her to know. Her own health is at risk since you've been having sex with her in a way that could have exposed her to the virus. Since you have a vasectomy, how are you going to explain to her why you need to start having sex with condoms and spermicidal foam? It would be wrong to simply stop having sex with her or continue in the old way.

Treatment for AIDS is improving, but chances are you may die before your children become adults. If your wife is infected with the virus, they may be deprived of their mother as well. This is not an easy thing to think about or talk about, but the two of you have got to make some plans for them. Counseling is available to help you and your wife deal with this crisis. My heart goes out to you in this difficult situation. But wishful thinking will not make your health problems go away. If you had a bad heart or cancer, I'm sure you wouldn't hide it from your spouse. Please talk to the folks at the closest AIDS foundation and find the strength to make the right choices.

✍

Q. I became very passionately involved with another woman before I got to know her very well. By asking a lot of questions, I have managed to piece together a picture of her prior life, and what I've found out leaves me with a question I can't ask her. Can I get AIDS from my girlfriend? She used to run with a very fast crowd, and apparently they did some bisexual experimentation with each other as well as shooting up cocaine. She doesn't do drugs now and is very healthy, and I would like us both to stay that way.

A. Known cases of AIDS among lesbians have almost all been attributed to IV drug use or having sex with an infected male partner rather than lesbian sex. However, some cases of sexual transmission of AIDS between women have appeared in the medical literature. So we know it's possible for women to give each other this disease. The CDC does not collect data on lesbians, so it's impossible to know how often this happens. Since medical authorities don't care about helping us, we have to protect ourselves.

It appears that it's much easier to get AIDS by sharing needles or by having sex that exposes you to infected semen than it is to get it during lesbian sex. However, your girlfriend has a higher chance of having been exposed to the AIDS virus than most lesbians. And she could pass that virus on to you.

The amount of virus found in vaginal secretions is low. However, during oral sex, HIV can enter your bloodstream via any raw gums, cuts, or sores in your mouth. No one has compared the amount of virus found in the bloodstream with the amount in menstrual blood. But you should assume that menstrual blood is much more risky to get in your mouth than vaginal fluids. Virus can also enter your body via trimmed cuticles, cuts on the hands, or any broken skin. It's essential to start practicing safe sex with your girlfriend now.

This means you have to talk about it. Historically, lesbians have assumed that they don't need to worry about venereal disease. But this assumption (although well-nigh universal) was false. Women can give each other herpes, crabs, some forms of vaginitis, syphilis, and more. Nowadays, there are few dykes who aren't aware of AIDS. Someone with your girlfriend's sophisticated background has probably already done a lot of reading and thinking about it. She may be relieved if you're the one who calmly and reasonably brings it up.

It can be strange to try to change the way you have sex. Let your passion help you get over any awkwardness. Not having to worry about staying healthy will enhance arousal. Keep the supplies that you need close to the bed so you don't have to jump up and hunt for them and interrupt the spontaneity of desire. Use latex gloves for lovemaking with your hands. Get some water-based lubricant like KY Jelly, because oily lubricants make rubber deteriorate. You can use latex dental dams (available from dental supply houses) during oral sex. When a dab of KY is placed on the side of the dental dam that goes against the clitoris and labia, it feels nice and slippery and easily transmits the erotic sensations of the lips and tongue. You may find that you need to change the way you do oral sex when you use a dental dam. You can usually make your motions more vigorous, and women who don't like having their bare clits sucked may find that this feels delicious through a dam.

You should not share sex toys. After use, they should be cleaned with boiling water, rubbing alcohol (the label should say it's a 70-percent solution), bleach, or hydrogen peroxide. Using condoms on dildos makes it easier to keep them clean.

Both of you should consider getting tested for the HIV antibody. There are treatments now that can help HIV-positive people stay healthy. If both of you turn up HIV-negative, you should still practice safer sex. There's no immunity to AIDS.

✍

Q. Lately I've been reading the labels on lubricants to make sure they are okay to use with condoms. I don't like KY. It dries up too fast. So I was really glad to see a container of a lube that used to be an old favorite of mine, only now it said "water-soluble." But when I read the ingredients it didn't seem to be any different — it's shortening with some glycerin and perfume. So I didn't buy it. What gives? Is this stuff going to eat rubber or not?

A. This is a new advertising gimmick, and I think whoever thought it up should be taken out and shot. Lubricants that contain petroleum products, mineral oil, or shortening are *not* water-based; they are oil-based, and they are *not* safe to use with condoms, gloves, or dental dams. You can make it easier to wash Crisco out of the sheets if you add some more air and some glycerin, and that justifies the claim that it's "water-soluble," but it is not "water-*based*." So even if a lube says it's water-soluble, read the ingredients!

Incidentally, what's this beef about KY drying out? Guys who used to think nothing of going through a five-pound can of Crisco with one trick are bitching because a little dab of KY won't last all the way through an eighteen-hour fuck. F'heavensake, quit being so cheap. Shove your hand under that tube and kneel on that sucker. Slop that goo on his butt and have at it.

Lubricants that are not manufactured by pharmaceutical companies are not approved by the FDA. There are no legal requirements about quality control. Although some manufacturers are responsible businessmen, some of these products contain harmful ingredients (like Lubraseptic, which was pulled off the market because it contained organic mercury compounds) or do not contain a uniform quantity of a specified ingredient, such as nonoxynol-9.

You'll get the most consistent results by purchasing products like KY or Today Personal Lubricant. If you want to use a spermicide, the only way you can make sure you have a product that contains the minimum effective level of 5 percent nonoxynol-9 is to buy a gel or foam approved for birth control purposes.

(P.S., if you're going to be plowin' long and hard, it don't hurt to pull out once in a while and change your rubber, either. Reduces the chances of breakage, and lets him get hunnnngry again.)

Getting older

Q. In recent months I've heard of clubs formed for the purpose of getting guys together to jack off. I'm intrigued by this kind of arrangement because it seems very safe but potentially quite exciting. However, I am also apprehensive. You see, I'm now in my mid-60s. Would I be welcome? I don't want to go only to experience rejection.

A. Every J/O club is different, but my impression is that they tend to give much less attitude than the old-style gay baths. There's more support for the idea of helping each other get off safely, which means more camaraderie and less discrimination. I can't give you any guarantes, but why not check it out? Chances are you'll have a good time.

✍

Q. Being over 70, I'm becoming frustrated because finding suitable partners has become so difficult. Middle-aged men or men my own age simply do not turn me on, nor do I find them attractive. Being still trim, in good health, active, and independent, I have a very healthy appetite for sex, particularly with a younger, attractive person.

I'm aware that there are young gay men around who do prefer older men. But how do I find them? I'm no sugar daddy, and at today's high fees for escorts, who can afford them? Paying for sex is not my cup of tea either. I'm still hoping to find someone I can relate to for a regular relationship.

A. Yes, there are younger gay men who prefer older men. Generally speaking, however, *they* will find *you*. This doesn't happen very often.

Why? Because there's a huge cultural gap between the generations that leaves most people of different ages with very little to talk about. And while you're trim and fit for a person of your age, you're going to have trouble keeping up with someone in his 20s. I don't want to be mean, but you must be realistic. Most young men have the same reaction to you that you have to men your own age. When you were 23, how many 65-year-olds did you bed?

Commercial sex has its drawbacks. But you don't express any interest in young men as individuals, only as members of the class you find sexually attractive. If encounters with live escorts are too expensive, you might have to content yourself with videotapes or magazines.

Now that I've uttered the cautionary statement, let's look on the bright side. There are young men who have the hots for older men. There's a possibility that a classified ad in one of the publications that caters to daddies or silver foxes (see the resource guide) might get the response you're looking for.

It's a pity that you're so limited, because I get many letters from hot, older gay men who want sex, affection, and more sex. There's nothing unusual about being over 70 and still having a libido; but if you reject people who are available to satisfy your needs, you should not feel too sorry for yourself when you are horny, lonely, and deprived. On the other hand, sex doesn't work when you try to do it with people you're not attracted to. So you'll have to resign yourself to hunting hard for the kind of man you really want.

✍

Q. I'm a young man of 26. I've been out since I was 16 and have always been attracted to older men, 49 and up. I have a lover 63 years of age and we have been together now, in a monogamous relationship, for almost four years.

One of the biggest problems I have is finding magazines, movies, videotapes, anything with older men. My partner has TV, movies, videotapes, magazines, and can drive through the university campus. I don't have any problem with this. But what about me?

I know only too well the drawbacks of being turned on by older men and I am very happy in this relationship, but just once in a while I would like to find some entertainment for me! Do you have any ideas?

A. See the resource guide for videos of older men.

✍

Q. I, too, am older (66), but contrary to the gent in his 70s, I much prefer men older than myself, much older as a matter of fact. At the present time I have two occasional visits, from an 88-year-old and a 90-year-old. They are both straight as a needle, but they sure do enjoy being serviced. I guess they miss their deceased spouses. If there are any older gents, gay or straight, out there who wish to be serviced, you can send them my way. The older the better. Older or elderly are completely left out when it comes to periodicals, newspapers, magazines, etc., and thus have no means of communication.

A. I'm sure that none of these gentlemen miss their spouses very much when they're visiting you. It's wonderful to get your letter.

✍

Q. I am in my 60s and wonder why people in our age bracket get sneered at by younger people. Don't they realize that someday, they will be our age also? I'm an active person, physically and sexually, and I get my share, although I prefer men over 50. I don't frequent gay bars, but on occasion have done so, and all I see are people frantically wanting to be noticed, getting high on drugs, and a lot of phoniness. Is this what makes our gay world go round today?

Another question. I have tried unsuccessfully to obtain video-tapes of older men. All that are offered in your publication and others feature young men who are practically "chicken." They turn me off. Don't the sellers of videotapes know there are some of us who prefer older men?

A. Of course all those young men know they will someday be your age! That's part of the reason why some of them are so frantically tricking only and obsessively with each other. They're entitled to this "get it while you can" attitude. But I agree with you that it's self-destructive to ignore the inevitability of age. Young gay people who can't look forward to being sexy, productive, middle-aged and old people must feel pretty grim about their own futures.

Our culture's obsession with youth and conflation of it with beauty is partially responsible. So is the homophobic stereotype of gay men as doomed, frivolous, suicidal substance abusers. One reason I continually urge older gay people to stay in touch with younger gays is to give the next generation a sense that they do have a history, they do have a future (if they'll slow down their drinking enough to preserve some brain cells to enjoy it), and not all of us are 18-year-old ribbon clerks or disco dance instructors.

Porn producers always try to make their product appeal to as many people as possible for the simple reason that they make more money that way. You aren't the only person with a minority interest who would like to see more high quality porn that features it. Your Adviser, for example, has yet to see an erotic film that features two butch dykes fucking in a pool of motor oil. Porn producers who are interested in a script for such a movie should contact me.

✍

Q. These days you hear so much about children abandoning their aging parents, I suppose I'm lucky to have both an attentive niece and a nephew (the children of my favorite sister). Each of them live within an hour's drive, and they visit me at least once a month. Lately, my arthritis has been bothering me more than usual, and the last time they visited, they came together and told me they had "decided" I should live with Jenny, my niece, since she has a fairly large house and my nephew lives in an apartment.

The problem is, I've already decided I want to live with my dearest friend and lover, a woman my own age. We were lucky to meet each other at the senior center, but at my age, I figured I had nothing to lose if I propositioned another woman — they could always chalk it up to senility! I've always been a lesbian, but I haven't had a serious relationship or considered living with anyone for more than twenty years.

How can I tell my young relatives that I am rejecting their kind offer because romance has graced my life once more? It really is sweet of them, and I don't want them to think I'm ungrateful. When I do move in with Emma, how do you think they will react? I want them to continue to visit me, but I'm afraid they will be hostile to her. I do wish people would not assume that sexuality ends at 65!

A. It seems to me that the assumption that old people have no sexuality could be useful if you want to avoid any homophobic reaction from your niece and nephew. Just tell them you realize you need company but need to keep your independence

190

and prefer the pace of people your own age. Have them meet Emma the way you would introduce any friend — over tea, at dinner, for brunch.

If you want to tell them you love Emma, you must be prepared for them to either assume this affection is completely platonic or be rather shocked about their aunt's daring behavior. But you have an edge on them because of your status as an elder. Kids who treat an aging relative this nicely probably won't get disrespectful and lippy with you. If they do, remind them to watch their manners. I've often found that a well-placed rap with a cane does wonders to bring people to their senses.

You certainly haven't lived this long just to allow some green (but well-meaning) relations to tell you how to live your life. I'm so happy to hear that you're in love, and I hope you and your new sweetheart enjoy many happy years together.

✍

Q. I am in my 60s. But am I old? Nonsense! In her mid-60s Lena Horne undertook a world singing tour. And look at her. Look at any number of prominent, high-profile people now in the public eye. Ronald Reagan is only one among many. The notion that 60 necessarily means "old" is horse-and-buggy. Last night I watched a rerun of the 1985 Mr. Universe contest and heard this statement: "Bodybuilding can be practiced at any age. Some men are still entering physique competitions at 65 and 75. Their bodies stay young. Age shows up only in their faces." But faces, like spirits, like weights, can be lifted.

When I was 29 I thought I would be old at 30. At 66 I know better. When I retired from teaching four years ago, I put myself on a regular weight-training program. When I look in the mirror today, I'm astonished at what I see. But what is even more astonishing, to me at least, is that I'm still making out with young men in their twenties. Dozens of them. And they call me. I do not call them. If I had made the common mistake and allowed myself to hate or envy them, is it not reasonable to expect they would respond in kind? But I could not hate them if I wanted to. I adore young male beauty. And young men, like people of all ages, love to be loved.

Some people have called me handsome, but I am not handsome. I have had a face-lift, and I can still pass for 52 "in the dark with the light behind me." But the point of this letter is that if my case is exceptional, it shouldn't be. Many men could enjoy the kind of active sex life I enjoy if they only realized that a man is not necessarily old at 60 or 70.

191

It was at 50 that I left New York (after two decades of living in Manhattan) and moved back to my hometown in the Bible Belt. And I'll tell you another thing — the widespread and oft-repeated myth that small towns are necessarily the death of gays is just another popular superstition like the belief that a man's sex life ends in his fourth decade. This small town has a public park where the cruising is better than Central Park was back in the forties and the fifties.

A. I suspect that the face-lift and weight training are not nearly as important as your determination to keep on enjoying all that life has to offer. The years are kinder to some of us than to others, but you are indeed proof that attitude makes all the difference. Maybe your letter will encourage other 40-plus readers to drop the self-pity and put themselves back into circulation. Glad to hear you can still get it up to cruising speed.

✍

Q. Could you advise your readers on locations where a gay person could retire and live comfortably on a limited income? Also, areas where older gay people are accepted. I realize this is a "tall order," but somewhere there must be a haven for older gays.

A. This is one question I am ashamed to say I can't answer. And you're not the first person who's asked me. There's obviously a great need for retirement communities where older gay men and lesbians can enjoy their golden years without giving up their sexuality. Entrepreneurs, take note!

✍

Q. I feel very foolish at age 50 sitting here writing this letter to you about my problem. At my age I should be able to solve it myself, but somehow I feel that I need an objective opinion.

In 1980 I met this man who is married and was advertising in a gay magazine to meet men. I broke my cardinal rule to never have anything to do with a married man. I was trying to get over a relationship that had just broken up after thirteen years and did not want to get involved with anyone. But we did become serious about one another. I sold my home, closed my business, and moved here to work in the store that *we* now own, to be able to work with him and for us to be able to be together. (He is 67 now.)

The problem for me seems to be this. I am spending more and more time alone and without his companionship. (He's with his wife.) It has been necessary for me to live alone for the last six and a half years. We decided that this would be a monogamous relationship from the start. He swears that he has not had sex with his wife in years. The sex is still good for both of us. But it's only rarely that we spend a night together. He ate dinner in my apartment once last year. This year that hasn't even happened. We will occasionally go out to eat together. Rarely is he available to get together with our friends who are gay. We see them in the store and that's just about it.

I don't feel that this man has dealt with his own sexuality, and I wonder if I should end the relationship as well as our partnership in the store. It seems to me that he is obviously happy in this situation. But I am feeling the pressures of living alone and without companionship that I need. I want a "home" again and someone to share it with.

For me to end this situation, there is so much involved. Please advise.

A. Why do you put the word "home" in quotes? Your idea of a home is every bit as valid as a heterosexual marriage — and a lot more valid than the relationship your lover has with his wife. You are entitled to the companionship you crave and a partner who can spend time with you and your friends after the store closes for the night.

This is a situation very few self-accepting gay men would tolerate. However, do not underestimate the hold this man has on your heart. You're going to need strong friends who will let you cry on their shoulders, and you may even need some counseling to sort out why you are in this situation and what it will take for you to feel strong enough to leave it.

Because your finances have become so entangled, I strongly advise you to see an attorney before informing your lover that you want out of the relationship and the business. At the age of 50, after years of hard work, you shouldn't have to start over from scratch.

Death

Q. I am HIV-positive, and my health is deteriorating. Although I intend to do everything possible to prolong my life and make it happy and productive, I do not want to linger in great pain if I am terminally ill. I'm especially afraid of having my mental faculties impaired and literally not being the same person that I am today.

It seems to me that either euthanasia or suicide is an ethical alternative to the suffering I have seen dear friends of mine undergo while well-meaning medical people could do nothing for them but prolong their agony.

A. This is a thorny moral dilemma for many of us. But I agree that the time to become informed and make decisions is before one is seriously ill and possibly unable to make an informed choice or act upon it. I absolutely do not advocate suicide; life is too precious. But death without dignity can be a mockery of life, and I believe it is the individual — not the state, a hospital, or their family and friends — who should have the authority to decide when it is time to let go.

Consult the resource guide for sources of information about the ethical, religious, and legal aspects of suicide and euthanasia. I also suggest that you talk to your doctor. He or she should be informed that you don't want to be in any pain and that you wish to be given any medication that's necessary to alleviate your suffering even if this will shorten your life. If it's solely a fear of pain and suffering that is making you contemplate suicide, you should know that it isn't necessary for anyone, even the terminally ill, to be in agony.

Consult with your attorney to find out if dying by your own hand would affect your personal arrangements — your will, life insurance benefits, etc. An attorney could also draw up a medical power of attorney that would allow a friend, lover, or family member to make decisions regarding what type of medical treatment you should receive if you are incapacitated and cannot express your own wishes.

✍

Q. I seem to be experiencing emotional changes, mostly depression, for some time due to the many AIDS deaths — not only friends but gay leaders and the everyday people I read about doing positive things for gay rights. They've become gay heroes to me, and when they succumb I really feel wrung out. I've started to turn inward emotionally. I turn to the obituaries in my gay newspaper, and the shock never seems to subside.

A. Our community is experiencing the same kind of devastation that befell the survivors of the world wars. Nothing will alleviate our grief completely because this tragedy is real and inescapable. Even if someone discovered a cure for AIDS tomorrow, it wouldn't bring the loved ones we've lost back to life.

But we don't have to make the epidemic even worse by denying it and refusing to practice safer sex, fragmenting our community by blaming parts of it that we don't like for the disease, or by becoming isolated and politically passive.

Depression usually contains some repressed anger. Letting the anger out is one way to break out of paralysis and withdrawal. The first thing your anger can do is motivate you to take really good care of yourself. Preserving your own health without giving up your sexuality is heroic. This includes preserving your mental health. Stop reading those damned obituaries for a few months. Give yourself a break from the constant onslaught of loss. You have a right to control the amount of upsetting information you have to process. You also have a right to concentrate on something else for a while. Dealing with AIDS is only one part of being gay. Get involved with community work to prevent the spread of AIDS and take care of those who have the disease, but pace yourself. Don't try to do everything and don't do AIDS work to the exclusion of everything else, or you'll burn out really fast.

AIDS is not going to disappear. When we are overwhelmed with grief, we have to take time to cry. When we are overcome with rage, we have to focus our anger at the appropriate targets — the people who have the money and the power to make things better. And when we're tired, we have to rest. I hate to employ military meta-

195

phors, but this is a lifelong battle, and you just can't do that without an occasional furlough.

✍

Q. My lover and I met in 1976. We had an open relationship until July 1985. In February 1987, he suddenly became ill, and on Friday the thirteenth he was diagnosed with AIDS. He died a week later. We were having unsafe sex until the week he got sick. How is it possible that I still test HIV-negative? How is it possible that he never showed any signs until he got pneumonia?

Remind readers about wills. My lover didn't like to discuss death and never made one. I don't have to tell you how his family reacted.

A. Your story proves a point that health educators often have to make with folks who claim that they don't need to worry about having safer sex because their partner is healthy. AIDS has such a long incubation period that there's no way to tell from someone's appearance whether they are sick or not. Sometimes (as in the case of your lover) death follows rapidly after diagnosis. It's possible that your lover had other symptoms — weight loss, night sweats, a fever, a persistent cough — and never noticed them or denied their existence.

Don't assume that because you test HIV-negative it's okay to go on having unsafe sex with other men. If you were exposed to the virus while having sex with your lover, it's possible that your body hasn't had enough time to manufacture antibodies that would show up on the test. Even if you have escaped exposure to HIV, you risk being exposed each time you have unsafe sex.

Everyone should have a will and a medical power of attorney. Unless you have a complicated estate, this is a routine matter that an attorney can handle inexpensively. Dying without a will puts an unfair burden on the loved ones you leave behind. A lover usually has absolutely no legal recourse against your family. Why make your partner dependent upon their good will? No one ever prolonged their life by refusing to put their last wishes on paper. I hope everyone will take care of this urgent matter immediately.

✍

Q. My lover and I recently went to our attorney to get our wills made. She suggested that we also fill out durable powers of medical attorney. I do not want to be resuscitated if I go into a coma, nor do I want to be kept alive by artificial means. I feel very strongly about this. I assumed that my lover would be the appropriate person to hold my medical power of attorney, but he seemed reluctant to sign. Finally he told me that he thinks doctors should do everything in their power to save a human life, and he does not want to tell the hospital that they have to unplug me from life support and let me die if there is any chance at all that I might live. He could not live with the guilt for "killing me," he says. I am stunned. My attorney is urging us to complete these forms as soon as possible. What should I do?

A. Make whatever bequest for your lover that you like in your will. But do not give him your medical power of attorney. It's important that this document give decision-making powers to someone who agrees with your wishes and will express them clearly, and if need be forcefully, to your caretakers.

The course of least resistance, of course, would be to pressure your lover into giving lip service to your demands and then let him sign the papers. But this would be a big mistake. It isn't fair to ask him to go against his own principles. Don't let this disagreement cause you to postpone completing these vital documents. Have the painful conversation with him that you know is necessary, locate someone else to hold your medical power of attorney, and get it executed as quickly as possible.

✍

Q. I'm a lesbian who has been doing home care for a good friend of mine (male) who has AIDS. Recently he has lost a great deal of weight because of diarrhea, and his doctor has told him he should be getting his affairs in order. He has asked me to help him end his own life. I don't object to this from any moral standpoint, but I have many, many questions about the practical details. And I'm not sure how I will cope emotionally with my grief. Not only will I have lost a friend, but to some extent I will be responsible for that loss.

A. We'll never know how many of the people who have loved and cared for PWAs have performed this last service for them as well. I suspect that many of the gentle and peaceful deaths PWAs have enjoyed at home were a gift from their friends or lovers. Nevertheless, in every state of this country, it is illegal to assist a suicide. This includes counseling or advising someone to commit suicide, procuring the medication, or assisting them in taking it. Prosecutions under these laws are rare, but when they do take place, they are very destructive. And these laws make it difficult for people to communicate honestly about this subject or act openly to fulfill a dying person's wishes for a comfortable, quick death. This is especially ironic because suicide itself is no longer illegal in most states.

Some doctors accept the existence of self-deliverance or assisted suicide; others feel that their Hippocratic Oath makes it impossible for them to assist in a patient's death or even hear a rumor about such a practice without launching an investigation. It would be helpful if a doctor could tell you which one of your friend's pain or sleeping medications would cause him to fall asleep and expire, and what kind of overdose would produce this effect, so you can make sure he doesn't accidentally take too much. But I have no way of predicting if your friend's physician would be comfortable with having even a theoretical, abstract conversation like this with you.

You're also going to need a doctor to sign the death certificate. The death certificate is important because it gives the cause of death, and many life insurance policies will not pay up if the holder commits suicide. Policies often have a two-year rider regarding suicide, which means policyholders will not be paid if they end their own life within two years of obtaining coverage.

Your friend is dying of AIDS. If he wasn't ill, he wouldn't consider suicide. You should get a firm grip on your codependent tendencies and realize that it's AIDS that is killing him, and nothing else. It's too easy for a person who is taking care of someone who's sick to start feeling responsible for the invalid's health. This is based on a false image of your own power. You can't save him. You can love him, feed him, bathe him, make him more comfortable, listen to him, and help him plan the rest of his life, but you can't prolong it. You also are not obligated to help him to die if you are emotionally incapable of handling the consequences. But let him know your decision soon.

Check the resources for sources of information. There is no universal right answer that I can give you. But if you examine your own heart, I'm sure you will discover the right course of action for you.

✍

Q. I'm a PWA who has struggled against this disease for three long years. Recently I had a good friend ask me, in what I'm sure he thought was a very tactful manner, if I'd made preparations to commit suicide "when the time came." I told him that I intend to go on fighting until the end. If I started thinking about dying, I would sink into depression and just give up. I've had to limit my activities, but I still love life, and I can't just turn my back on it. My friend seemed to think I was being thickheaded. Now I'm wondering if everyone with a terminal illness is now expected to shoot themselves or take a fatal dose of poison!

A. This is probably the most personal decision a person can make. No one else has a right to influence your choice in this matter. There most certainly is not a consensus that the terminally ill ought to do away with themselves, just as there is no consensus that suicide or euthanasia is always wrong. You are very clear about wanting to wait until the natural moment of death comes, so that must be the right choice for you.

However, you should talk this over in more detail with your physician. He or she can tell you some of the other choices you may need to make about what type of health care you'd like to receive. Do you want to be put on a respirator? If you're in a coma, do you want them to continue to give you IV nutrition and hydration? It's best to make these decisions now and put them in written, legal form so they can guide your doctors and nurses if you're so sick that you're unable to tell them what you'd like them to do.

✍

Q. There might be others in my position. When I was 18 years old I met the most handsome man, also 18, I have ever seen. He told me that very night that he was going to marry me. Well, that is exactly what happened. We remained together for fourteen wonderful years. Many tried to part us. However, it only brought us closer together. Our sex life was great. We never went one day without making love to and with one another. There was no role-playing, we did it all sexually. He was my life and I was his.

He was killed as we entered into our fifteenth year of being married. That was four years ago. My problem is that I can't stand for anyone to even touch me sexually. I need people. I need to make passionate love again, even if it's only for one night. I'm still considered good-looking, I have plenty of money, and I own my own company. My problem is that I can't really let go of my lover. I'm not sure that I want to. Yet I know how empty and pointless my life is.

A. It can be very difficult to get over the death of a loved one. Widowed partners often find it impossible to imagine being intimate with anyone other than the spouse they have lost. Permitting oneself to enjoy sex with another seems disloyal or unfaithful to the memory of the departed loved one.

Nevertheless, you are right to feel that you need to renew the sexual part of your life. If your partner could speak to you, I'm sure he would tell you the time has come to stop expressing your sorrow at his death in this manner. He would tell you that he does not need you to allow a part of yourself to die to know you love him and remember him.

Perhaps you hold imaginary conversations with your lover, to tell him things you think he would want to know. Why not ask him if he wants you to continue to be celibate and in mourning? I would be surprised if he doesn't "tell" you to start going out again, and that it's no crime to want another man to touch you. If you had died and left him behind, isn't that what you would tell him?

Of course you will never have the same experience with another man, even if you find someone you love very much. Time has probably erased many of your memories of less-than-perfect moments you spent together. Don't expect a new friend to compete with the past. Don't look for someone who is a copy of your dead love. But do look for someone new. If your life is going to be meaningful, you need to give and receive love.

A compassionate gay therapist could probably help you complete the process of grieving for your deceased spouse. Widowhood is hard enough for straight couples whose relationships are recognized and valued by society, who have a traditional process for mourning, and whose friends help them re-enter society as a single person. Bereaved gay men and lesbians are often not even recognized as being widowed, and this makes it even more difficult to come out of isolation.

✍

Q. I am writing in regard to the man whose lover of fifteen years was killed. I wanted to pass on my thoughts since I was in this situation myself. I had a relationship with a man for eight years that sounded much like this man's relationship. It was truly beautiful — sharing, warm, learning, and loving. He was killed in a car accident by a drunk driver, and my life was destroyed.

I had so much anger, hate, and sorrow I was unable to do much of anything. Through a good psychotherapist I was able to redirect those negative feelings into positive ones and make a better life for myself. I slowly learned to open up to other men. It was hard and painful. I found myself putting my energy into my work. This made me very successful, but I was alone.

I sincerely hope that he obtains the help that is needed to piece his life back together. I'm sure he has a lot to share with another man. I know I would not have been able to do this without professional help.

A. Often gay people assume that the resources of trained professionals — lawyers, therapists, couples counselors, even medical doctors — are only available to or useful for straights. The truth is that when you are in deep trouble you will usually be able to recover much more quickly with the advice and support of an expert who knows the way out of a particular quagmire.

Unfortunately, when overwhelmed by grief or anger, it's well-nigh impossible to figure out a practical course of action. Friends can be so helpful here. There are problems that a heart-to-heart talk with a close friend can solve; but there are also times when a friend should say, "I think you need to talk to an expert." A friend who will go to the trouble of locating a qualified professional is a gem.

Even if no gay switchboard exists in your area to give you the names of gay or nonhomophobic straight professionals, it's still imperative to get counseling, medical help, or legal advice if you need it. Nonjudgmental doctors, lawyers, and therapists exist everywhere. A wise person prepares for a crisis by finding out who these people are *before* disaster strikes.

✍

Q. I am up in years (mid-70s) and have a large collection of video hard-core tapes that I still enjoy viewing. I'm planning to update my will and would like to leave my collection to some gay organization or gay person who will enjoy them after I'm gone. I would be grateful to you if you could name someone I could contact or name as the party in my will to inherit the collection.

A. Your collection may be of interest to a gay archive. Some of the biggest archives are listed in the resource guide. The *Gayellow Pages* has a more complete listing. An archive might also like to receive letters, photos, and any other material that documents your life as a gay person. History isn't just the artifacts and biographies of famous people. Gay and lesbian archives are devoted to passing on a sense of who we are to future generations of young gay men and lesbians. Too many gay seniors die and have their letters and photo albums thrown out by insensitive families. This material is precious to our community. Some archives have oral history projects, so they might want to tape an interview with you, if you'd be willing to take the time to do that. Since these repositories of gay and lesbian history hardly ever receive grants and are often cramped for space, they are always happy to receive donations or bequests to fund their vital work.

✍

Q. My family contains a plethora of elderly aunts and uncles, so the loss of a fairly close family member happens more frequently than I'd like. My problem is that although my mom, dad, brothers, sisters, and a few same-age cousins know I'm gay and are very friendly with my lover, the rest of the family and friends do not. Out of respect for my family, my lover feels it is his place to at least pay a visit to the wake and extend condolences to my family. When my great-aunt, whom I was very close to, passed away, we both attended the funeral. Although my family hasn't said anything about it, I'm wondering if maybe I'm pushing things a bit. Should my lover accompany me on these occasions?

A. If your family hasn't said anything, I don't think you should go borrowing trouble. It sounds like they are more comfortable with your lover being at these events than you are. Why?

A funeral is not like a wedding, which people attend by invitation only. It is a time of grief and mourning, and anyone who feels sincere sympathy should express it by attending. It is also appropriate for people who were not necessarily close to the dear departed, but who are close enough to the survivors to lend them valuable sympathy and emotional support, to attend. This is a comfort to those who were left behind. I give your lover a lot of credit for being willing to be at your side through times of sorrow as well as enjoying the happy, fun times with you.

✍

Q. My ex-lover, who has been one of my best friends ever since we broke up ten years ago, has recently asked me to be responsible for his memorial service. I have no idea when this is likely to be necessary since he is a fit gentleman of 65. Nevertheless, since I am in my early 50s, it seems likely I will outlive him. What is involved in planning a memorial service? I want to do the right thing, but how?

A. Talk this over with your friend. A memorial service (a gathering of friends and relatives of the departed individual held after burial or the disposition of ashes) is usually a little different than a funeral, which is held when someone's body or ashes are actually interred (put into a grave or a memorial vault, scattered, or otherwise conveyed to a final resting place). Find out which your friend prefers, and encourage him to make arrangements now with a mortuary or crematorium.

If your friend is religious, contact his pastor, priest, or rabbi, and see what assistance they can offer you and if they have a suitable space for a service. Get your friend to provide you with a list of the folks he'd like to have notified in the event of his death. Find out where he keeps his current address book so you can update this list later if you must. Ask him who he'd like to have as speakers. These should be people who know him well and will be able to help everyone who is present remember his achievements and abilities.

It's customary to play music, so find out what kind of pieces your friend would like to have played. It's thoughtful to have a guest book for people to sign, which can then be given as a keepsake to his significant other or a close family member, whichever seems most appropriate. I always appreciate it when copies of a good photograph are made available. There are always people who meant to get a picture of their friend and somehow never found the time, and this is the easiest way to make sure they have something to remember him by. Depending on where the funeral or memorial service is held, it may or may not be appropriate to offer refreshments afterward.

A memorial service is held to allow people to summon all their memories of someone they cared for and say good-bye to that person. It's also their last chance to do something thoughtful and useful for their departed friend. So you want to make the service consistent with their character. You don't want to have a religious service for an atheist or ignore religion for someone who was devout. You don't want to paint that person in a false light or run them down. There's nothing sadder than a censored funeral, where the official (i.e., heterosexual, sanitized-for-the-family) version of a gay man or lesbian's life is recited from the pulpit while their grieving gay friends and lovers (if any are even present) sit still and are silent. So don't be afraid to give this service any personal touches that are true to the gay way your friend lived his life.

Solidarity

Q. I would like to know why lesbians act like and look like men when supposedly what they want is another lady. I mean, if you want to be with another girl, then you are rejecting men, so why are so many of my lesbian friends so butch? Some of them would be really nice-looking girls if they would fix themselves up, but when I suggest this they just laugh at me.

A. Usually a butch lesbian doesn't have much choice about how other people perceive her. When I came out, the only person who was surprised was me. My family and practically everybody who knew me had been assuming I was a dyke long before I knew it.

From time to time, I pour myself into a black dress, and after years of practice I can pull it off. I enjoy playing with a feminine image from time to time, but it's an act. I feel like I'm in drag.

When I wear my leather jacket, a t-shirt, jeans, and boots, I feel sexy and at ease because my personal appearance is consistent with how I feel about myself. The women I find attractive think I *am* a "really nice-looking girl" when I'm dressed this way, so hey, who am I to argue or complain? The only people who've ever told me I look like a man are men. I guess competition makes them bitchy. Other women know exactly who I am and what I can do for them. This erotic language doesn't make any sense to you because you're not the intended audience.

Your butch friends know what will get them some pussy. Better give up on arguing them out of that! By having short hair and wearing "masculine" clothes, a butch is not saying, "I am a man," she is saying, "I know you itch, and I know how to scratch it. Come here, little honey, I can turn you inside out quicker, deeper, harder, and longer than any silly old straight boy."

✍

Q. I have a lesbian roommate. We went to the same college, and I'm really glad to have somebody I know in the big city. We don't see each other real often — we both have lovers — but we try to get together for dinner once a week or so. Every now and then she cancels everything and has "cramps." I have always politely said "okay" and made other plans. Please don't laugh at me. If I had had sisters when I was growing up, maybe I would know what she was talking about, but I don't. I can't ask her, it's too personal!

A. About once every twenty-eight days, if a woman has not conceived (gotten pregnant), the lining of the uterus sloughs off and is shed, along with the unfertilized egg, in the form of menstrual blood. This lining is perpetually going through a cycle of growth, expulsion, and renewal. The presence of a fertilized egg in the uterus stops this process, and the uterine wall becomes part of a system that feeds nourishment to the fetus via the placenta and umbilical cord and filters out wastes.

Most women experience a slight degree of discomfort when they're menstruating. If your roommate feels bad enough to cancel social plans, she has dysmenorrhea or menstrual pain or cramps. This pain can be caused by several different things, and every woman who has cramps has her favorite home remedies — dolomite, raspberry leaf tea, a hot-water bottle, back rubs, masturbation, painkillers, or drugs like Motrin or Ponstel that inhibit the body's production of prostaglandins, hormone-like substances that make the uterus contract painfully.

The idea of menstruation freaks a lot of men out because the only time they bleed is when they're injured. It's not at all the same thing. Relatively little blood is shed over the three to eight days a woman has her period — only about two to four tablespoons. There's a myth that menstruating women smell bad, but normal personal hygiene is enough to make it impossible for anyone to detect the fact that a woman is having her period. Some women suffer from PMS (premenstrual syndrome), which makes them rather grumpy and moody just before the flow begins, but in my experience, women with PMS are no more irrational than a man who has just been told, "Your dick is too small" or "I'm tired of being your secretary. I want a raise and a vice presidency."

205

Next time your roommate tells you she has cramps, if you say, "Yuck, I'm sorry, can I get you anything? Want a hot bath or a back rub?" she will probably love you forever. Then the next time you run out of rubbers in the middle of a hot date, maybe you can talk her into running down to the drugstore so you don't have to put your clothes back on.

✍

Q. My best friend (a gay man) took me out to dinner last week and did something I never in a million years expected to hear from him, of all people. He propositioned me. His reason was that he feels he never really gave sex with women a fair trial and now that there's a "health crisis" it has made him rethink being exclusively gay. I was so surprised and upset it was all I could do to choke out a relatively polite rejection. I have always enjoyed his friendship because I like men, but in trying to socialize with straight men I find that sex always becomes an issue. Being a lesbian, this was extremely distasteful to me. Now I wonder if I can ever trust my so-called gay friend again.

A. Cut your friend some slack. Anxiety about AIDS has put so much stress on many gay men that they don't always think clearly about what they're doing. It's hard to respond logically to something so scary. If anything, his offer to share sex with you was probably prompted by the fact that he likes and trusts you, not by wanting to use or pressure you.

Rather than abandon a friendship that obviously means a lot to you, call him up and talk this out. Suggest that you could do him more good by listening to the impact the AIDS epidemic has had on his life than by having sex with him. You might also tell him just how strongly you are opposed to the idea of having sex with a man and ask him not to bring it up again. If he can't honor your lesbian identity, there's no basis for friendship here.

✍

Q. What is the appropriate response for a lady to make when she is walking through the town's only mixed gay bar, toward her friends, and overhears a man say loudly, "I smell fish"?

A. A lady should turn toward the source of the comment, wrinkle her nose, announce, "I smell pansies," and then continue walking toward her friends.

$Q.$ We've been trying to increase our female membership to 50 percent of total membership, but try as we might, we never seem to get there. For every woman who joins, we have two men join. I was therefore intrigued to read in a recent column of yours that there are more gay men than gay women. Perhaps this is our problem. If this is true, perhaps we need to set a more reasonable goal for percentage of female membership. I would be interested in knowing what the ratio of gay men and women are compared to the population. We keep hearing 10 percent for both sexes.

$A.$ I don't know where that 10 percent figure comes from. I keep hearing Kinsey quoted as a source, but Kinsey didn't exactly say that. What he did was challenge the notion that there was a tiny minority of strange perverts who had sex only with members of their own gender. In their 1948 *Sexual Behavior in the Human Male*, Alfred C. Kinsey and his associates stated:

> Since only 50 percent of the male population is exclusively hetero-sexual throughout its adult life, and since only 4 percent of the population is exclusively homosexual throughout its life, it appears that nearly half (46 percent) engage in both heterosexual and homo-sexual activities, or reacts to persons of both sexes, in the course of their adult lives.

In the 1953 follow-up volume, *Sexual Behavior in the Human Female*, the Kinsey group reported that the incidence of homo-sexuality among women was one-third to one-half less than that among men. Of course, these figures may have changed in the half-century that's elapsed since these data were gathered.

Part of the problem is that Kinsey was studying sexual behavior, not sexual identity. As we all know, there are plenty of people who identify as heterosexual who have gay sex, and even some folks who self-identify as gay, but are actually celibate or have opposite-sex partners. Another problem is that since these studies, which were conducted in the forties and fifties, sexual behavior has probably changed significantly, but nobody has undertaken the kind of broad, systematic study that Kinsey and his associates performed.

There are sociological techniques that might be useful for estimating gay population based on attendance at gay male and lesbian bars, but to my knowledge, nobody has ever tried to do this.

So nobody knows exactly how many gay men or lesbians there are. It's only an opinion, but if your organization is attracting half as many women as men, I think you're doing well.

That doesn't mean you can stop trying to do better, though. A successful coalition is based on mutual understanding and working toward shared goals. More lesbians will be encouraged to join your group if women are visible in leadership positions and your activities or goals clearly reflect lesbian as well as gay male needs.

✍

Q. My sister is also gay. I just found this out recently. She came out to me before visiting me and my lover. Naturally, we were all excited and wanted to go bar-hopping together. We had a good time at the largest place in town, which is mixed, although a lot more men go than women. But I also wanted to go to one of her places, so I had asked a lesbian friend of mine for a list of lesbian bars. Would you believe we were asked to leave? My sister was embarrassed and I was so angry, I'm afraid I said a few things I shouldn't have (sexist). When I told my lesbian friend about this, she said I should have expected it. I wish she had given me some warning, and I still don't think this was right.

A. I don't either. It's sex discrimination to keep men out of a lesbian bar or women out of a gay men's bar. A court case about this got the Duchess closed in New York. Of course, there is a problem with straight men harassing lesbians or with obnoxious straight people crashing gay bars and destroying the ambience. But they should be removed because they're rowdy, not because of their gender. The bar you visited should be more careful. This could get them into considerable legal trouble.

However, given that this is the way the real world operates, I suggest you do things a little differently the next time you want to visit a lesbian bar with your sister or a woman friend. Call all of the bars up. Explain your situation. Ask if you are welcome. If a town is large enough to have more than one lesbian bar, there will usually be at least one place that welcomes gay men (or even straight men, if they behave).

Mixed groups that want to attend gay male spaces that are usually sex-segregated (the trendiest disco, a leather bar) should do the same thing. Until you try to get your sister and her lover into one of *your* bars, you may not realize how prevalent separatism is in the gay male community. The idea of women wanting women-only social space is much more controversial than men-only institutions, but in fact there are a lot of gay men who have little or nothing to do with women or are up-front misogynists.

While I recognize that lesbians and gay men have many political issues in common and share much of our culture, we also need our own social institutions and activist organizations. It's important to recognize the areas where we do have different needs if we're going to build any kind of stable partnership with one another. It's every bit as legitimate for lesbians to want women-only space to cruise, flirt, dance, and hang out in as it is for gay men to have men-only J/O clubs or baths, bike clubs, and bars.

✍

Q. During my twenties, I was exclusively lesbian. Now I've started to experiment with straight sex. I don't know if this makes me a bisexual or what, and probably won't know until I've had some more experience. But there may not be any more experience because I've been very disappointed with my male partners. They aren't unappealing, but they're *fast*. By the time I'm warmed up, they think it's all over. Is there any way to prolong the lovemaking?

A. My subjective experience is that men and women pace sex very differently. Because women can have multiple orgasms, lesbian sex is usually structured to give both partners as many orgasms as possible. Men usually come more quickly than women, and then they have to wait a while before they can get it up again. Most of them just fall asleep rather than engage in foreplay or amusing conversation. When gay men want to make sex last, they tend to try to delay their orgasms as long as possible. Very few straight men have ever thought of such an outrageous thing. If you want a good male lover, you'll have to seduce a gay man or take a straight boy under your wing and tutor him. He may be somewhat startled to find himself doing Cunnilingus 101, a seminar on female masturbation, and the dildo-and-vibrators workshop, but all of the other women in his life will bless your name forever. Incidentally, you *do* know enough to use condoms when you sleep with penis-people, don't you?

✍

Q. Is it possible for a gay man to become a lesbian? Ever since I came out I've been looking for one man I can settle down with and grow old together. That's all I want. But it seems to me that all the long-term lovers I know are women. Men are obsessed with sex and are always swapping partners. My lesbian friends don't seem to be having a lot of sex, but I would gladly trade that for some stability.

A. There are so many stereotypes in your letter that it's making me dizzy. There's a grain of truth in the widely accepted idea that gay men are more promiscuous than lesbians, but there are a lot of people who don't fit these neat little categories. I've known a lot of trashy dykes, and I've known a lot of very married gay men. Couples sometimes tend to withdraw from the bar scene and live more privately. Maybe that's why most of the men you know are bachelors.

Many, many couples find that they have sex less frequently the longer they stay together. This is why many, many couples break up. So I wouldn't recommend de-emphasizing sex as a way to have a long-term relationship. It's never a good idea to let your sweetheart start thinking of bed as a place to do nothing but sleep.

I have no idea why you're doing so poorly in the gay male marriage sweepstakes, but I think your chances would be even worse in the lesbian lottery. Have you considered cruising older men, men who aren't the hottest thing in the bar, men who are quiet, men who seem lonely, or men who are looking for friends instead of bagging the limit on their License to Cruise?

☞

Q. Why are gay men obsessed with the size of their partner's penis? It seems like every time one of my friends falls in love, he has to brag about how well hung his new stud is. I can't imagine telling everybody that the new woman in my life has a humongous clit. I don't cruise women for their crotches.

A. The size of your partner's clitoris probably has relatively little to do with how it feels to have sex with her. But there's a big difference between trying to swallow five inches and eight or take a dick that's four inches around versus six inches around up the ass. Besides, in our society, men with big cocks are assumed to be virile. When you're bragging about your new sweetie, you want to talk him or her up. Although there are some gay men who prefer small penises, the boastful phrase, "My new lover has an adorable cock like a tiny, pink shrimp" isn't usually going to make the competition jealous.

I absolutely refuse to subscribe to that broad and sweeping theory that gay men are genitally oriented and lesbians care more about the Whole Person. It may take a lot of work to get a dyke to be candid with you, but most of us have preferences about tit size, get turned on to the size and shape of somebody's ass, etc. As for cruising crotches — have you ever been at the gym and had a girl with muscular thighs in a pair of Spandex shorts spot you while you were on your back doing flat flyes? No? Well, you go do that, then we'll talk.

So much that's derogatory and disgusting has been written about women's genitals that I think lesbians are naturally reluctant to say or even think anything that isn't cunt-positive. So I certainly can't say that there is such a thing as an ugly cunt, but there are some that I like putting my face in a lot more than others. I have certain preferences about internal capacity as well.

✍

Q. I live in a collective household of three gay men and one lesbian. I wanted to do something nice for our lesbian roommate for Christmas, so I bought her a vibrator. Well, when it came time to sit by the tree and unwrap our presents, she was *not* pleased! She threw the poor little thing across the room like an Apollo rocket. The bottom came off, and I had to duck to avoid being brained by the batteries. I don't get it. I got the idea from her in the first place! (I overheard her telling her lover over the phone that she wanted one.) Now she hardly speaks to me unless it's to call me a "sexist," and I don't even dare ask her to do her share of the dishes. Please save my household from further acrimony and misunderstanding!

A. Cheer up, honey. You did not do a Bad Thing. But hell hath no fury like a woman given the *wrong* kind of vibrator. This matter is a mystery to men. When I worked at Good Vibrations, San Francisco's feminist vibrator store, nice guys would often wander in, eager to buy their lady friends a "buzzer." Inevitably, no matter what I said, they would head for the phallic or wand-shaped, battery-operated vibrators, certain that this would do the trick. A week later, they would be back, firmly in tow of their girlfriend or wife, who wanted to exchange the battery-operated vibrator for one that plugged in, wasn't phallic-shaped, and gave much stronger vibes.

Of course, there's really no such thing as the "wrong" kind of vibrator. Some women (and men too) prefer the battery-operated kind. They're more portable, don't vibrate as strongly, are easier to use for insertion, and cost much less.

Some lesbians (not all, but some) have ambivalent or negative feelings about phallic objects. Your roommate is probably calling you "sexist" because you assumed such an object would be erotically pleasing to her. This doesn't mean you are sexist. When we're trying to turn someone else on, most of us do for or to them what we most like ourselves. This gives the other person a chance to react and reveal what they really do like, and then some learning and negotiation can take place.

This communication process becomes hurtful only if one partner refuses to pay attention to the other partner's response. ("You don't really want me to do this with my fingers instead of my tongue. I like it this way, so this is the best way, and if I just keep doing it long enough, you'll like it too.") And there's going to be a fight if one partner blames the other for not anticipating their desires. ("If you weren't such a sexist pig, you would read my mind and see that I want a Panabrator with a rabbit-fur cozy!")

You meant well, and I do think your roommate owes you an apology. She should dry her eyes, glue the little rocket ship back together, and give it to you or save it in her erotic hope chest for the day when she meets a woman who will like it. Then you should both go through the resource list for more information about sex toys and places to order them through the mail.

✍

Q. Is there something about male sexuality — perhaps the structure of the XY chromosome — that makes them more susceptible to sexual deviation? It seems to me that most "perverted" sexual acts are carried out by men. Men are the child molesters, drag queens, sadomasochists, transsexuals, etc. Women seem to be more stable and less prone to having a disturbed gender identity or being sidetracked by a fetish.

A. You're confusing the behavior of the majority with normalcy and conflating both of those concepts with sexual health. I'm not even sure we know what the majority of people really do. Any study of sexual behavior that I've ever read indicates that there are a lot more men and women having gay sex, indulging their fetishes, and having kinky fantasies than you'd think if you walked down the street and saw everybody in their best got-to-go-to-work-at-the-office clothes. I suspect that this is one reason why homosexuals and other sexual minorities are so persecuted. The majority doesn't want its dirty laundry being aired in public. It wants a bunch of private playgrounds where the ostensibly normal can have their libidinous cake and eat it too. When you consider how few married women are orgasmic, how many marriages are marred by domestic violence or incest, and how many married men are having furtive, anonymous gay sex, how can you equate heterosexuality with sexual health?

We live in a patriarchal culture. Men receive a disproportionate amount of attention. What men think, want, buy, pay for, prefer, do, and need is always given priority. There are women who are pedophiles, transsexuals, transvestites, sadomasochists, fetishists, etc. But the repression of female sexuality, economic inequality, and the threat of violence make it much more difficult for a woman to discover the nature of her own desire, especially if it is "deviant," and then act upon it. It still isn't really "normal" for women in this culture to have an independent sexuality at all. We're supposed to get pleasure out of pleasing others. *That's* sick.

As a radical pervert, I have my own bias in these matters. But I'm simply unable to agree with your judgmental dismissal of anyone who's "being sidetracked by a fetish." What you do to get off (or want to do but don't dare) has absolutely nothing to do with whether or not you are a good person. Where your sexual preferences come from — their genetic, physiological, social, or psychological origins — also has nothing to do with whether or not you're a decent human being. What matters is what you do with your desire.

Do you love yourself? Do you treat your partners well? Are you as honest with others as you can be without threatening your own survival? Do you strive to educate others and make their lives easier? Do you defend yourself and other members of your community against violence or prejudice? Do you live without exploiting or oppressing others? Are you kind, tolerant, ethical, and forgiving?

These are the questions that matter, not "Do you put on lipstick and then jack off to visions of plump calves in black silk stockings with seams?" or "Are you unable to get off with anybody over the legal age of consent in Great Britain?" or "Do you fall in love only with people who will give you a spanking?"

Resources

How to use this list

All information was current as we went to press. However, change is inevitable. Many of these groups exist on volunteer energy and small budgets. So please enclose a stamped, self-addressed envelope (SASE) when you write for information. When appropriate, include an "over-21" statement. Sometimes a publication or organization does *not* want its full title on correspondence. When this is true, I have given the acronym first and spelled the full title out after the mailing address. Listings are alphabetical by topic. This creates some interesting juxtapositions which I hope will not offend anyone. Furthermore, I hope no one will be mean-spirited enough to begrudge the fact that listings for topics that it's difficult to find information about are sometimes longer than more mainstream interests.

✍

Addiction and compulsive behavior

It's easy to find local chapters of Alcoholics Anonymous, Al-Anon, Narcotics Anonymous, Overeaters Anonymous, and many other self-help, twelve-step groups just by looking in your telephone book. Once you call the local contact number, you can usually obtain a list of meetings in your area which indicates groups with a gay or lesbian focus. Twelve-step groups traditionally do not charge any dues or membership fees, and they are anonymous and confidential.

• Alcoholic Anonymous, P.O. Box 459, Grand Central Station, New York, NY 10163. *Alcoholics Anonymous* (now in its third edition; affectionately known as the "Big Book") looks intimidating, but I enjoyed it. The personal accounts are honest, and it has a humble tone that is lacking in some of the New Age works about addiction. There's a whole industry of self-improvement books that use bastardized forms of AA's twelve-step program in attempts to cure just about everything. Some of these books are so vague they sound like horoscopes. Anybody could fit into their parameters of the new kind of addiction the author purports to have discovered. By contrast, AA stays focused on alcoholics helping other alcoholics to stay sober, without preaching or false promises, just for today. And they've helped millions of people.

• Al-Anon Family Group Headquarters, P.O. Box 862, Midtown Station, New York, NY 10018-0862.

• Narcotics Anonymous, World Service Office, Inc., P.O. Box 9999 Van Nuys, CA 91409.

• Overeaters Anonymous. Organized much like Alcoholics Anonymous for people with eating disorders. Call (213) 542-8363 for the local chapter nearest you. You can also obtain general information about OA by sending a long, self-addressed, stamped envelope to them at 4025 Spencer St., Suite 203, Torrance, CA 90503.

• Sexual Compulsives Anonymous. In Los Angeles/Orange County, call (213) 859-5585. In New York, call (212) 439-1123. Other local chapters exist. Check your phone book or write to: SCA Southern California, 4470-107 Sunset Blvd., No. 520, Los Angeles, CA 90027, or SCA New York, P.O. Box 1585, Old Chelsea Station, New York, NY 10013-0935. Enclose SASE.

• *SCA: A Program of Recovery*, $5.25 to SCA/ISO Literature, P.O. Box 931181, Hollywood, CA 90093.

• Pride Institute, 1-800-54-PRIDE. Residential treatment program for alcohol or other chemical dependencies. For lesbians and gay men. Also provides local referrals.

AIDS: *General information*

• *Newsline*, PWA Coalition, 31 W. 26th St., New York, NY 10010, (212) 532-0568. Free to PWAs, $35 a year to everyone else. Great 'zine. Also lists services for women.

• *Bulletin of Experimental Treatments for AIDS*, P.O. Box 2189, Berkeley, CA 94702-0189. A quarterly publication of the San Francisco AIDS Foundation. Call (415) 863-AIDS in San Francisco or 1-800-327-9893 elsewhere for subscription information.

• Drug Information and Clinical Trial Hotline, 1-800-874-2572. English and Spanish. Monday–Friday, 9 a.m.–7 p.m., Eastern Standard Time.

• *Condom Sense*, The Condom Resource Center, P.O. Box 30564, Oakland, CA 94604, (415) 891-0455. Newspaper format publication filled with wit and wisdom. Includes table of condom sizes. $2 for single copy. Lots of other educational material available.

AIDS: Information for men

• PIA, P.O. Box 1501, Pomona, CA 91769. *Positive Image* is a monthly newsletter for HIV-positive men. Personal ads. Send SASE for more information.

• PF, P.O. Box 4262, Boulder, CO 80306-4262. *Positive Friends* is a contact and information club for HIV-positive men. Free information with SASE.

• *Living With AIDS: A Guide to the Legal Problems of People with AIDS*, Lambda Legal Defense and Education Fund, 666 Broadway, New York, NY 10012. $3.95. Mostly helpful for gay male residents of New York City. Does not include issues pertinent to female PWAs like reproductive rights and access to experimental treatments. Does not address IV drug users' concerns — for example, the widespread discrimination against HIV-positive people who want to get into drug treatment programs.

• *How to Have a JO Party in Your Own Home*, Buzz Bense, 894 Folsom St., San Francisco, CA 94107. $3 plus over-21 statement. This is a practical guide that will get your party off to a great start. Let's take safer sex into our own hands!

AIDS: Information for women

• *Making It: A Woman's Guide to Sex in the Age of AIDS*, Cindy Patton and Janis Kelly (Firebrand Books, 1987). $3.95 plus $1.50 postage and handling from Firebrand Books, 141 The Commons, Ithaca, NY 14850. Free to institutionalized women. English and Spanish text (translated into Spanish by Papusa Molina). Illustrations by Alison Bechdel. Clear information for heterosexual, bisexual, and lesbian women. Includes good advice for IV drug users and sex workers and a resource list.

• *AIDS: The Women*, ed. Ines Rieder and Patricia Ruppelt (Cleis, 1988). A moving anthology, the only work of its kind.

• *Women, AIDS, and Activism*, the ACT UP/New York Women and AIDS Book Group (South End Press, 1990).

• *Current Flow*, a short lesbian safer-sex video, Gay Men's Health Crisis, Shorts, 129 W. 20th St., New York, NY 10011, $5 plus $2 postage. State that you are over 18. They also have two pamphlets, "Women Need to Know About AIDS" (English and Spanish), heterosexually oriented, and the best safe-sex pamphlet for lesbians, "Women Loving Women," English only, lesbian-oriented. They're 35 cents apiece from Myrtle Graham, (212) 337-3697, or write GMHC at the above address to the attention of publications orders.

• *Women and AIDS: A Survival Kit,* University of California, Extension Media Center, 2176 Shattuck Ave., Berkeley, CA 94704. Heterosexually oriented, multicultural video. Good information presented in a format that will help women talk about safe sex with their male partners. To rent, call (415) 642-0460, $35. To buy, call (415) 642-5578, $195.

• "Lesbians and AIDS: What's the Connection?" (English only) and "Women and AIDS" (English and Spanish, heterosexually oriented), pamphlets available for 10 cents apiece from Impact AIDS, Inc., 3692 18th St., San Francisco, CA 94110, (415) 861-3397. They have a wide range of educational materials about AIDS.

• Association for Women's AIDS Research and Education (AWARE), San Francisco General Hospital, 995 Potrero, Building 90, Ward 95, San Francisco, CA 94110, (415) 476-4091. Clinical study of HIV-positive women, women in the sex industry, and women at risk for HIV infection because of multiple partners or high-risk partners. Testing, counseling, and referrals for study participants. All services free and anonymous.

• Women's AIDS Network, c/o San Francisco AIDS Foundation, P.O. Box 6182, San Francisco, CA 94101-6182, (415) 864-4376, extension 2007. Monthly meetings for women involved in providing AIDS services. A packet of articles about AIDS, women, and children available for $12.

• Women in Crisis, Inc., 133 W. 21st St., 11th Floor, New York, NY 10011, (212) 242-4880. AIDS education primarily for black and Hispanic women in East Harlem and the southwest Bronx.

• Women and AIDS Resource Network, P.O. Box 020525, Brooklyn, NY 11202, (718) 596-6007. Resources for women and children affected by HIV disease. Counseling, referrals, and education.

Anti-violence resources

• *Victims No Longer: Men Recovering from Incest and Other Sexual Child Abuse,* Mike Lew (Perennial/Harper & Row, 1990). Includes a resource list. This book is mentioned here because so far it is the only text to address this issue. I have several problems with it, however. One is that Lew extends the definition of incest to include any sex between a young person and an authority figure. He also believes that any sex between an adult and a younger person is abusive and nonconsensual. The resource list at the end is a good idea, but by including groups that offer "support" for victims of "ritual abuse," Lew lends credence to long-discredited media scare campaigns about Satanic cults that are supposedly kidnapping, torturing, and raping children. However, don't think this means *Victims No Longer* isn't worth reading. The survivors'

217

accounts are moving, and I was amazed by their strength and honesty. The message of the book — that survivors can heal themselves and have happy lives — will give badly needed hope to anyone who is trying to recover from the trauma of a violent childhood.

• *Naming the Violence: Speaking Out about Lesbian Battering,* ed. Kerry Lobel (Seal Press, 1986). A compassionate and helpful book.

• New York City Gay and Lesbian Anti-Violence Project, 208 W. 13th St., 3rd Floor, West Wing, New York, NY 10011, (212) 807-0197. Publishes *Newsline.*

• Lambda Project Oasis, a program for lesbians and gay men who are victims of domestic violence, sponsored by Victim Services Anonymous, (718) 447-5454. Monday–Friday, 9–5 p.m. VSA Hotline for other times, (212) 577-7777.

• Men Overcoming Violence, 54 Mint St., Suite 300, San Francisco, CA 94103, (415) 626-MOVE. Peer counseling and support group for men who batter. Can make referrals.

• World Services Office, Incest Survivors Anonymous, P.O. Box 5613, Long Beach, CA 90805-0613. Send #10 SASE for information. State in a letter that you are an incest survivor and a nonperpetrator. Perpetrators, researchers, and journalists are not allowed at their meetings. $15 check for literature.

• National Coalition against Domestic Violence, 1012 14th St. N.W., Suite 807, Washington, DC 20005, (202) 638-6388. No direct services (i.e., no counseling or shelter). They are a national clearinghouse of information, provide referrals, and work to establish public policy.

• *Voices of Battered Lesbians,* a half-hour audiocassette created by survivors. For more information, contact the Lesbian Caucus of the Massachusetts Coalition of Battered Women Service Groups, 107 South St., 5th Floor, Boston, MA 02111, (617) 426-8492.

Archives

For a more complete list of gay or lesbian archives, see *The Gayellow Pages,* listed under "Gay Guides," below.

• International Gay and Lesbian Archives, P.O. Box 38100, Los Angeles, CA 90038-0100, (213) 854-0271 or 662-9444.

• International Gay History Archive, Village Station, P.O. Box 2, New York, NY 10014, (212) 625-6463.

• June L. Mazer Lesbian Collection, 626 N. Robertson Blvd., West Hollywood, CA 90069, (213) 659-2478. An archive devoted to lesbian herstory and culture.

• Lesbian Herstory Archives, P.O. Box 1258, New York, NY 10016, (212) 874-7232. Call Wednesday and Thursday nights. Visits by appointment only. Founded in 1974.

Bisexual support

• *Bisexuality: A Reader and Sourcebook,* ed. Thomas Geller (Times Change Press, 1990). A thought-provoking anthology that includes an international resource list.

• *Bi Any Other Name: Bisexual People Speak Out,* ed. Loraine Hutchins and Lani Kaahumanu (Alyson Publications, 1991).

• *Eidos,* P.O. Box 96, Boston, MA 02137-0096, (617) 262-0096. Quarterly tabloid advocating sexual freedom for women, men, and couples of all sexual orientations. $30 for four issues.

• Bi-POL, 584 Castro St., Box 422, San Francisco, CA 94114, (415) 775-1990. Recently sponsored a national conference.

• Bisexual/Gay Information and Counseling Service, 599 West End Ave., Suite 1A, New York, NY 10024, (212) 496-9500, 9 a.m.– 9 p.m. EST, Monday–Friday. Nonprofit agency that provides information and counseling.

Books

If there's no local gay, lesbian, or feminist bookstore in your area, you can call 1-800-343-4002 to get a twenty-page, illustrated catalog of books from A Different Light. They carry many of the books mentioned here or will special order them for you.

Coming out: General

• *Coming Out to Your Parents,* Parents of Gays, Box 15711, Philadelphia, PA 19103. SASE gets you a single free copy. Additional copies are 25 cents.

• *One Teenager in Ten: Writings by Gay and Lesbian Youth,* ed. Ann Heron (Alyson Publications, 1982).

• *Young, Gay and Proud,* ed. Sasha Alyson (Alyson Publications, 1980). A resource guide for gay and lesbian youth. High school reading level.

• *Gay American History: Lesbians and Gay Men in the USA,* Jonathan Katz (Thomas Y. Crowell, 1976). The fact that this history is drawn from original documents makes it even more powerful. Items pertaining to lesbians are marked with a woman's symbol.

• Federation of Parents FLAG, Administration and Program Office, P.O. Box 27605, Washington, DC 20038, (202) 638-4200. Many local chapters. Organization for parents and friends of lesbians and gays. Write with SASE for local referral.

• National Gay Alliance for Young Adults, P.O. Box 190426, Dallas, TX 75219-0426, (214) 701-3455. Newsletter.

Coming out: Information for men
• *Are You Still My Mother?*, Gloria Gussback (Warner, 1985).
• *Coming Along Fine*, Wes Muchmore and William Hanson (Alyson Publications, 1986).
• *Revelations*, ed. Wayne Curtis (Alyson Publications, 1988). A collection of gay male coming-out stories.
• *Reflections of a Rock Lobster*, Aaron Fricke (Alyson Publications, 1981). An autobiography of a gay teen.
• *What Teenagers Should Know about Homosexuality and the AIDS Crisis*, Morton Hunt (Farrar, Straus & Giroux, 1987).

Coming out: Information for women
• *Being Lesbian*, Lorraine Trenchard (GMP, 1989). A short, simple, yet wide-ranging guide for the young woman who is coming out.
• *Lesbian/Woman*, Del Martin and Phyllis Lyon (Bantam, 1972). This book by two of the founders of the modern lesbian feminist movement is a good way for young American lesbians to get an overview of the history of their own community since the fifties.
• *A Restricted Country*, Joan Nestle (Firebrand Books, 1987). In poetic fiction and stirring essays, Joan Nestle (a founder of New York's Lesbian Herstory Archives) talks about butch–femme relationships and lesbian bar culture in the fifties and what this history means for women today. Nestle's work is by turns erotic, tragic, and empowering.
• Ambitious Amazons, P.O. Box 811, East Lansing, MI 48826, (517) 371-5257 (call noon to midnight only). They publish *Lesbian Connection*, the oldest and largest lesbian magazine in the U.S. News, reviews, readers' letters, local "contact dykes," ads for lesbian businesses. Bimonthly. $18 (more if you can afford it, less if you can't). Checks should be made payable to Elsie Publishing Institute and sent to Ambitious Amazons. Do *not* put "Lesbian Connection" on the envelope.
• Naiad Press, P.O. Box 10543, Tallahassee, FL 32302, (904) 539-9322. Write or call for a free catalog. The oldest and biggest publisher of lesbian literature in the world.

Computer BBS
• The Backroom, America's largest gay and lesbian computer information service, active since 1984. Computer access to AIDS

220

and health news, on-line games, high-res graphics, on-line chat (24-hour phone lines), private mail, on-line travel agency, on-line bookshop, XXX stories, general interest articles, and lesbians on-line. Founder and national coordinator of GayCom (the national gay/lesbian communications network). To log on for subscription information, call (718) 849-1614 with your modem set on the following communications parameters: 8 data bits, no parity, 1 stop bit, full duplex. If you log on using the name AIDS News, you can access this information for free. Logging on using the name GLAAD Info will get you the latest media watches from that organization for free. These two free services are available from 7 a.m. to 7 p.m., Eastern Standard Time. The Backroom carries a current listing of gay and lesbian BBSs.

Contact publications for men

• BC, P.O. Box 1501, Pomona, CA 91769. *Ball Club Quarterly* "for men who have' em and men who want 'em." Lots of personal ads, fiction, drawings, and photos. A labor of love, always comes out on time. $30 for four issues (includes your ad). Back issues (for members only) are $7. State you are over 21.

• *RFD*, P.O. Box 68, Liberty, TN 37095. Country men. Stories, ads. Subscriptions $15.

• *Country Exchange*, P.O. Box 381, Sibley, LA 71073. Contact club for rural and small-town gay men.

• Ganymede Press, Box 5325, Harrisburg, PA 17110. They publish *Daddy*, $34/eight quarterly issues. Stories about hot daddies (35–65), daddy/son personals, and more. Send over-21 statement and make check out to Ganymede Press.

• *The Advocate*, P.O. Box 4371, Los Angeles, CA 90078, (213) 871-1225. Call for subscription info. National news, features, classified ads.

Contact publications for women

• *The Wishing Well*, P.O. Box 713090, Santee, CA 92072-3090. Sample $5. To answer ads, you must purchase a membership, which entitles you to four issues and your own ad. Hundreds of descriptions by women all over the country. Bimonthly. Seventeen years of helping women meet other women.

Couples

• *Partners*, P.O. Box 9685, Seattle, WA 98109, (206) 329-9140. Newsletter for gay and lesbian couples. Twelve issues, $36. Send SASE for resource list. Recently sponsored an interesting study of lesbian and gay couples.

- *Couples: A Gay and Lesbian Newsletter on Coupling*, TWT Press, P.O. Box 155, Boston, MA 02124-0002. Monthly, $27/year.
- *A Legal Guide for Lesbian and Gay Couples*, 2nd edition, Hayden Curry and Dennis Clifford, attorneys (Nolo Press). $14.95.
- *Lesbian Passion: Loving Ourselves and Each Other*, JoAnn Loulan (Spinsters Books, 1987).
- *The Lesbian Erotic Dance: Butch, Femme, Androgyny, and Other Rhythms*, JoAnn Loulan (Spinsters Books, 1990).
- *The Male Couple's Guide to Living Together*, Eric Marcus (Harper & Row, 1988).
- *The Male Couple*, David McWhirter (Prentice-Hall, 1984).

Cross-generational sex
- North American Man-Boy Love Association, P.O. Box 174, Midtown Station, New York, NY 10018, (212) 807-8578. Publishes the *NAMBLA Bulletin*.
- *The Age Taboo: Gay Male Sexuality, Power and Consent*, ed. Daniel Tsang (Alyson Publications, 1981).

Death
- The National Hemlock Society, P.O. Box 11830, Eugene, OR 97440-3900. A not-for-profit organization trying to get wider support for the right to choose to die with dignity. For a $20 ($15 seniors) membership fee, you receive the *Hemlock Quarterly*, a free copy of the Living Will and a Durable Power of Attorney for Health Care. Call (503) 342-5748 for a list of their publications. They cannot give you advice or counseling over the phone since it is illegal for them to do so. They sell a book entitled *Let Me Die Before I Wake* and reprints of their January 1988 newsletter. These publications include drug dosage tables.

Disability
- *Able-Together*, P.O. Box 931028, Los Angeles, CA 90093. Quarterly publication for disabled or nondisabled gay people who want to correspond or meet.
- *Dykes, Disabilities and Stuff*, P.O. Box 6194, Boston, MA 02114. Also a Boston support group.
- *Disability Rag*, P.O. Box 145, Louisville, KY 40201. Lesbian publication.
- *With the Power of Each Breath: A Disabled Women's Anthology*, ed. Susan E. Browne, Debra Connors, and Nanci Stern (Cleis Press, 1985). Somebody needs to put together a similar collection for disabled gay men.

• SIECUS, listed under "Raising Children," has a bibliography called "Sexuality and the Developmentally Disabled" for $2.88. They're always generating new material, so inquire about other publications they may have.

• Lavender Tapes, 1125 Veronica Springs Road, Santa Barbara, CA 93105, (805) 682-4047. Lesbian books on tape.

• EDGE, P.O. Box 305, Village Station, New York, NY 10014, (212) 246-3811, ext. 292. Education in a Disabled Gay Environment. Their support group provides local services only. Call them to discuss how you can start your own local chapter.

• Center for Independent Living, 2539 Telegraph Ave., Berkeley, CA 94704, (415) 841-4776. Services for disabled people. Can provide referrals to similar agencies in other parts of the U.S.

• Recordings for the Blind, 20 Roszel Road, Princeton, NJ 08540, (609) 452-0606. WATS line for orders, 1-800-221-4792, 8:30 a.m.–4:30 p.m. EST. After hours, you can leave a message.

• Womyn's Braille Press, Inc., P.O. Box 8475, Minneapolis, MN 55408, (612) 872-4352. Feminist literature for the blind and other print-disabled people. Over five hundred books on tape and in braille. Quarterly newsletter, $10–$50 (sliding scale). Need volunteers.

Gay guides

• *Gayellow Pages,* Renaissance House, P.O. Box 292, Village Station, New York, NY 10014. $10 for 1991 national edition. Provides an overview of the entire gay and lesbian community in the U.S. and Canada. Organizations, bars, mail-order businesses, gay businesses, and everything else are listed.

• *Places of Interest International Gay Guide* (for men and women), $12.50, Ferrari Publications, P.O. Box 37887, Phoenix, AZ 85069, (602) 863-2408. Also *Places for Men,* $11; *Places of Interest to Women,* $9; and *Inn Places,* $14.95. Ferrari's guides are intended for the traveler, so their focus is on events and places you can go to have fun, rather than organizations. Includes maps.

• *Bob Damron's Address Book,* P.O. Box 11270, San Francisco, CA 94101-7270, (415) 255-0404. $12.95 plus $4.50 postage and handling. California residents, add 7 percent sales tax. Includes information about cruisy areas (parks, beaches, rest stops, and the like).

Impotence

• Center for Male Sexual Dysfunction, Beth Israel Hospital, Manhattan, (212) 420-2000.

• Impotents Anonymous, 119 S. Ruth St., Maryville, TN 37801, (615) 983-6064. Call for information about local chapter.

• Impotence Information Center, American Medical Systems, Dept. USA, P.O. Box 9, Minneapolis, MN 55440, (800) 843-4315. They have a list of urologists specializing in impotence treatment.

• Surgitek/Medical Engineering Corp., booklet on impotence, 3037 Mt. Pleasant St., Racine, WI 53404, (800) 558-4321. They manufacture penile implants and can refer you to physicians in your area familiar with the product.

• 24-hour-a-day hotline, (312) 725-7722. Established by Sheldon Burman of the Male Sexual Dysfunction Institute in Chicago.

Infantilism

• DPF, 3020 Bridgeway, No. 164, Sausalito, CA 94965. Diaper Pail Fraternity. Personal ads, information about businesses that cater to adult babies.

• ABC Designs, P.O. Box 741, Jaffrey, NH 03452-0741, (603) 532-6237, Monday–Friday, 8:30 a.m.–4:30 p.m. EST. Clothing for the incontinent.

• Infantae Press, P.O. Box 12466, Seattle, WA 98111. They publish the *Play Pen* and other magazines of interest.

• Edley, P.O. Box 429, Sanbournville, NH 03872. Clothing for the incontinent.

• J.K. Personal Products, P.O. Box 13383, Scottsdale, AZ 85267, (602) 948-0901. A wide range of vinyl and latex panties for adults and some other waterproof, "sanitary" clothing. Reasonable prices and good service.

Legal

• Committee to Preserve our Sexual and Civil Liberties, P.O. Box 1592, San Francisco, CA 94101-1592. Originally formed to protest closure of the baths in San Francisco, their newsletter *Journal of Sexual Liberty* ($10/year) covers a wide range of sex news. Annual conference.

• *National Attorney Directory of Lesbian and Gay Rights,* Gay Legal Advocates and Defenders (GLAD), P.O. Box 218, Boston, MA 02112. (617) 426-1350. Attorneys listed are not necessarily gay. $15.

• Lambda Legal Defense and Education Fund, 666 Broadway, New York, NY 10012, (212) 995-8585. They take test cases to further the cause of lesbian and gay rights.

Married gays

• Wives of Gay Men, P.O. Box 8898, Pittsburgh, PA 94565. Support group for spouses (male or female) of gay persons.

• MGM Club, 175 Fifth Ave., Suite 2300, New York, NY 10010. Club for married gay men. Discreet and confidential. $5 for information and application.

Miscellaneous fetishes and special interests

• Hot Ash, c/o AWS, P.O. Box 20147, London Terrace Station, New York, NY 10011. Cigar-smoking studs and their smoky-eyed slaves.

• Cigar Studs, P.O. Box 712311, Los Angeles, CA 90071. "For men who turn on to men who smoke them!!!" Include SASE.

• *Rubbersheets,* 1044 23rd St., San Diego, CA 92103. Newsletter for men into rubber.

• *Jack's Number Two,* P.O. Box 542253, Houston, TX 77254-2253. Personal ads and short fiction for guys into scat. Send $10 with an over-21 statement for a sample copy.

• *Small, Etc.,* The Small Club, P.O. Box 294, Bayside, NY 11361. For gay men who are small in size or height and their fans.

• Send SASE to P.O. Box 72455, Corpus Christi, TX 78472 for information about another club for small men and their admirers.

• Second Skin Books, 521 Rue St. Philip, New Orleans, LA 70116. *Foreskin Restoration (Uncircumcision),* $14.95 plus $1.25 postage.

• BUFF, P.O. Box 1501, Metairie, LA 70004-1501. Brothers United for Future Foreskins. Publish a pamphlet about how to gradually stretch the skin left after circumcision.

• *Trust,* Alamo Square Press, P.O. Box 14543, San Francisco, CA 94114. Handballing newsletter. $15/quarterly subscription. Includes a free classified ad. Make check payable to Alamo and include a statement that you are over 21 and won't be offended by sexually explicit material.

• Palm Drive Video, P.O. Box 3653, San Francisco, CA 94110. Send SASE and a signed statement you are over 12 for a free brochure. Many offbeat subjects, redneck men, construction workers, wrestling cops. Definitely not your typical vanilla, surferboy flicks.

People of color: AIDS resources

• BWMT National Task Force on AIDS Prevention, 273 Church St., San Francisco, CA 94114, (415) 255-8378. Risk reduction, research, and evaluation of HIV/AIDS issues as they relate to gay men of color. Information and referrals to local services.

• People of Color against AIDS Network (POCAAN), 1200 S. Jackson, Suite 25, Seattle, WA 98144-2065, (206) 322-7061. Multiracial educational coalition that provides training about AIDS/ HIV infection, develops educational materials for the Latino, Black, Asian/Pacific Islander, and Native American communities, and works with existing AIDS programs on issues pertaining to people of color.

• San Francisco Black Coalition on AIDS, P.O. Box 11908, San Francisco, CA 94103, (415) 553-8197. Helpline at (415) 553-8600. Dedicated to fighting the AIDS epidemic in the African American community.

• National Native American AIDS Prevention Center, 6239 College Ave., No. 201, Oakland, CA 94618, (415) 658-2051. Nonprofit agency that provides training and technical assistance to tribes, the Indian Health Service, and public health service regarding prevention of AIDS. Information department provides educational material including videos. Nonhomophobic.

American Indian AIDS Institute, 333 Valencia St., Suite 200, San Francisco, CA 94103, (415) 626-7639.

• Minority AIDS Project, 5149 W. Jefferson Blvd., Los Angeles, CA 90016, (213) 936-4949. Anonymous testing, call (213) 737-4120 for appointment.

• African American Men's Health Project, 74 New Montgomery, No. 600, San Francisco, CA 94105, (415) 597-9137. Research and intervention project in San Francisco and the East Bay. Interested participants call. Black gay and bisexual men only, 18-39.

• GAPA Community HIV Project, 2261 Market St., No. 447, San Francisco, CA 94114. Safer-sex workshops for gay and bisexual Asian/Pacific Islander men. Michael Foo, (415) 512-3400.

• Asian AIDS Project, 300 4th St., Suite 401, San Francisco, CA 94107, (415) 227-0946. An AIDS education organization.

Also see other listings under AIDS and call your local AIDS service organizations. Many of them have task forces or support groups for racial and ethnic minorities.

People of color: General

• *AMALGAM,* P.O. Box 543, Prudential Station, Boston, MA 02199, (617) 499-9535. Quarterly subscription $12. Published by the Alliance of Massachusetts Asian Lesbians and Gay Men, a social, cultural, and political organization.

• *BLK,* P.O. Box 83912, Los Angeles, CA 90083-0912, (213) 410-0808. Monthly news magazine featuring material of interest to the black lesbian and gay community. Free in major metropolitan areas. Subscriptions $18/year, sample $2.

• *Pyramid Periodical: Journal for Gay People of Color,* P.O. Box 1111, Canal St. Station, New York, NY 10013. Quarterly magazine that includes poetry, short stories, essays, graphics, Third World gay news.

• If you're traveling in a new city and would like to find a bar or club that isn't just wall-to-wall white faces, check out *Places of Interest* (listed under "Gay Guides"). They try to indicate patrons' race/ethnicity. I have mixed feelings about this. I hope it helps people to make rewarding social/sexual connections and doesn't facilitate discrimination.

• American Indian Gays and Lesbians, P.O. Box 10229, Minneapolis, MN 55458-3229.

• Gay American Indians, P.O. Box 56474, New York, NY 10163.

• We Wah and Bar-Chee-Ampee, (212) 260-5617 or (212) 675-2848. The New York City Lesbian and Gay Native American Group.

• Asian/Pacific Lesbians and Gays, 7985 Santa Monica Blvd., No. 109-443, Los Angeles, CA 90046, (213) 664-4356.

• Asians and Friends — Chicago, P.O. Box 11313, Chicago, IL 60611, (312) 248-2444.

• Asians and Friends — New York, P.O. Box 6628, New York, NY 10163-6023, (212) 673-2596.

• *Trikone*, P.O. Box 21354, San Jose, CA 95151, (408) 270-8776. Newsletter for gay and lesbian South Asians. $10/six issues. Pen friends, news, local contacts.

• Gay African Americans of Westchester, 172 Ravine Ave., No. 30, Yonkers, NY 10701-1843, (914) 376-0727.

• Gay and Lesbian Arabic Society (GLAS), P.O. Box 4971, Washington, DC 20008. Founded in 1989 as a support network, coming-out group, and social forum. Has chapters in Los Angeles, San Francisco, Detroit, and New York. Write with SASE for contact info. Newsletter $10/year.

• Gay Asian Pacific Alliance, P.O. Box 421884, San Francisco, CA 94142.

• Black Gay and Lesbian Leadership Forum, P.O. Box 29812, Los Angeles, CA 90027 (213) 666-5495. AIDS Prevention Team conducts safe-sex workshops and trains facilitators. Sponsors social events, fundraisers, and publishes *The Black Forum.*

• National Black Gay and Lesbian Conference, 3924 W. Sunset Blvd., No. 1, Los Angeles, CA 90029, (213) 6766-5493. Facilitated by the Black Gay and Lesbian Leadership Forum.

• National Latino and Latina Lesbian and Gay Organization, P.O. Box 44483, Washington, DC 20026, (202) 544-0092. Promotes coalition, AIDS risk-reduction program for gay Latinos, Latina lesbian health project.

People of color: Men's resources
• *Other Countries*, P.O. Box 3142, Church St. Station, New York, NY 10008-3142, (212)505-0506. A black gay men's writing

organization. Workshops, journal, performances, outreach, and speaking.

• *BGM*, The Blacklight Press, P.O. Box 9391, Washington, DC 20005. Black gay men's literary magazine. $5.95 each plus $1.50 postage.

• *Quarterly Interchange*, P.O. Box 42502, San Francisco, CA 94101. Quarterly magazine. Free forty-word classified ad with $20 subscription. State that you are over 21.

• Barangay, P.O. Box 691985, West Hollywood, CA 90069, (213) 869-8033, ext. 345. Or call Ed or Jose at (818) 584-5936. Filipino gay men's support group — the name means "extended kinship group."

• National Association of Black and White Men Together, 584 Castro St., Suite 140, San Francisco, CA 94114, (415) 431-1976. Many local chapters. Write them with business-sized SASE for complete list. Newsletter and computer bulletin board (300, 1200, or 2400 baud, n, 8, 1). Also sponsors National Task Force on AIDS Prevention.

• Chulo Productions, Juan Mendez, (213) 665-0539. Social club for Latinos and their admirers.

• Committee of Black Gay Men, P.O. Box 865, Brooklyn, NY 11202.

• Gay Men of African Descent, P.O. Box 2519, New York, NY 10185-0021, (718) 802-0162 or 756-1548.

People of color: Women's resources

• *Phoenix Rising: The Asian/Pacifica Sisters Newsletter*, P.O. Box 170596, San Francisco, CA 94117. Subscriptions $10/year ($15 with membership). Make check out to Asian/Pacifica Sisters. Published by that organization, a social and support group for Asian and Pacific Islander lesbians and bisexual women in the Bay Area.

• *Shamakami*, P.O. Box 643, Cambridge, MA 02238. Subscriptions $10/year. Newsletter by and for South Asian American lesbians.

• ALN, P.O. Box 322, Rajdamnern, Bangkok 10200, Thailand. Asian Lesbian Network, international networking organization.

• *ALOEC Newsletter*, P.O. Box 850, New York, NY 10002, (212) 517-5598. Subscriptions $5/year. Published by Asian Lesbians of the East Coast, a political, social, and support network of Asian Pacific lesbians.

• *Aché: A National Journal for Black Lesbians*, P.O. Box 6071, Albany, CA 94706, (415) 824-0703. Bimonthly. $10-25/year (sliding scale).

• *Phoenix Rising,* P.O. Box 31631, Oakland, CA 94604, (415) 750-3385. Asian lesbian newsletter.

• WIM Publications, 3601 Crowell Road, Dept. 100, Turlock, CA 95380, (209) 667-0966. Woman in the Moon is a publishing company owned by a black woman, publishes material of interest to black lesbians. Catalog free with two first-class stamps.

People of size

• Affiliated Bigmen Clubs, 584 Castro, Box 139, San Francisco, CA 94114. Send SASE for the club nearest you.

• Girth and Mirth Club of New York, P.O. Box 10, Pelham, NY 10803-0010. They publish *Fat Apple Review* and help host an annual conference for big men and their admirers.

• *The Big Ad,* 44 Monterey Blvd., Box 38, San Francisco, CA 94131. Personals for the full-framed man and his admirer. $3 for the current issue.

Piercing

• Gauntlet, 8720 Santa Monica Blvd., Los Angeles, CA 90069, (213) 657-6677. Catalog $3 plus over-21 statement. Jewelry for body piercings, publications, piercings done on premises in Los Angeles and San Francisco. Can sometimes make referrals in other areas.

• Raelynn Gallina, P.O. Box 20034, Oakland, CA 94620, (415) 655-2855. Lesbian-owned business offering piercing and jewelry. Brochure $1 plus legal-sized SASE.

Pornography: General

• *An Annotated Bibliography of Quality Erotica,* David Steinberg, Red Alder Books, P.O. Box 2992, Santa Cruz, CA 95063, (408) 426-7082, $4.

• C. J. Scheiner, 275 Linden Blvd., No. 2B, Brooklyn, NY 11226, (718) 469-1089. A reliable and knowledgeable rare book dealer specializing in erotica. Annotated catalog $2.

Pornography for men

• Asian Videos Available, Seibu Productions, P.O. Box 5215, Redwood City, CA 94063. Illustrated catalog $1 and over 21 statement.

• Black Forest Productions, P.O. Box 46628, Los Angeles, CA 90050. Black men. Send SASE, over-21 statement.

• International Wavelength, 2215-R Market St., No. 829, San Francisco, CA 94114, (415) 749-1100. Brochure pack $5 and over-21 statement. Erotic U.S.- and foreign-produced videos, magazines, and photo sets featuring Asian and Latin men.

• True Blue Productions, 70A Greenwich Ave., New York, NY 10011. Brochure $2 and over-21 statement. Videos featuring Asian men.

• *First Hand*, P.O. Box 1314, Dept. V, Teaneck, NJ 07666. Sample $3. Monthly sex magazine for gay men.

• *In Touch for Men*, 7216 Varna Ave., North Hollywood, CA 91605. $35/twelve issues. Nude male photos, fiction, other departments.

• *Advocate MEN, Male Pictorial,* and *Fresh MEN*, Liberation Publications, P.O. Box 4371, Los Angeles, CA 90078, (213) 871-1225. Write for subscription info. Magazines that feature nude men, erotic gay male fiction.

• Colt Studio, P.O. Box 1608, Studio City, CA 91614. Send over-21 statement, $7 for introductory folio.

Pornography for women

• *On Our Backs*, 526 Castro St., San Francisco, CA 94114, (415) 861-4723. Bimonthly "entertainment for the adventurous lesbian." $28/year in U.S. Personal ads. X-rated lesbian videos. Worth buying for the ads alone, which give you a fairly complete picture of what's available for lusty dykes.

• *Bad Attitude*, P.O. Box 110, Cambridge, MA 02139. Lesbian fiction, poetry, and nonfiction about sexuality and sexual politics.

• Tiger Rose Distributing, P.O. Box 609, Cotati, CA 94931. Erotic videos by and for lesbians.

Prisoners

• Dignity Prison Ministry, Attention: Eric Anderson, Coordinator, 1500 Massachusetts Ave. N.W., Suite 11, Washington, DC 20005, (202) 861-0017. Finds pen pals for gay and lesbian prisoners. Huge backlog of mail. They try to respond with a month, but it can take up to a year to get a pen pal. If you are not incarcerated and want to help, please write!

• Prisoner Project, *Gay Community News*, 62 Berkeley St., Boston, MA 02116, (617) 426-4469. Mike Riegele, coordinator. Free pen-pal ads and copies of *GCN*. Information on services available to prisoners, used books, information packets on AIDS, TV/TS issues, how to get in and out of protective custody, exercises, gay liberation. Donations needed!

• ACLU National Prison Project, 1875 Connecticut Ave. N.W., Suite 410, Washington, DC 20009, (202) 234-4830. Class-action suits over prison conditions and related issues in federal and state institutions. Information and referrals. Journal and other publications, including a handbook of prisoners' rights and AIDS information for prisoners and administrators.

• *NOMMO,* 112C Kerckhoff Hall, 308 Westwood Plaza, Los Angeles, CA 90024. News magazine published by Africans in America. Subscriptions $16 (general), $10 (prisoners). Free if you can't afford it, but they do need donations.

• *Resist Newsletter,* 1 Summer St., Somerville, MA 02143, (617) 623-5110. Free to prisoners, $7.50/year to individuals who are not incarcerated, $15/year to libraries. Donations requested. Lists other publications and prisoners' rights groups.

• Ex-Con's Support Group for Gay and Bi Men, P.O. Box 421331, San Francisco, CA 94142, or call Steve Fryer, (415) 252-0802. BBS in planning stages.

Also see Renaissance, listed under "Transsexuals and Transvestites."

Raising children

• *Daddy's Roommate,* Michael Willhoite (Alyson Publications, 1990). A hardbound, 32-page, full-color picture book for young children.

• *Heather Has Two Mommies,* Lesléa Newman, black-and-white illustrations by Diana Souza (Alyson Publications, 1989).

• *A Kid's First Book about Sex* and *The Playbook for Kids about Sex,* both by Joani Blank and illustrated by Marcia Quackenbush (Down There Press/Yes Press). This press also offers *The Sexuality Library, Jr.: A Mail Order Catalog of Sex Books for Kids, Teens and Parents,* free with SASE, 1210 Valencia St., San Francisco, CA 94110, (415) 550-7399. Includes Spanish texts.

• *Changing Bodies, Changing Lives,* Ruth Bell (Random House, 1987).

• *Boys and Sex* or *Girls and Sex,* revised editions, Wardell B. Pomeroy, Ph.D. (Dell, 1981). Useful books for parents to read before they embark upon educating their children about human sexuality.

• Sex Information and Education Council of the U.S. (SIECUS), 130 W. 42nd St., Suite 2500, New York, NY 10036, (212) 819-9770. They have a publication called *Current Books on Sexuality* that has some good listings for children, preteens, and teens, $2.88. A complete set of all twelve of their bibliographies is $17.25.

• Lesbian Mothers Resource Network, P.O. Box 21567, Seattle, WA 98111, (206) 325-2643. Emotional support, information, and attorney referrals for lesbians regarding custody cases, adoption, and donor insemination.

• *The New Our Bodies Ourselves,* the Boston Women's Health Collective (Simon & Schuster, 1984). This comprehensive guide to women's health unfortunately has no male equivalent. Good sections on donor insemination and trying to determine the sex of one's unborn child.

Religious organizations

N.B.: There are so many of these organizations, I can't include them all here. For a more complete list, see *The Gayellow Pages*, listed under "Gay Guides," above, or *The Alyson Almanac* (Alyson Publications, 1989).

• Affirmation, P.O. Box 46022, Los Angeles, CA 90046, (213) 255-7251. National office of this organization for lesbian and gay Mormons. Write or call for information about local chapters.

• American Baptists Concerned, 870 Erie St., Oakland, CA 94610-2268, (415) 465-8652.

• Dignity, 1500 Massachusetts Ave. N.W., No. 11, Washington, DC 20005, (202) 861-0017. Gay and lesbian Catholics.

• Integrity, Inc., P.O. Box 19561, Washington, DC 20036-0561, (718) 720-3054. Contact this national office for local chapters of the lesbian and gay ministry of the Episcopal church.

• National Gay Pentecostal Alliance, P.O. Box 1391, Schenectady, NY 12301-1391, (518) 372-6001.

• Universal Fellowship of Metropolitan Community Churches, 5300 Santa Monica Blvd., No. 304, Los Angeles, CA 90029, (213) 464-5100. Send SASE for the MCC church nearest you. They also sell books relevant to gay Christians.

• World Congress of Gay and Lesbian Jewish Organizations, P.O. Box 18961, Washington, DC 20036.

Seniors

• SAGE, 208 W. 13th St., New York, NY 10011, (212) 741-2247. Senior Action in a Gay Environment (SAGE), a multiservice agency for lesbian and gay seniors.

• *Chiron Rising*, 4864 Luna, No. 191, Phelan, CA 92371. For older gay men and their admirers. Fiction, personals, hot graphics featuring silver foxes. They also have videos. This publication also includes a lot of material about gay men who are not stereotypically young, white, slender, and pretty. They have an inclusive attitude, and their ads are great. Send $9.98 for current issue or SASE for more information.

• *Holiday Bulletin*, P.O. Box 1208, Minneapolis, MN 55458. Correspondence club for older men and those who appreciate them. Send $1 for latest bulletin.

• Prime Timers, P.O. Box 291, Midtown Station, New York, NY 10018. Send SASE for a list of branches in other cities. This club for older men and their admirers sponsors a lot of fun activities.

• *Golden Threads*, P.O. Box 3177, Burlington, VT 05401-0031, (802) 658-5510. Contact publication for lesbians over 50 and their younger friends. Annual Provincetown celebration in June.

• *Broomstick*, 3543 18th St., No. 3, San Francisco, CA 94110, (415) 552-7460. A publication by, for, and about women over 40.

Sex manuals

• *Anal Pleasure and Health: A Guide for Men and Women*, Second Edition, Jack Morin, Ph.D. (Yes Press, 1986).

• *Men Loving Themselves: Images of Male Self-Sexuality*, Jack Morin, Ph.D. (Down There Press, 1980). A photo essay about male masturbation. Features men of all sexual orientations and many races.

• *The Joy of Gay Sex*, Dr. Charles Silverstein and Edmund White (Fireside/Simon & Schuster, 1977). Out of print. Check used bookstores. Apparently the challenge of updating this book to include the AIDS epidemic was too much for the publisher. Mentioned here because there is no good, current sex manual for gay men in print. However, *Gay Sex: A Manual For Men Who Love Men*, by Jack Hart, is scheduled to appear in the fall of 1991, from Alyson Publications. If it's good, it will help fill a long-felt need.

• *Men Loving Men: A Gay Sex Guide and Consciousness Book*, Mitch Walker (Gay Sunshine, 1977). This badly dated book was radical for its time. Why has no one written a good sex manual for gay men coming out and staying out in the '90s? Publishers are probably assuming that gay men are teaching each other everything they need to know about sex. But if that's true, why am I still getting questions like, "How do you give a good blowjob?" and "Why does anal sex hurt when I'm using lots of spit?"

• *Lesbian Sex*, JoAnn Loulan, illustrated by Barbara Johnson (Spinsters Books, 1984). Two sections were written by other lesbian therapists. A useful and accurate but very sober book about lesbian sexuality that should not offend anyone but the most die-hard antiporn activist. Sexual minorities within the lesbian community are only briefly mentioned. The focus is on the couple, twelve-step programs, healing from sexual abuse, and Making It (the relationship) Work. Do not expect to be titillated.

• *Sapphistry: The Book of Lesbian Sexuality*, 3rd edition, Pat Califia (Naiad Press, 1988).

Sexual problems and therapy

• *Welcome to the Club*, Dean Worbois, BoisLine, Box 8182, Boise, ID 83707, (208) 344-1311. $3. A booklet for men who are piss-shy.

• San Francisco Sex Information, (415) 621-7300. Well-trained volunteers who are very knowledgeable about human sexuality take your call 3–9 p.m., Monday–Friday.

• American Association of Sex Educators, Counselors, and Therapists (AASECT), 11 Dupont Circle, N.W., No. 220, Washington, DC 20036, (202) 638-0103.

• SIECUS, listed under "Raising Children," has a list of sexual dysfunction clinics and training programs for sex therapists, $4.60. Check with them for other resources.

• Institute for the Advanced Study of Human Sexuality, 1523 Franklin, San Francisco, CA 94109, (415) 928-1133. A private graduate school and research center. They do not do phone counseling, but do have a referral list.

• *For Yourself: The Fulfillment of Female Sexuality*, Lonnie Garfield Barbach (Signet, 1975). A book for preorgasmic women. How to become orgasmic by learning how to masturbate.

• *Sex for One: The Joy of Self-Loving*, Betty Dodson (Crown, 1987). Dodson is the high priestess of jilling off, and her iconoclastic book has shocked both men and women into looking at sex and romance in a whole new light.

Sex toys

• Good Vibrations, 1210 Valencia St., San Francisco, CA 94110. Catalog $2. A feminist vibrator store that also sells dildos, harnesses, lubricants, and many other erotic accessories. Inquiries from men are welcome.

• Eve's Garden, 119 W. 57th St., Suite 420, New York, NY 10019. Catalog $2. Silicone dildos that retain body heat and have a unique texture. Other goodies.

• Stormy Leather, 1158 Howard St., San Francisco, CA 94103, (415) 626-1672. Leather, latex, and lingerie. Inventors of a special harness to hold a dental dam in place, freeing your hands for more interesting chores. They also sell dental dams. Catalog $4.

Sex workers

• *Sex Work: Writings of Women in the Sex Industry*, ed. Frederique Delacoste and Priscilla Alexander (Cleis Press, 1987). In poems, short stories, essays, and personal narratives, sex workers talk about themselves, their jobs, the law, and the future.

• *The Whore Stigma: Female Dishonor and Male Unworthiness*, Gail Pheterson, Ph.D. (Ministerie van Sociale Zaken an Werkgelengenheid, The Netherlands, 1986). English language. Both of these books are available from COYOTE.

• COYOTE, 333 Valencia St., Room 101, San Francisco, CA 94103, (415) 558-0450. Sponsors California Prostitutes Education Project (CAL-PEP), devoted to AIDS prevention and education among Bay Area prostitutes and IV drug users. *Prostitutes and AIDS: Scapegoating and the Law,* an information packet, available for $12.25. California residents add 7.25 percent sales tax. They have many other pertinent publications.

• PONY, P.O. Box 1331, Old Chelsea Station, New York, New York, 10011, (212) 713-5678. Prostitutes of New York.

Solidarity

Lesbians who wish to understand their gay male friends better should read the following publications or books:

• *Fag Rag,* P.O. Box 331, Kenmore Station, Boston, MA 02215.

• A gay male sex manual — if you can find one — and one of the gay men's porn magazines.

• *PWA Newsline,* listed under "AIDS: General."

Gay men who wish to understand their lesbian friends better should read the following:

• *Off Our Backs,* 2423 18th St. N.W., 2nd Floor, Washington, DC 20009, (202) 234-8072. A doctrinaire and self-righteous lesbian news journal that you have to read if you want to understand why lesbian culture often seems obsessed with political correctness and devoid of humor or fun. Monthly. $17/year.

• *On Our Backs,* listed under "Pornography." Two magazines could not be more different.

• One of the lesbian books listed under "Sex Manuals."

S/M

• *Drummer,* monthly magazine devoted to gay male S/M. Desmodus, Inc., Box 11314, San Francisco, CA 94101-1314. $50 a year bulk rate, $70 first class. *Drummer* publishes (in three parts, one updated part in each issue) an international resource list of *all* clubs and organizations that cater to leather or S/M men and women. Desmodus also publishes *DungeonMaster,* a newsletter for those interested in training the male bottom, and *The Sandmutopia Guardian and Dungeon Journal,* an excellent, pansexual technical journal of S/M. The latter magazines are $4.95 apiece plus postage/handling, but Desmodus has a minimum order of $10, so get two of them for $13.50 postpaid.

• The National Leather Association, Box 17463, Seattle, WA 98107-0463. Annual conference. Newsletter, *First Link,* has a national calendar of events. Write with SASE for membership information, list of local chapter.

• *Skin Two,* BCM Box 2071, London WC1N 3XX. Glossy, kinky, pansexual, high-fashion fetish magazine from Great Britain. Wonderful resource list for those lucky enough to be traveling (and shopping) in England and Europe. Subscriptions are 30 pounds overseas (60 airmail), and have to be payable in British funds. Appears irregularly. It may be easier for you to order single copies from Constance Enterprises, below.

• Constance Enterprises, P.O. Box 43079, Upper Montclair, NJ 07043. Send SASE for their list of American and European fetish publications. They also manufacture English school canes.

• *The Leather Journal,* 7985 Santa Monica Blvd., No. 109-368, West Hollywood, CA 90046. $23/six bimonthly issues.

• The Outbound Press, Inc., 496A Hudson St., Suite 167, New York, NY 10014. They publish *Bound and Gagged,* a fine little magazine of gay male bondage, $30/six issues. Include over-21 statement and make check payable to Outbound Press.

• *The Lesbian S/M Safety Manual,* ed. Pat Califia (Lace/Alyson Publications, 1988). Contains basic safety information useful to anyone who wants to experiment with bondage or other forms of consensual power exchange.

Transsexuals and transvestites: General

• *Man and Woman, Boy and Girl,* John Money and Anke A. Ehrhardt (Johns Hopkins University Press, 1973). A classic exploration of the relationships between gender, society, and biology.

• DeVrey catalog, free by calling (516) 623-6211. Elastic undergarments to flatten or pad various parts of your torso, hips, etc.

Transsexuals and transvestites: Female-to-male

• *Information for the Female-to-Male Crossdresser and Transsexual,* Lou Sullivan, $8.95 plus $1 postage/handling from Ingersoll Gender Center, 1812 E. Madison, Seattle, WA 98122-2843, (206) 329-6651. Practical and supportive information about making temporary, reversible changes in your physical appearance and the more permanent process of taking male hormones or having surgery to accomplish sex reassignment.

• Integrity, c/o S.G., P.O. Box 615, Tenafly, NJ 07670. An FTM support group.

• *FTM,* P.O. Box 40897, San Francisco, CA 94110-0897. Send a donation if you can. FTM publishes a newsletter that lists other groups and resources and sponsors meetings.

• *Transexuality-Jude,* a 28-minute film in which an FTM counselor describes his own surgery. Focus International, 14 Oregon Drive, Huntington Station, NY 11746, (516) 549-5320.

Available for purchase in 16mm ($345) or video ($99), or for rental ($50).

Transsexuals and transvestites: Male-to-female

• Lee's Mardi Gras Boutique, 400 W. 14th St., 3rd Floor, New York, NY 10014, (212) 645-1888. $2 to be put on mailing list. A department store (really, this is a huge place) for the cross-dresser and female impersonator. Shoes, lingerie, dresses, breast forms, makeup, and a helpful and flirtatious staff. A lot of "real girls" and big women shop here for their lingerie because of the fabulous selection.

• Renaissance Education Association, P.O. Box 552, King of Prussia, PA 19406, (215) 630-1437, 24 hours. A TV/TS group that publishes *Renaissance News*. Nonhomophobic and does outreach to prisoners.

• International Foundation for Gender Education, P.O. Box 367, Wayland, MA 01778, (617) 899-2212. Publishes *TV/TS Tapestry Journal*.

• J2CP, P.O. Box 184, San Juan Capistrano, CA 92693. Information packet.

• *Transformations: Crossdressers and Those Who Love Them*, Mariette Pathy Allen (Dutton, 1989). An amazing photo essay about cross-dressers and their partners. Allen took the time to include personal statements from the people she photographed, and the range of experience represented is amazing. Includes a few women cross-dressed as men.

Other books of interest from
ALYSON PUBLICATIONS

MACHO SLUTS, by Pat Califia, $10.00. Pat Califia, the prolific lesbian author, has put together a stunning collection of her best erotic short fiction. She explores sexual fantasy and adventure in previously taboo territory — incest, sex with a thirteen-year-old girl, a lesbian's encounter with two cops, a gay man who loves to dominate dominant men, as well as various S/M and "vanilla" scenes.

THE ALYSON ALMANAC, $9.00. How did your representatives in Congress vote on gay issues? What are the best gay and lesbian books, movies, and plays? When was the first gay and lesbian March on Washington? With what king did Julius Caesar have a sexual relationship? You'll find all this, and more, in this unique and entertaining reference work.

LAVENDER LISTS, by Lynne Y. Fletcher and Adrien Saks, $9.00. This all-new collection of lists captures many entertaining, informative, and little-known aspects of gay and lesbian lore: 5 planned gay communities that never happened, 10 lesbian nuns, 15 cases of censorship where no sex was involved, 10 out-of-the-closet law enforcement officers, and much more.

THE TWO OF US, by Larry J. Uhrig, $7.00. Any two people trying to build a fulfilling relationship today face some major hurdles. A gay or lesbian couple faces even more potential problems. Here, Larry Uhrig, pastor of the Metropolitan Community Church in Washington, D.C., draws on his experience counseling gay couples to provide a practical handbook about how to make a gay relationship work.

ONE TEENAGER IN TEN, edited by Ann Heron, $4.00. One teenager in ten is gay. Here, twenty-six young people from around the country discuss their experiences: coming out to themselves, to parents, and friends; trying to pass as straight; running away; incest; trouble with the law; making initial contacts with the gay community; religious concerns; and more. Their words will provide encouragement for other teenagers facing similar experiences.

GAYS IN UNIFORM, edited by Kate Dyer, $7.00. Why doesn't the Pentagon want you to read this book? When two studies by a research arm of the Pentagon concluded that there was no justification for keeping gay people out of the military, the generals deep-sixed the reports. Those reports are now available, in book form, to the public at large. Find out for yourself what the Pentagon doesn't want you to know about gays in the military.

BROTHER TO BROTHER, edited by Essex Hemphill, $9.00. Black activist and poet Essex Hemphill has carried on in the footsteps of the late Joseph Beam (editor of *In the Life*) with this new anthology of fiction, essays, and poetry by black gay men. Contributors include Assoto Saint, Craig G. Harris, Melvin Dixon, Marlon Riggs, and many newer writers.

COMING OUT RIGHT, by Wes Muchmore and William Hanson, $8.00. Every gay man can recall the first time he stepped into a gay bar. That difficult step often represents the transition from a life of secrecy and isolation into a world of unknowns. The transition will be easier for men who have this recently updated book. Here, many facets of gay life are spelled out for the newcomer, including: coming out at work; gay health and the AIDS crisis; and the unique problems faced by men who are coming out when they're under 18 or over 30.

BI ANY OTHER NAME, edited by Loraine Hutchins and Lani Kaahumanu, $12.00. Hear the voices of over seventy women and men from all walks of life describe their lives as bisexuals. They tell their stories — personal, political, spiritual, historical — in prose, poetry, art, and essays. These are individuals who have fought prejudice from both the gay and straight communities and who have begun only recently to share their experiences. This ground-breaking anthology is an important step in the process of forming a community of their own.

DOC AND FLUFF, by Pat Califia, $9.00. The author of the popular *Macho Sluts* has written a futuristic lesbian S/M novel set in a California wracked by class, race, and drug wars. Doc is "an old Yankee peddler" who travels the deteriorating highways on her big bike. When she leaves a wild biker party with Fluff (a cute and kinky young girl) in tow, she doesn't know that Fluff is the property of the bike club's president. *Doc and Fluff* is a sexy adventure story but it also confronts serious issues like sobriety, addiction, and domestic violence.

BETWEEN FRIENDS, by Gillian E. Hanscombe, $8.00. The four women in this book represent radically different political outlooks and sexualities, yet they are tied together by the bonds of friendship. Through their experiences, recorded in a series of letters, Hanscombe deftly portrays the close relationship between political beliefs and everyday lives.

REVELATIONS, edited by Wayne Curtis, $8.00. For most gay men, one critical moment stands out as a special time in the coming-out process. It may be a special friendship, or a sexual episode, or a book or movie that communicates the right message at the right time. In *Revelations,* twenty-two men of varying ages and backgrounds give an account of this moment of truth. These tales of self-discovery will strike a chord of recognition in every gay reader.

TESTIMONIES, edited by Sarah Holmes, $8.00. Twenty-two women of widely varying backgrounds and ages give accounts of their journeys toward self-discovery. The stories portray the women's efforts to develop a lesbian identity, to explore their sexuality, and to build a community with other lesbians.

THE GAY BOOK OF LISTS, by Leigh Rutledge, $8.00. Rutledge has compiled a fascinating and informative collection of lists. His subject matter ranges from history (6 gay popes) to politics (9 perfectly disgusting reactions to AIDS) to entertainment (12 examples of gays on network television) to humor (9 Victorian "cures" for masturbation). Learning about gay culture and history has never been so much fun.

LESBIAN LISTS, by Dell Richards, $9.00. Lesbian holy days is just one of the hundreds of lists of clever and enlightening lesbian trivia compiled by columnist Dell Richards. Fun facts like uppity women who were called lesbians (but probably weren't), banned lesbian books, lesbians who've passed as men, herbal aphrodisiacs, black lesbian entertainers, and switch-hitters are sure to amuse and make *Lesbian Lists* a great gift.

SUPPORT YOUR LOCAL BOOKSTORE

Most of the books described above are available at your nearest gay or feminist bookstore, and many of them will be available at other bookstores. If you can't get these books locally, order by mail using this form.

Enclosed is $_____ for the following books. (Add $1.00 postage when ordering just one book. If you order two or more, we'll pay the postage.)

1. _____

2. _____

3. _____

name: _____ address: _____

city: _____ state: _____ zip: _____

ALYSON PUBLICATIONS
Dept. H-69, 40 Plympton St., Boston, MA 02118

After December 31, 1992, please write for current catalog.